First World War
and Army of Occupation
War Diary
France, Belgium and Germany

56 DIVISION
Divisional Troops
'B' Squadron 2 King Edward's Horse
2 October 1915 - 13 June 1919

WO95/2940/1

The Naval & Military Press Ltd
www.nmarchive.com
Published in association with The National Archives

Published by

The Naval & Military Press Ltd

Unit 10 Ridgewood Industrial Park,

Uckfield, East Sussex,

TN22 5QE England

Tel: +44 (0) 1825 749494

www.naval-military-press.com

www.nmarchive.com

This diary has been reprinted in facsimile from the original. Any imperfections are inevitably reproduced and the quality may fall short of modern type and cartographic standards.

Contents

Document type	Place/Title	Date From	Date To
Heading	WO95/2940/2		
Heading	56 Division Troops 280 Brigade RFA (Formerly 1/1 London Bde) 1915 Oct-1919 Jun		
Heading	56 Div Troops Attached 36 & 38 Divs 1/1st London Bde R.F.A. Oct Dec 1915		
Heading	280 Bde RFA 56 Div Formerly 1/1st London Brigade R.F.A. Statement To Accompany War Diary		
Heading	1/1 London Bde R.F.A. Nov Vol II 1915 Oct-1915 Dec		
Miscellaneous	1st London Division T.F. Circular Letter War Diaries & Statements	13/01/1915	13/01/1915
Miscellaneous	Appendix to H.Q. Vol 1 London Artillery (attached XXXVI Division) Statement by C.R.A. 1/1st London Divisional Artillery.	05/07/1915	05/07/1915
Heading	36th Division 1/1st London Bde. R.F.A. Vol I Oct 15 Dec 15		
War Diary	Bordon	02/10/1915	02/10/1915
War Diary	Southampton	03/10/1915	03/10/1915
War Diary	Havre	04/10/1915	04/10/1915
War Diary	St. Sauveur	05/10/1915	05/10/1915
War Diary	Colincamps	09/10/1915	19/10/1915
War Diary	Bertrancourt	19/10/1915	19/10/1915
War Diary	St. Sauveur	20/10/1915	20/10/1915
War Diary	Canaples	22/10/1915	22/10/1915
War Diary	Vert-Galand	25/10/1915	25/10/1915
War Diary	Halloy-Les-Pernois	28/10/1915	28/10/1915
War Diary	Lambres	11/12/1915	12/12/1915
War Diary	Merville	19/12/1915	19/12/1915
War Diary	Rincq (Aire)	24/12/1915	24/12/1915
Heading	War Diary Of 1/1 London Brigade R.F.A. From 1st To 31st October		
Heading	War Diary Of 1st London Brigade R.F.A. From 1st November 1915 To 30th Nov 1915		
War Diary	Longvillers	28/11/1915	28/11/1915
Heading	War Diary Of 1/1 London Brigade R.F.A. (Attached 38th West Div) From 1st December To 31st December 1915		
Heading	16th Division 1st London Brigade R.F.A. 1916 Jan-1916 Feb		
War Diary	Ecquedecques	01/01/1916	01/01/1916
War Diary	Fosse No.7 De Bethune (Near Quality St) Loos Sector	03/01/1916	25/01/1916
War Diary	Lieres	26/01/1916	26/01/1916
War Diary	Farm No.7 Lieres	27/01/1916	27/01/1916
War Diary	Lieres	24/02/1916	24/02/1916
War Diary	Fontaine-Sur-Somme	24/02/1916	25/02/1916
War Diary	Halloy-Les-Pernois	27/02/1916	27/02/1916
Heading	1/1st London Brigade R.F.A. (T.F) War Diary For March 1916		
War Diary	Candas	12/03/1916	12/03/1916
War Diary	Rebreuve-Sur-Canche & Rebreuviette	14/03/1916	14/03/1916
War Diary	Rebreuve S/c	18/03/1916	19/03/1916

War Diary	Arras (Vicinity Of)	22/03/1916	24/03/1916
Heading	1/1 London Brigade R.F.A. War Diary For April 1916		
War Diary	Arras (Vicinity Of)	02/04/1916	13/04/1916
War Diary	Frevent	15/04/1916	15/04/1916
War Diary	Arras (Vicinity Of)	19/04/1916	26/04/1916
War Diary	Arras	01/04/1916	28/04/1916
Heading	280th (City Of London) Brigade R.F.A. Formerly 1/1st London Brigade R.F.A. War Diary For May 1916		
War Diary	From Rebreuve & Rebreuviette to Pas & Souastre	08/05/1916	08/05/1916
War Diary	Sailly-Au-Bois	10/05/1916	16/05/1916
War Diary	Pas	17/05/1916	17/05/1916
War Diary	Sailly-Au-Bois	19/05/1916	25/05/1916
War Diary	Sailly-Au-Bois & Pas	28/05/1916	28/05/1916
War Diary	Hebuterne & Pas	28/05/1916	28/05/1916
War Diary	Sailly-Au-Bois	30/05/1916	30/05/1916
War Diary	Arras	01/05/1916	29/05/1916
Heading	War Diary For June 1916 280th (City of London) Bde R.F.A. (T.F.)		
War Diary	From Vicinity Of Arras To Pas	01/06/1916	03/06/1916
War Diary	Vicinity Of Sailly & Hebuterne	03/06/1916	14/06/1916
War Diary	Pas to Henu	15/06/1916	15/06/1916
War Diary	Vicinity Of Sailly & Hebuterne	15/06/1916	28/06/1916
Heading	280 Bde RFA Appendix 6 Vol 7 War Diaries-June 1916		
War Diary	Vicinity Of Sailly & Hebuterne	29/06/1916	30/06/1916
War Diary	Vicinity of Hebuterne	19/06/1916	30/06/1916
War Diary	Hebuterne	01/06/1916	30/06/1916
Operation(al) Order(s)	Operation Order No. 1 Northern Group By Lieut Colonel L.A.C. Southam Commanding Northern Group	22/06/1916	22/06/1916
Miscellaneous	Schedule		
Operation(al) Order(s)	Operation Order No. 2 By Lieut Colonel L.A.C. Southam Commanding Northern Group	23/06/1916	23/06/1916
Miscellaneous	O.C. Batteries	23/06/1916	23/06/1916
Operation(al) Order(s)	Operation Order No. 3 By Lieut Colonel L.A.C. Southam Commanding Northern Group	27/06/1916	27/06/1916
Operation(al) Order(s)	Operation Order No. 4 By Lieut Colonel L.A.C. Southam Commanding Northern Group	29/06/1916	29/06/1916
Miscellaneous	Schedule		
Heading	War Diary For July 1916 Of 280th (City of London) Bde R.F.A.		
War Diary	In The Field	01/07/1916	01/07/1916
War Diary	Hebuterne	01/07/1916	03/07/1916
War Diary	Fonquevilliers	04/07/1916	16/07/1916
War Diary	Sailly-Au-Bois	19/07/1916	27/07/1916
War Diary	Vicinity Of Sailly & Hebuterne	01/07/1916	03/07/1916
War Diary	Sailly To Souastre	04/07/1916	04/07/1916
War Diary	Henu To Pas	12/07/1916	12/07/1916
War Diary	Souastre To Pas	13/07/1916	13/07/1916
War Diary	Bienvillers	14/07/1916	14/07/1916
War Diary	Pas To Sailly	19/07/1916	19/07/1916
War Diary	Vicinity Of Sailly & Hebuterne	20/07/1916	24/07/1916
War Diary	Pas Huts To Gaudiempre	25/07/1916	25/07/1916
War Diary	Vicinity Of Sailly & Hebuterne	25/07/1916	31/07/1916
Operation(al) Order(s)	Operation Order No. 5 By Lieut Colonel L.A.C. Southam Commanding Northern Group	30/06/1916	30/06/1916
Miscellaneous	Artillery Narrative-Northen Group	01/07/1916	01/07/1916

Miscellaneous	A/770	17/07/1916	17/07/1916
Miscellaneous	A/657	06/07/1916	06/07/1916
War Diary	Vicinity Of Fonquevillers	03/07/1916	31/07/1916
War Diary	Fonquevillers	05/07/1916	14/07/1916
War Diary	Bienvillers	15/07/1916	30/07/1916
War Diary	Fonquevillers	04/07/1916	12/07/1916
War Diary	Sailly	13/07/1916	19/07/1916
Heading	56th Divisional Artillery 280th Brigade Royal Field Artillery August 1916		
War Diary	Vicinity Of Sailly & Hebuterne	01/08/1916	01/08/1916
War Diary	Sailly & Bienvillers	02/08/1916	02/08/1916
War Diary	Vicinity Of Bienvillers & Fonquevillers	02/08/1916	15/08/1916
War Diary	Bienvillers To Fme De La Haie	16/08/1916	16/08/1916
War Diary	Vicinity Of Hebuterne & Fonquevillers	16/08/1916	30/08/1916
War Diary	Chateau De La Haie To Gaudiempre	30/08/1916	31/08/1916
Miscellaneous	A/Battery		
War Diary	E 20a68 93 Near Fonquevillers	16/08/1916	29/08/1916
Miscellaneous	B Battery		
War Diary	Bienvillers	16/08/1916	30/08/1916
Miscellaneous	C Battery		
War Diary	Sailly (K13a9.9)	02/08/1916	31/08/1916
Miscellaneous	D Battery		
War Diary	In The Field	06/08/1916	16/08/1916
Miscellaneous	56th Division	19/08/1916	19/08/1916
Heading	56th Divisional Artillery 280th (City Of London) Brigade R.F.A. September 1916		
War Diary	Gaudiempre	01/09/1916	01/09/1916
War Diary	Gaudiempre To Occoches Of Vicinity	01/09/1916	02/09/1916
War Diary	Occoches To Coisy	03/09/1916	03/09/1916
War Diary	Coisy To Daours	04/09/1916	04/09/1916
War Diary	Daours To Vicinity of Bray-Sur-Somme	05/09/1916	07/09/1916
War Diary	Vicinity Of Maricourt & Hardecourt	07/09/1916	12/09/1916
War Diary	Vicinity Of Hardecourt	12/09/1916	22/09/1916
War Diary	Vicinity Of Hardecourt & Guillemont & Ginchy	22/09/1916	30/09/1916
War Diary	Morval	30/09/1916	30/09/1916
Operation(al) Order(s)	Operation Order No. 1 By Lieut Colonel L.A.C. Southam Commanding Northern Group	09/09/1916	09/09/1916
Operation(al) Order(s)	Prichtel's Group Operation Order No. 4	08/09/1916	08/09/1916
Operation(al) Order(s)	Operation Order No. 2 By Lieut Colonel L.A.C. Southam Commanding Northern Group	11/09/1916	11/09/1916
Operation(al) Order(s)	Operation Order No. 3 By Lieut Colonel L.A.C. Southam Commanding Northern Group	14/09/1916	14/09/1916
Miscellaneous	Barrages		
Miscellaneous	Objectives		
Operation(al) Order(s)	Operation Order No. 4 By Lieut Colonel L.A.C. Southam Commanding Northern Group	18/09/1916	18/09/1916
Operation(al) Order(s)	Operation Order No. 5 By Lieut Colonel L.A.C. Southam Commanding Northern Group	24/09/1916	24/09/1916
Miscellaneous	Life Group Schedule Of Barrages		
Miscellaneous		25/09/1916	25/09/1916
Operation(al) Order(s)	Operation Order No. 2 Right Central Artillery Right Group	24/09/1916	24/09/1916
Miscellaneous	Reference Right Group Operation Orders No. 2	24/09/1916	24/09/1916
Miscellaneous	Confirmation Of Amendments To Operation Order No. 2		

Operation(al) Order(s)	Right Centre Divisional Artillery Right Group Operation Order No. 1	23/09/1916	23/09/1916
War Diary	Somme Front	08/09/1916	20/09/1916
War Diary	Bray	08/09/1916	10/09/1916
War Diary	Mariecourt	11/09/1916	19/09/1916
War Diary	Leuze Wood	20/09/1916	20/09/1916
War Diary	In The Field	08/09/1916	19/09/1916
War Diary	Vicinity Of Ginchy & Morval (Somme Front)	01/10/1916	31/10/1916
Heading	War Diary For November 1916 280th (City Of London) Bde R.F.A. (T.F.)		
War Diary	Somme Front To Daours	01/11/1916	01/11/1916
War Diary	Daours To Talmas	02/11/1916	02/11/1916
War Diary	Daours To Amplier	03/11/1916	03/11/1916
War Diary	Amplier To Rebreuve & Rebreuviette	04/11/1916	04/11/1916
War Diary	Rebreuve To Neuville St Vaast Front	05/11/1916	06/11/1916
War Diary	Vicinity Of Neuville-St. Vaast	06/11/1916	30/11/1916
Miscellaneous	Warning Order	04/11/1916	04/11/1916
Operation(al) Order(s)	Operation Order No. 37 by Brigadier-General R.J.G. Elkington C.M.G. Commanding 56th Divnl Artillery	04/11/1916	04/11/1916
Heading	War Diary December 1916 280th (City of London) Brigade R.F.A. (T.F.)		
War Diary	Vicinity Of Neuville St Vaast	01/12/1916	01/12/1916
War Diary	Laresset & Acq To Raimbert	02/12/1916	02/12/1916
War Diary	Raimbert To St. Floris	03/12/1916	03/12/1916
War Diary	Vicinity Of Vieille Chapelle & Richebourg St Vaast	04/12/1916	10/12/1916
War Diary	Laventie	10/12/1916	31/12/1916
Operation(al) Order(s)	Operation Order No. 4 By Lieut Colonel L.A.C. Southam Commanding Northern Group	23/12/1916	23/12/1916
Miscellaneous	O.C. Batteries	24/12/1916	24/12/1916
Operation(al) Order(s)	Operation Order No. 4 Schedule		
Miscellaneous	Trench Mortar Programme		
Miscellaneous	O.C. Batteries	25/12/1916	25/12/1916
Miscellaneous	Operation Order No. 4 Schedule		
Heading	War Diary January 1917 280th (City Of London) Bde R.F.A.		
War Diary	Laventie	01/01/1917	31/01/1917
Heading	War Diary 280th (City of London) Bde RFA February 1917		
War Diary	Laventie	01/02/1917	28/02/1917
Heading	War Diary March 1917 280th (City of London) Bde R.F.A.		
War Diary	Laventie	01/03/1917	05/03/1917
War Diary	Calonne	06/03/1917	06/03/1917
War Diary	Estree Blanche	07/03/1917	07/03/1917
War Diary	Anvin	08/03/1917	08/03/1917
War Diary	Ligny-Sur-Canche	09/03/1917	09/03/1917
War Diary	Lucheux	10/03/1917	14/03/1917
War Diary	Simencourt	15/03/1917	15/03/1917
War Diary	Simencourt & Achicourt	16/03/1917	17/03/1917
War Diary	Achicourt	18/03/1917	19/03/1917
War Diary	Achicourt & Agny	20/03/1917	20/03/1917
War Diary	Agny	21/03/1917	25/03/1917
War Diary	Agny & Mercatel	26/03/1917	29/03/1917
War Diary	Mercatel & Beaurains	30/03/1917	31/03/1917
Heading	War Diary 280th Bde RFA April 1917		
War Diary	Beaurains & Mercatel	01/04/1917	11/04/1917

War Diary	Mercatel & Neuville Vitasse	11/04/1917	16/04/1917
War Diary	Neuville Vitasse & St. Martin Sur Cojeul	17/04/1917	24/04/1917
War Diary	Heninel & St. Martin Sur Cojeul	25/04/1917	30/04/1917
Heading	War Diary 280th Bde R.F.A. May 1917		
War Diary	Heninel	01/05/1917	27/05/1917
War Diary	Mercatel District	28/05/1917	31/05/1917
Heading	War Diary June 1917 280th Bde RFA		
War Diary	Mercatel & Heninel	01/06/1917	05/06/1917
War Diary	Heninel	06/06/1917	13/06/1917
War Diary	St. Martin & Heninel	14/06/1917	25/06/1917
War Diary	Mercatel	26/06/1917	27/06/1917
War Diary	Hendecourt	28/06/1917	30/06/1917
War Diary	Beaumetz	01/10/1917	31/10/1917
Heading	War Diary Original 280th Brigade RFA Nov 1917		
Miscellaneous	Herewith War Diary For Month Of November 1917	30/11/1917	30/11/1917
War Diary	Demicourt	01/11/1917	30/11/1917
Heading	280th Bde R F A War Diary December 1917		
War Diary	Boursies	01/12/1917	31/12/1917
Heading	War Diary January 1918 Original		
War Diary		01/01/1918	31/01/1918
Heading	280 Bde War Diary February 1918		
War Diary	Bethencourt Etc.	01/02/1918	28/02/1918
Heading	55th Div. War Diary Headquarters 280th Brigade R.F.A. March 1918		
Heading	280 Bde R F A War Diary For March 1918 Vol 28		
War Diary	Gavrelle	01/03/1918	31/03/1918
Miscellaneous	Right Group Report Of The Operations	28/03/1918	28/03/1918
Miscellaneous	Intelligence Report Of Liaison Officer Right Battalion		
Heading	56th Divisional Artillery 280th (City Of London) Brigade R.F.A. April 1918		
War Diary	Gavrelle	01/04/1918	07/04/1918
War Diary	Agny	08/04/1918	30/04/1918
Heading	280th (City Of London) Brigade R.F.A. War Diary May 1918 Original		
War Diary	Agny	01/05/1918	17/05/1918
War Diary	Dainville	18/05/1918	31/05/1918
Heading	Original War Diary June 1918 Vol 31		
War Diary	Dainville	01/06/1918	30/06/1918
Heading	War Diary 280th (City of London) Brigade R.F.A. July 1918		
Miscellaneous	Herewith Original Of War Diary For Month Of July 1918	01/08/1918	01/08/1918
War Diary	Dainville	01/07/1918	20/07/1918
War Diary	Berneville	21/07/1918	21/07/1918
War Diary	Frevin Capelle	22/07/1918	31/08/1918
Heading	War Diary Sept 1918 280 Bde RFA Vol 34		
War Diary		01/09/1918	30/09/1918
Heading	War Diary October 1918 280 Bde R.F.A.		
War Diary		01/10/1918	31/10/1918
Miscellaneous	Herewith Original Of War Diary For Month Ending November 30 1918	30/11/1918	30/11/1918
War Diary	Thient (Sheet 51 A. N.E)	01/11/1918	30/11/1918
Miscellaneous	Herewith Original Of War Diary For Month Ending December 31st 1918		
War Diary	Goegnies Chaussee	05/12/1918	05/12/1918
Heading	War Diary January 1919		

Miscellaneous	Herewith Original Of War Diary For Month Ending January 31st 1919	31/01/1919	31/01/1919
War Diary	Goegnies-Chaussee	07/01/1919	07/01/1919
Miscellaneous	Various Re-Organizations Of The 280th Brigade R.F.A.		
Miscellaneous	Herewith Statement Regarding The Various Re-Organizations Of The Brigade Required By You	21/02/1919	21/02/1919
Miscellaneous	History Of The 280th (City Of London) Brigade RFA		
Miscellaneous			
War Diary	Goegnies-Chaussee		
Miscellaneous	Reference S.C. 451/27	20/03/1919	20/03/1919
Miscellaneous	Record of Instances of Gallant Conduct on the Part of the Artillery During the Recent War.		
Miscellaneous	Reference SC 451/27		
War Diary	Goegnies-Chaussee	01/03/1919	19/03/1919
War Diary	Flenu	25/03/1919	29/03/1919
Miscellaneous	Diary Of Events Of 56th. Division	10/04/1919	10/04/1919
War Diary	Flenu	24/05/1919	13/06/1919

WO 95/2940/2

BEF

56 DIVISION TROOPS

280 BRIGADE RFA
(FORMERLY 1/1 LONDON BDE)

1915 OCT. — 1919 JUN

(MISSING? 1917 JULY AUG & SEP)

Box ~~2801~~ 2940

56 DIV. TROOPS

ATTACHED 36 + 38 DIVS

1/1st London Bde R.F.A

Oct - Dec 1915

2940

~~2193~~

4 280 BDE RFA 56 DIV

Finney 1/1st LONDON BRIGADE R.F.A.

Statement to accompany War Diary
%%%

NIL

Warren Heath
Ipswich
31st August 1915

H. N. Clark Major
Commanding 1/1st London Bde R.F.A.

56

36th

XI corps (mostly 38th Div) 11.12.15
16th Div 1.1.16.
56th Div 24.2.16.

1/1 London Bde R.F.A.

No [illegible]

Vol II

1915 OCT — 1915 DEC

2290

Copy to O.C. 1st Lond Bty RGA 13.1.15

CRA

1st LONDON DIVISION T.F. G/38/8.

CIRCULAR LETTER.

WAR DIARIES & STATEMENTS.

The following notes on the writing of War Diaries (Army Form C.2118), and War Diary Statements are issued for information :-

1. A general entry covering a period of more than 24 hours should not be made.

2. Daily Meteorological observations should not be made, except so far as they affect military training and operations.

3. The War Diary is the Diary of a Unit not of an individual officer, so that entries should not be made in the 1st Person.

4. The object of War Diaries as given in F.S.Regns., Part II, Section 140, para. 1, should be borne in mind. The Diary should be a chronicle of events, containing the information asked for in F.S.Regns., Part II, Section 140, para.5, Sub-headings i - ix. Subheading X should be dealt with in the War Diary Statement.

5. Each entry in the War Diary should be initialled by an officer.

6. The War Diary and the War Diary Statement must be signed by the Officer Commanding the Unit.

7. The name of the unit should be inserted on the top sheet of the War Diary and on the front page of the War Diary Statement.

8. The use of Appendices is given in F.S.Regns., Part II, Section 140, para. 7.

9. Criticisms and suggestions should not be made except in so far as they serve the purpose mentioned in F.S.Regns., Part II, Section 140, para. 1, Subheading II.

10. War Diaries are essentially confidential documents and must be treated as such. See F.S.Regns., Part II, Section 140, paras. 1, 3, 4, also King's Regns., para. 1861.

11. Should War Diaries and War Diary Statements not reach Headquarters on the appointed day, they should be accompanied by a written statement explaining the reason for the delay in their despatch.

Fred. W. Bewsher: Lieut.
Attached General Staff,
1st London Divn., T.F.

Crowborough,
13/1/15.

Appendix to H.Q. Vol 1. London Artillery (attached XXXVI Division

STATEMENT BY C.R.A. 1/1st LONDON DIVISIONAL ARTILLERY.

DIVISION. 1st London Division.

MOBILIZATION CENTRE. London.

TEMPORARY WAR STATION. Full details given in October 1914 Statement.

CONCENTRATION AT WAR STATION. No further remarks.

ORGANIZATION FOR DEFENCE. These Artillery units are very short of horses, and would have considerable difficulty in moving the whole of their equipment and ammunition. As a temporary measure until remounts are supplied, arrangements have been made to impress horses and civilian harness (where this is possible) from farmers and firms in the vicinity of units' stations.

TRAINING. This is progressing satisfactorily. The personnel of these first line units are fit for servive abroad. Horses, harness, field telephones and G.S.Wagons &c, are required to complete.

Several officers have been attached for a fortnight's course of instruction to batteries at the front, and the experience gained by these officers is of great assistance to the units concerned. ~~50% of~~ 25% of the 2nd line units are attached to brigades for training.

46
47
100
193

1 field battery complete has been sent to No.3 training school at Kettering for the purpose of being used as a training battery for other Artillery units.

A Howitzer battery has been sent to the barracks at IPSWICH for the purpose of training 10 officers and 100 gunners of 1(b) Reserve Brigade R.F.A.

One battery is stationed at Lord's Cricket Ground London and is being used as a training battery for Territorial officers of the London Division. Instruction is being given to men of Infantry Units in Cold Shoeing. Each Unit also has a certain number of its own men under instruction. Several Officers have attended Telephone Courses.

Discipline. On the whole the discipline has been very good. No particular offence is prevalent.

Administration. Ordnance Services. Satisfactory. A great deal of extra clerical work is caused by Units being constantly called upon to render Indents for Equipment &c, which have previously been submitted. The Ammunition on charge of Units is well cared for and good reports have been received from Ordnance Inspecting Officer.

Billetting:- Satisfactory except in a few cases

Supply of Remounts. Remounts are urgently required. The 1/1st London Brigade R.F.A. is 72 horses short of its establishment, the 1/2nd London Brigade R.F.A. is 112 short and the 1/3rd London Brigade is about 100 short.

The 1/4th London Howitzer Brigade R.F.A. and the 1/1st London Battery R.G.A. are also considerably under their establishment.

This shortage of horses greatly interferes with the mobility of these Units.

Organization into Home and Imperial Service. All ranks are for Imperial Service.

F. Beaver.

Red House Park,
Ipswich,
5.7.15.

Colonel,
Commanding
1/1st London Divisional Artillery.

36th Division

121/7432

1/1st London Bde: RFA.

Vol I

Oct 15
1
Dec 15

Instructions regarding War Diaries and Intelligence Summaries are contained in F. S. Regs., Part II. and the Staff Manual respectively. Title Pages will be prepared in manuscript.

Secret

WAR DIARY
or
~~INTELLIGENCE~~ SUMMARY
(Erase heading not required.)

Army Form C. 2118

Place	Date	Hour	Summary of Events and Information	Remarks and references to Appendices
BORDON	2/10/15	–	Brigade proceeded by units to SOUTHAMPTON for embarkation.	
SOUTHAMPTON	3/10/15	–	Brigade embarked.	
HÄVRE	4/10/15	–	Brigade disembarked and entrained.	
ST SAUVEUR	5/10/15	–	Brigade went into billets after detrainment at LONGUEAU + journey by road via AMIENS.	
COLINCAMPS	9/10/15	–	Firing Batteries of 1st 2nd + 3rd Batteries arrived for attachment to 29th Brigade R.F.A. 4th Division. Guns run into alternative positions of 29th Brigade after sunset. Horses + wagons to wagon line at BERTRANCOURT	
"	12/10/15	–	Fire opened by 1st 2nd + 3rd Batteries – various points registered. (40 rounds fired in all)	
"	14/10/15	–	Fire opened by 1st Bty (35 rounds) + 3rd Bty (48 rounds)	
"	16/10/15	–	3rd Bty fired 18 rounds shrapnel + 20 rounds H.E. (on salient of German lines)	
"	18/10/15	–	1st Bty fired 34 rounds shrapnel + 8 rounds H.E. 2nd Bty fired 65 rounds shrapnel + 8 H.E	
"	19/10/15	–	2nd Bty fired 12 rounds H.E.	
BERTRANCOURT	"	–	Batteries evacuated positions of 29th Brigade after sunset + parked at BERTRANCOURT for the night.	
ST SAUVEUR	20/10/15	"	Batteries returned to ST SAUVEUR	
CANAPLES	22/10/15	–	Brigade moved from ST SAUVEUR to CANAPLES + adjoining village of HALLOY-LES-PERNOIS, to be in 107th Inf. Bde Billeting area	
VERT-GALAND	25/10/15	4 pm.	Inspection by H.M. the King at VERT-GALAND FARM on AMIENS-DOULLENS road.	
HALLOY-LES-PERNOIS	28/10/15	–	Brigade H.Q moved from LE CHATEAU, CANAPLES to L'ECOLE, HALLOY-LES-PERNOIS.	

L. A. C. Southam

LT: COL; COMDG;
1/1st LONDON BRIGADE. ROYAL FIELD ARTILLERY.

30. 10. 15.

Instructions regarding War Diaries and Intelligence Summaries are contained in F. S. Regs., Part II. and the Staff Manual respectively. Title Pages will be prepared in manuscript.

WAR DIARY ~~or~~ ~~INTELLIGENCE SUMMARY~~

(Erase heading not required.)

Army Form C. 2118

Place	Date	Hour	Summary of Events and Information	Remarks and references to Appendices
LAMBRES	11 & 12 DEC. 1915	NIGHT	Brigade arrived & went into billets after journey from LONGVILLERS (entraining at PONT REMY) on change of Division from 36th (3rd Army) to 38th (1st Army).	
MERVILLE	19 DEC 1915	1 pm	Brigade arrived & went into billets between LE CORBIE & LE SART on HAVERSKERQUE - MERVILLE road on change of area.	
RINCQ (AIRE)	24 DEC 1915	NOON	Brigade arrived & went into billets on change of area (Bde HQ, 1st Bty, 2nd ", Amn Colmn) at RINCQ; 3rd Bty at WARNE	

31/12/15.

L. A. C. Southam

LT: COL; COMDG;
1ST LONDON BRIGADE. ROYAL FIELD ARTILLERY.

1875 Wt. W593/826 1,000,000 4/15 J.B.C. & A. A.D.S.S./Forms/C. 2118.

56 DIV

attached 36 DIV

CONFIDENTIAL

WAR DIARY

of

1/1 London Brigade R.F.A.

From 1st to 31st October.

2293

36th Div.

Confidential

War Diary

of

~~[illegible]~~
1st London Brigade RFA.

from 1st November 1915 to 30th Nov. 1915

Instructions regarding War Diaries and Intelligence Summaries are contained in F. S. Regs., Part II. and the Staff Manual respectively. Title Pages will be prepared in manuscript.

WAR DIARY
or
~~INTELLIGENCE SUMMARY~~
(Erase heading not required.)

Army Form C. 2118

Place	Date	Hour	Summary of Events and Information	Remarks and references to Appendices
LONGVILLERS	28/11/15	11 am	BRIGADE arrived + went into billets on change of area from CANAPLES and HALLOY-LES-PERNOIS.	

L. A. C. [signature]
LT: COL; COMDG;
1/1st LONDON BRIGADE, ROYAL FIELD ARTILLERY.

1875 Wt. W593/826 1,000,000 4/15 J.B.C. & A. A.D.S.S./Forms/C. 2118.

War Diary

of

1/1 London Brigade R.F.A.
(attached 38th Welsh Div)

from

1st December to 31st December 1915

ATTACHED 16TH DIVISION

1ST LONDON BRIGADE R.F.A.

~~JAN 1916 ONLY~~

1916 JAN – 1916 FEB

Jan '16 only

Instructions regarding War Diaries and Intelligence Summaries are contained in F. S. Regs., Part II. and the Staff Manual respectively. Title Pages will be prepared in manuscript.

WAR DIARY
or
INTELLIGENCE SUMMARY

(Erase heading not required.)

Army Form C. 2118

Place	Date	Hour	Summary of Events and Information	Remarks and references to Appendices
ECQUEDECQUES	1/1/16	1 pm.	Brigade arrived and went into billets on change of Division from 38th to 76th.	
FOSSE No. 7 DE BETHUNE [illegible] LOOS SECTOR	3/1/16		[illegible] Bde, OC Units + Adjt reconnoitred positions &c to be taken over from French Batteries of 18 French Div (LOOS SECTOR). Bde to being attached to 47 Div + forming part of LOWE group.	
	5/1/16		Reconnaissance of communications by Bty Staffs	
"	6/1/16	4.30 pm	One Section of each Bty relieved corresponding Sections of French Batteries. Bde H.Q. established at ~~[illegible]~~ LES BREBIS	
"	7/1/16	4.30 pm noon	Remaining Section of each Bty relieved remaining Sections of French Batteries. Sections arriving previous day registered. Amm: Column arrived HOUCHIN. [illegible] CHALK PIT WOOD – PETIT SAINS road [illegible] by French [illegible] at 6 pm	
"	8/1/16		Registration ~~of Batteries completed~~ LOWE group (consisting of 6th Lon, 1st Lon Bdes) now in position ~~Batteries~~ covering the front of 141st Inf Bde. Registration completed	
	9/1/16		Retaliation at request of Inf.	
		11 am	Bombardment by 5" How. 3rd Londons took part + made excellent shooting. Commended by GOC RA 4th Corps.	
	10/1/16		During day enemy shelled our front line, 2nd line + communication trenches continuously. We retaliated at request of Infantry.	
	11/1/16		Enemy shelled trenches during day. We retaliated + in the majority of cases enemy ceased firing.	
		2 - 4.30 pm	Enemy shelled LOOS at frequent intervals. OC 2nd Bty reports that generally speaking his retaliation did not stop enemy shelling LOOS.	
	12/1/16		Practically no firing from either side during the morning owing to the number of balloons up. In the afternoon the light was bad. Firing on trenches M 5 a M 6 a seemed to stop the enemy shelling LOOS sector.	
		1 - 2 pm	Western end of the DOUBLE CRASSIER shelled.	
	13/1/16		During the day there was a certain amount of firing on the front line trenches of right subsection of LOOS Sector. In every case firing ceased on batteries retaliating. Batteries continued to register various points	
		3.30 pm	All batteries concentrated fire on Railway as ordered at intervals during the night. Batteries fired on their night lines.	

1875 Wt. W593/826 1,000,000 4/15 J.B.C. & A. A.D.S.S./Forms/C. 2118.

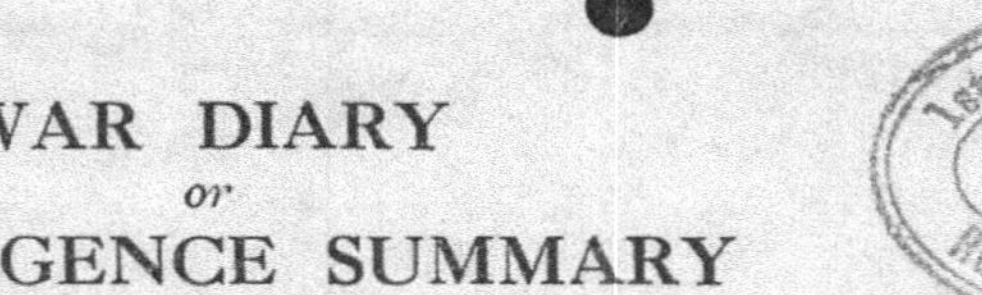

WAR DIARY
or
INTELLIGENCE SUMMARY
(Erase heading not required.)

Army Form C. 2118

Place	Date	Hour	Summary of Events and Information	Remarks and references to Appendices
FOSSE No. 7 DE BETHUNE (near QUALITY ST) LOOS SECTOR	14/1/16	8-10.30 AM	Shelled right LOOS subsection at intervals. 3rd Bty claim to have hit a suspected machine gun emplacement at G 36 d 9 2	
		10.45 PM &	German relief apparently taking place & at request of Inf. Batteries fired on their right line.	
	15/1/16	12.30 AM		
			Quite a lot of retaliation during the day for enemy shelling on front & 2nd line trenches. Germans shelled LENS-BETHUNE road intermittently. Fire on the main road at N 7 a 3.0 caused enemy to cease firing.	
		10 AM & 11 AM	LOOS heavily shelled	
			The new Inf. Bde took over from the 141st Bde a slightly different front, entailing the Rt. Batt. HQ becoming the centre, the centre the left, & a new right. This caused some trouble with wires but the communication was satisfactorily maintained.	
	16/1/16		2nd & 3rd Batteries registered their new zones. 2nd Bty took new O.P. At frequent intervals all day enemy shelled our front line trenches from M 5 b 8.2 to M 5 a 4.4	
		8-10.30 AM	Enemy shelled front line trenches just north of Chalk pit to half way down the copse. Four balloons up opposite LOOS sector during day. These appeared to be lowered.	
	17/1/16		Quietest day in LOOS sector since taking over. The enemy hardly shelled at all except a little on our front line trenches. Many aeroplanes up which may have accounted for this.	
	18/1/16		German artillery very active probably owing to absence of our aeroplanes. 3rd & 5th Batteries fired on front line trench M 5 d 7½ 9½ to M 5 d ½ 6 which was effective in causing the enemy to cease firing. During the day up to about 2.45 PM each Battery retaliated on the enemy's support & communication trenches.	

Instructions regarding War Diaries and Intelligence Summaries are contained in F. S. Regs., Part II. and the Staff Manual respectively. Title Pages will be prepared in manuscript.

WAR DIARY
or
INTELLIGENCE SUMMARY
(Erase heading not required.)

Army Form C. 2118

Place	Date	Hour	Summary of Events and Information	Remarks and references to Appendices
	19/1/16		Enemy shelled our trenches in LOOS sector at frequent intervals during day. Our retaliation was successful in causing hostile fire to cease each time.	
		12 noon	Test concentration on the copse as practice against the mine going up. This was successful & the batteries got off their rounds very quickly.	
	20/1/16		Quality St. Fosse No 7 & LENS-BETHUNE Road were heavily shelled this morning. Enemy fire on our trenches in LOOS sector with Field guns & 4.2 was fairly active throughout the day. In every case retaliation followed & was successful. Batteries registered points outside their allotted zones with a view to possible concentration of fire.	
	21/1/16		There was a certain amount of shelling during day in LOOS sector more especially in the centre subsection. Batteries retaliated & were successful in causing enemy to cease fire each time.	
	22/1/16		During day only slight intermittent firing on front & support trenches in LOOS sector more especially in M 5 a & b. Battery positions (Fosse 7) heavily shelled all day. Guns shelling Battery positions were – 4.2 from CITE ST PIERRE 5.9 from DOUVRAIN & a 4.2 (very high velocity) from HULLUCH direction. This gun must be very near German front line trench as ~~the arrival of the shelling~~ judged by the sound of the discharge. 2nd 15 pdr No 2070 damaged by direct hit on roof of gun pit & withdrawn. Replaced 4pm by gun from 5th Lond Bde.	
	23/1/16	2 AM	Mine fired. GOC 47th Div commended preparations made by & resultant co-operation of 47 Div Arty. The 3 Batteries of the Bde fired 667 rounds during the ½ hours.	
			Very quiet during day. A little hostile shelling on M 5 a & b; otherwise no shelling in LOOS sector or Battery positions at Fosse 7. German aircraft active in morning. ~~Flashes observed in [illegible]~~	

1875 Wt. W593/826 1,000,000 4/15 J.B.C. & A. A.D.S.S./Forms/C. 2118.

Instructions regarding War Diaries and Intelligence Summaries are contained in F. S. Regs., Part II. and the Staff Manual respectively. Title Pages will be prepared in manuscript.

WAR DIARY
or
INTELLIGENCE SUMMARY
(Erase heading not required.)

Army Form C. 2118

Place	Date	Hour	Summary of Events and Information	Remarks and references to Appendices
	24/1/16		Enemy artillery very active during day. Intermittent firing on front lines & communication trenches.	
			O.C. Orderly Officer & Bty Commanders of 3rd London Bde visited positions preparatory to taking over from 1st London Bde. Battery Commanders returned same night.	
	25/1/15	11.30 AM to 4 PM.	Enemy shelled LOOS sector very steadily & at times the bombardment was intense, especially LOOS PYLONS & houses south of Crassier. Enemy aircraft very active all day. Much work has been done on saps in M 5d & M 5c in front of German front line.	
		3 PM.	Main LOOS-MAROC communication trench was shelled with enemy howitzers (40–50 shells)	
			1st Batty fired as Retaliation	
			2nd " to shew new zone to Relieving battery from 3rd Bde	
			3rd " on suspected M.G. emplacement & signs of new work.	
		Evening	First sections of 3rd Lon Bde arrived & corresponding sections of batteries of 1st Lon Brigade withdrew, leaving 1st Brigade guns in position for use of 3rd Lon Bde.	
	[illegible]		~~[illegible]~~ First sections of batteries moved off from wagon lines & travelled during night.	
LIERES	26/1/16	4 AM	First sections of batteries arrived & went into billets previously occupied by 3rd Lon Bde	
"	"		Amn Column moved from HOUCHIN	
			Bde HQ established at LIERES	
From No 7		Evening	Remaining sections of batteries withdrawn on relief by 3rd Lon Bde. Guns left in position.	
LIERES	27/1/16	4 AM	Remaining sections arrived & went into billets	

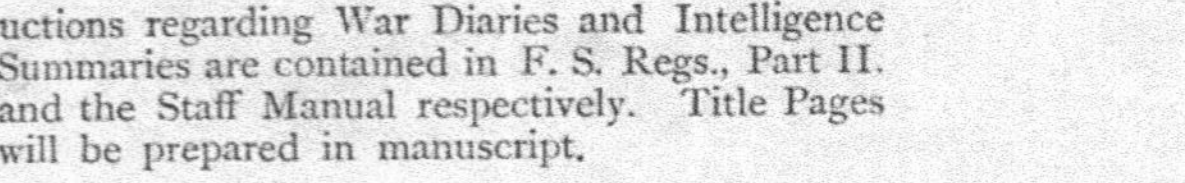

1875 Wt. W593/826 1,000,000 4/15 J.B.C. & A. A.D.S.S./Forms/C. 2118.

1/1st LONDON BRIGADE RFA (TF)

Army Form C. 2118.

Instructions regarding War Diaries and Intelligence Summaries are contained in F. S. Regs., Part II. and the Staff Manual respectively. Title Pages will be prepared in manuscript.

WAR DIARY
or
~~INTELLIGENCE~~ SUMMARY
(Erase heading not required.)

Place	Date	Hour	Summary of Events and Information	Remarks and references to Appendices
LIERES	24.2.16	MORNING	Brigade left 16th Division for 56th Division, proceeding to BERGUETTE where it entrained, thence by rail to PONT-REMY for detrainment.	
FONTAINE-SUR-SOMME	24.2.16 to 25.2.16	11 P.M. to 9 A.M.	Brigade arrived after detrainment & went into billets.	
HALLOY-LES-PERNOIS	27.2.16	3 PM	Brigade arrived and went into billets, having marched via LONGPRE with 167th INF. BDE. group, due to move of 56th Division on its way to join remainder of 6th Corps.	

[illegible] Major

~~LT. COL.~~ COMDG.
1st LONDON BRIGADE, ROYAL FIELD ARTILLERY.

1/1st LONDON BRIGADE RFA (T.F.)

WAR DIARY FOR MARCH 1916

56th from 16th 24.2.16.

1/1 London Bde R.F.A.

Vol IV

56

Instructions regarding War Diaries and Intelligence Summaries are contained in F. S. Regs., Part II. and the Staff Manual respectively. Title Pages will be prepared in manuscript.

WAR DIARY
or
INTELLIGENCE SUMMARY
(Erase heading not required.)

1/1st LONDON BRIGADE R.F.A. (T.F.)

Army Form C. 2118

Place	Date	Hour	Summary of Events and Information	Remarks and references to Appendices
CANDAS	12/3/16	12.30 P.M.	Brigade arrived and went into billets, having moved from HALLOY-LES-PERNOIS under 56th Divisional Orders en route for VIth CORPS area.	
REBREUVE-SUR-CANCHE + REBREUVIETTE	14/3/16	2.30 P.M.	Brigade arrived and went into billets in area S. of RIVER CANCHE (2nd Battery at REBREUVIETTE).	
REBREUVE S/C	18/3/16		MAJOR H N. CLARK (commanding 3rd CITY OF LONDON BATTERY) proceeded to ENGLAND to take up a command at home.	
"	19/3/16		CAPT. G. C. J. BRADY (BDE AMMn COLUMN) posted to command 3rd BATTERY vice MAJOR H N. CLARK	
	"		CAPT W. L. W. BIRD (1st BATTERY) posted to command BDE. AMMn COLUMN vice CAPT. G C J BRADY.	
ARRAS (VICINITY OF)	22/3/16	10 AM.	Battery Commanders, 1st + 2nd BATTERIES, with two other officers per Battery reported to CRA 14th Division + proceeded to reconnoitre positions in neighbourhood S.W. of ARRAS.	
"	24/3/16		Following above-mentioned reconnaissance the following parties proceeded to selected positions to prepare gun emplacements &c. – 1st Battery – Battery Commander + two other Officers; 42 other ranks 2nd " – do – do ; 40 " "	

L. A. C. Southam

LT: COL; COMDG;

1/1st LONDON BRIGADE. ROYAL FIELD ARTILLERY.

1875 Wt. W593/826 1,000,000 4/15 J.B.C. & A. A.D.S.S./Forms/C. 2118.

ORIGINAL.

56

Vol V

1/1st LONDON BRIGADE R F A

WAR DIARY FOR APRIL 1916

56

Instructions regarding War Diaries and Intelligence Summaries are contained in F. S. Regs., Part II. and the Staff Manual respectively. Title Pages will be prepared in manuscript.

WAR DIARY
~~or~~
~~INTELLIGENCE SUMMARY~~
(Erase heading not required.)

1/1ST LONDON BRIGADE RFA (T.F.)

Army Form C. 2118.

Place	Date	Hour	Summary of Events and Information	Remarks and references to Appendices
ARRAS (VICINITY OF)	2/4/16		Two guns + limbers, 1/2ND City of London Battery, left REBREUVIETTE for party already in line (attached 14TH DIV. ARTY) + were placed during the night in the gun emplacements just prepared	DIARY OF 1/2ND City of LONDON BATTERY RFA is attached
-do-	4/4/16		Two guns + limbers 1/1ST City of London Battery and 302 rounds per gun left REBREUVE for party already in the line (attached 14TH DIV. ARTY) + were placed during the night in gun emplacements just prepared. Ammunition wagons returned to REBREUVE	— 1/1ST City of London Battery RFA has not fired during the month
-do-	5/4/16		Remaining two guns + limbers 1/1ST City of London Battery + 302 rounds per gun left REBREUVE for party in the line + were placed in new gun emplacements during the night. Ammn wagons returned to REBREUVE	
-do-	6/4/16		Ammunition (302 rounds per gun) taken up for the two guns of 1/2ND City of London Battery placed in position during night of 2nd/3rd April. Ammn wagons returned to REBREUVE	
-do-	13/4/16		Remaining section of 1/2ND City of London Battery + 657 rounds left REBREUVIETTE for the party in the line. Guns placed in the new gun emplacements + ammunition dumped during night. Ammunition wagons returned to REBREUVE	
FREVENT	15/4/16	7 PM	93RD BATTERY RFA (commanded by MAJOR G. S. COOPER) + sub section of BDE AMMN COLUMN arrived by train, to make Brigade up to strength of four 4-gun Batteries (New Establishment) and marched into billets at REBREUVIETTE.	
ARRAS (VICINITY OF)	19/4/16		O.C. Bde. with Adjutant + other Officers, proceeded to reconnoitre positions in the line, at present occupied by 14TH DIV ARTY.	
-do-	26/4/16		O.C. Bde. with Adjutant + other Officers, made further reconnaissance of positions occupied by 14TH DIV ARTY.	

L. A. C. Southam
LT: COL; COMDG,
1/1ST LONDON BRIGADE, ROYAL FIELD ARTILLERY.

ORIGINAL

APRIL 1916

1/2nd CITY OF LONDON BATTERY RFA

Army Form C. 2118

Instructions regarding War Diaries and Intelligence Summaries are contained in F. S. Regs., Part II. and the Staff Manual respectively. Title Pages will be prepared in manuscript.

WAR DIARY
or
~~INTELLIGENCE SUMMARY~~
(Erase heading not required.)

Place	Date	Hour	Summary of Events and Information	Remarks and references to Appendices
ARRAS	1.4.16		Work on Left Section positions being sufficiently advanced the two guns of this section were sent up for. ~~Left X~~.	
	2.4.16	9pm.	Guns arrived under charge of Lieut. Redfern and were placed into position. Communication was established with Observation Station.	
	3.4.16		Adverse atmospheric conditions made observation difficult.	
	4.4.16		Registration postponed.	
	5.4.16		Two points on German front line W. of BEAURAINS registered for each gun of Left Section.	
	7.4.16	1pm	From the direction of MERCATEL 2 rounds of 5.9" were fired on the cross roads in rear of Left Section positions.	
	9.4.16		Two further points on German front line System W. of BEAURAINS registered for each gun of Left X.	
	13.4.16		Work having been sufficiently advanced at Right X positions, guns were brought up and placed into position.	
	16.4.16		Two further points on German front line system W. of BEAURAINS registered for each gun of Left Section, & checked old registrations.	
	23.4.16		Two further points on German front line W. of BEAURAINS registered by No. of gun.	
	26.4.16		Checked registrations on change of weather & found guns shooting about 10% longer.	
	27.4.16	5pm	Left X fired 40 rounds Shrapnel in combined shoot with other batteries on front line system W. of BEAURAINS with excellent results. No. 3 gun was taken out of its pit & placed into old French position at 7pm. across the road from whence gun could be brought to bear on CAMBRAI Road.	
	28.4.16		Five points on CAMBRAI road registered by No. 3 gun from old French position.	

[signature] Major,
[illegible] London Battery,
[illegible]

1875 Wt. W593/826 1,000,000 4/15 J.B.C. & A. A.D.S.S./Forms/C. 2118.

ORIGINAL

56

280th (CITY OF LONDON) BRIGADE RFA

formerly 1/1st LONDON BRIGADE RFA

Vol 6

WAR DIARY FOR MAY. 1916.

ORIGINAL

Instructions regarding War Diaries and Intelligence Summaries are contained in F. S. Regs., Part II. and the Staff Manual respectively. Title Pages will be prepared in manuscript.

WAR DIARY
~~or~~
~~INTELLIGENCE SUMMARY~~

(Erase heading not required.) For month of MAY 1916

280th (CITY OF LONDON) BDE RFA
formerly 1/1st LONDON BDE RFA

Army Form C. 2118

Place	Date	Hour	Summary of Events and Information	Remarks and references to Appendices
From REBREUVE + REBREUVIETTE to PAS + SOUASTRE	8/5/16	7 AM	Brigade moved out of station owing to 56th Division changing from VI Corps to VII Corps and proceeded to billets at PAS with Bde HQ in SOUASTRE. 1st + 2nd London Batteries, in the line at ARRAS (attached 14 Div. Arty.) remain there until further orders, their wagon lines moving with the Brigade to PAS.	Diary of 1/2nd City of London Bty (now 280/B Bty) is attached.
SAILLY-AU-BOIS	10/5/16	Afternoon	O.C. Bde accompanied C.R.A. on reconnaissance of ground East of SAILLY-AU-BOIS for Battery positions	
do	11/5/16	morning	O.C. Bde with Adjutant + Battery Commanders (3rd London Bty + 93rd Bty RFA) reconnoitred ground and selected two positions.	
	11/5/16		Under authority of W.O. letter No 9/General No/6051 (S.D.2) 6 May 1916 the designation of the Brigade becomes 280th (City of London) Brigade RFA, the nomenclature of Batteries being changed as follows:- 1st City of London Battery to 280/A 2nd " " " 280/B 3 " " " 280/C 93rd Battery RFA 280/D	
SAILLY-AU-BOIS	12/5/16	~~10 AM~~	Two Officers + 40 other Ranks from each Battery (C + D) arrived at positions with material for preliminary work. Billets taken in SAILLY until cover is made.	Map Refce FRANCE SHEET 57D NE Edition 2A 1/20,000
do	13/5/16	morning	Commenced excavations for gun pits - C Bty at K.13.a. 8½. 9½ D Bty at K.14.c. 2½. 1½ Further reconnaissance made in direction of FONQUEVILLERS by OC Bde, Adjutant, + Officer of B Bty for positions for other Batteries.	
do	16/5/16	morning	Reconnaissance by OC Bde + O.C. B Bty.	
PAS	17/5/16	12 noon	The Bde Ammn Column came under command of OC 56 Div. Ammn Column in accordance with scheme of re-organisation of Bde + Div Ammn Columns. (Auth. G.H.Q memo O.B. 818 of 6/5/16).	
SAILLY-AU-BOIS	19/5/16	morning	Reconnaissance by OC A Bty.	
do	25/5/16		Preliminary working party of 1 Officer + 15 Other Ranks from B Bty (the Battery itself being still in the line near ARRAS) proceeded to commence digging gun pits at K.2.a 6.3. Billets taken in SAILLY until cover is made.	

1875 Wt. W593/826 1,000,000 4/15 J.B.C. & A. A.D.S.S./Forms/C. 2118.

280TH (CITY OF LONDON) BDE RFA
formerly 1/1ST LONDON BDE RFA

Army Form C. 2118

Instructions regarding War Diaries and Intelligence Summaries are contained in F. S. Regs., Part II. and the Staff Manual respectively. Title Pages will be prepared in manuscript.

WAR DIARY

~~or~~

~~INTELLIGENCE SUMMARY~~

(Erase heading not required.) For month of MAY 1916 (SHEET 2)

Place	Date	Hour	Summary of Events and Information	Remarks and references to Appendices
SAILLY-AU-BOIS + PAS	28/5/16	1 P.M.	280/D Battery (previously 93rd Battery RFA) transferred to 283 Bde as 283/A Battery, but remains at disposal of OC 280 Bde for digging & preparing positions.	
HEBUTERNE + PAS	28/5/16	1 P.M.	283/B Battery (previously 1/11th LONDON (HOW.) Battery) under command of CAPT. E.R.C. WARRENS, transferred to this Brigade & re-numbered 280/D Battery. This Battery is engaged in preparing positions in HEBUTERNE, at K.9.c.6.4. Wagon line at PAS.	
SAILLY-AU-BOIS	30/5/16		Preliminary working party of 1 Officer + 12 Other Ranks from A Bty (the Battery itself being still in line near ARRAS) commenced work on position at K.14.c.2½.4½. Billets taken in SAILLY until cover is made.	

31 – 5. 1916

L. A. C. Southam
Col.
Comdg 280th (City of London) Bde RFA

1875 Wt. W593/826 1,000,000 4/15 J.B.C. & A. A.D.S.S./Forms/C. 2118.

WAR DIARY
or
INTELLIGENCE SUMMARY
(Erase heading not required.)

280/B Battery RFA (formerly 1/2nd City of London Battery RFA)

Army Form C. 2118.

Instructions regarding War Diaries and Intelligence Summaries are contained in F. S. Regs., Part II. and the Staff Manual respectively. Title Pages will be prepared in manuscript.

Place	Date	Hour	Summary of Events and Information	Remarks and references to Appendices
ARRAS	1.5.16	5 p.m.	Fired 40 rds H.E. in a combined Group shoot on the enemy front line trenches W. of BEAURAINS	
		7.30"	20 rds Shrapnel were fired on the CAMBRAI RD.	
	2.5.16	5 p.m.	Existing registrations on CAMBRAI RD were checked and a further point registered.	
		6.30"	Small party of enemy were observed on CAMBRAI RD: 2 rds. Shrapnel were fired which dispersed them.	
	3.5.16	7 p.m.	The CAMBRAI RD kept under observation. A small working party was engaged & dispersed.	
	5.5.16		Fired 9 rds Shrapnel in special test on H 19 C. 3.8½, with other Batteries.	
	7.5.16		Fired on working party on CAMBRAI RD.	
	8.5.16		ditto	
	13.5.16		Participated in combined shoot directed against G.35. d. 6. 1.	
	17.5.16		Participated in Group shoot on BEAURAINS trenches at about M.4 d. 7.6 & M. 4. d. 7.10.	
	20.5.16		Participated in Group shoot on enemy front line & support trenches from M.4 d. 6 4 6 to ACHICOURT BEAURAINS RD	
	26.5.16	3.0 p.m.	Group shoot on trenches from M.4 d. 6. 9½ to M.5 a 5.6½.	
	29.5.16	3.0 p.m.	Group shoot on Sap at G.36. C. 0 6. Fired 300 rds Shrapnel, wire cutting front cut in hostile wire in front of Sap. Fired 100 rds Shrapnel, wire cutting lane of 15 yards	

F. W. Fisher Lt
for O.C. 2nd City of London Battery,
Royal Field Artillery.

2449 Wt. W14957/M90 750,000 1/16 J.B.C. & A. Forms/C.2118/12.

ORIGINAL

56

Vol 7

WAR DIARY FOR JUNE 1916

280TH (CITY OF LONDON) BDE R.F.A (TF)

Instructions regarding War Diaries and Intelligence Summaries are contained in F. S. Regs., Part II. and the Staff Manual respectively. Title Pages will be prepared in manuscript.

WAR DIARY
~~or~~
~~INTELLIGENCE SUMMARY~~
(Erase heading not required.)

280TH (CITY OF LONDON) BDE. RFA (T.F) — Army Form C. 2118

JUNE 1916

Place	Date	Hour	Summary of Events and Information	Remarks and references to Appendices
From vicinity of ARRAS to PAS	1/2 June 1916	During night	280/A & 280/B Batteries (temporarily attached to VII Corps) withdrew from positions in vicinity of ARRAS.	
PAS	2/3 June 1916	During night	280/A & 280/B Batteries marched from WANQUETIN to PAS to rejoin Brigade	
Vicinity of SAILLY & HEBUTERNE	3/6/16		Further parties of 280/A & 280/B Batteries proceeded to augment initial parties preparing gun positions. All Batteries continuing preparation of positions; 93rd Battery attached for such purpose; 280/D (How) Battery temporarily detached for tactical work and in action at HEBUTERNE (See War Diary for May – entries on 28/5/16.)	
do			280/B Battery ordered by 56 DIV. ARTY to hand over position already commenced & start fresh position at E. 26. a. 40. 15.	
do	9/6/16	night	280/C Battery gave up position in preparation & came into action at E. 25. a. 65. 00 taking over position & guns of 109th Battery RFA being temporarily attached to the group in action	
	14/6/16		Northern Group, 56 DIV. ARTY. in course of formation – to consist of 93rd 280/A 280/B and 280/C 18 pr Batteries and 282/D (4.5 How) Bty	
PAS to HENU	15/6/16	morning	Wagon lines moved from PAS to HENU, arriving 12 noon	
Vicinity of SAILLY & HEBUTERNE	15/16 June	night	3 guns 282/D Bty taken into position.	
	16/6/16	10 AM	Brigade (& northern Group) H.Q. established at SAILLY, having moved up from SOUASTRE. Horses & details left at SOUASTRE	
do	do	12.45 to 1.30 PM	Registration carried out by 282/D Battery – 24 rounds.	
	16/17 June	night	Remaining guns of 282/D Bty & all guns of 93rd Bty brought into position	
	17/6/16	9.30 to 11.5 AM	Registration by 282/D Bty – 24 rounds	
		11.30 AM to 4 PM	do " 93rd Bty – 95 "	

1875 Wt. W593/826 1,000,000 4/15 J.B.C. & A. A.D.S.S./Forms/C. 2118.

280th (CITY OF LONDON) BDE RFA (T.F)

Army Form C. 2118

Instructions regarding War Diaries and Intelligence Summaries are contained in F. S. Regs., Part II. and the Staff Manual respectively. Title Pages will be prepared in manuscript.

WAR DIARY

~~or~~

~~INTELLIGENCE SUMMARY~~

(Erase heading not required.)

JUNE 1916 (Sheet ii)

Place	Date	Hour	Summary of Events and Information	Remarks and references to Appendices
Vicinity of SAILLY & HEBUTERNE	17/18 June 1916	night	Guns of 280/A & 28/B Batteries brought into position	
	18/6/16	9 AM	Northern Artillery Group, 56 DIV. ARTY. takes over (Y sector) section of line FIT to FEVER facing N.E side of HEBUTERNE. 280/C Bty rejoins group.	
		12 noon to 6 PM	Registration carried out by 282/D Bty – 38 rounds; 280/B Bty – 62 rounds; 280/C Bty – 33 rounds; 93rd Bty – 108 rounds.	
		11.20 PM	Salvo by 280/C Bty as retaliation, at request of Infantry.	
	19/6/16	12.45 to 1.15 AM	282/D fired on MINENWERFER at request of Infantry, & again at various times during ensuing day	
		11.45 to 11.55 AM	282/D fired 13 rounds checking registration.	
		2 to 4 PM	Registration by 93rd Bty – 37 rounds.	
			280/A Battery ordered to leave group for Wire-cutting group; position to be evacuated. Reconnaissance made for new position	See War Diary of 280/A Bty (while with Wire cutting Group 56 DA) for further particulars
	20/6/16	1.20 to 4.20 PM	282/D Bty – Checking registration, particularly on position of MINENWERFER observed at K5c 00.15 – 20 rounds	
		3 to 4 PM	280/B Bty Registration of enemy front line system, 52 rounds.	
	21/6/16	morning	282/D Bty fired on MINENWERFER at various times at request of Infantry	
		Afternoon	93 Bty fired 61 rounds – 18 Retaliation; 43 verification of previously registered targets	
			280/B Bty – 39 " – Registration of 2nd & 3rd lines & support trenches.	
	22/6/16	12.10 AM to 12.45 AM	282/D Bty – 10 " – on MINENWERFER, K5c 00 25 in retaliation	
			Conference OC group & Bty Commanders re scheme for forthcoming active operations	
	23/6/16	12 noon	93 Bty fired 32 rounds – verification of registrations.	
		3.30 to 5 PM	93rd Bty + 282/D fired 23 rounds on points in conjunction with registration of Heavy guns.	
		3.30 to 7.30 PM	280/B fired 48 rounds & 280/C 37 rounds – Registration of selected points in zone.	
		midnight	282/D & 280/C fired 4 & 9 rounds respectively at request of infantry	

1875 Wt. W593/826 1,000,000 4/15 J.B.C. & A. A.D.S.S./Forms/C. 2118.

280TH (CITY OF LONDON) BDE RFA (TF)

Army Form C. 2118

Instructions regarding War Diaries and Intelligence Summaries are contained in F. S. Regs., Part II and the Staff Manual respectively. Title Pages will be prepared in manuscript.

WAR DIARY

~~or~~

~~INTELLIGENCE SUMMARY~~

(Erase heading not required.)

JUNE 1916 (Sheet iii)

Place	Date	Hour	Summary of Events and Information	Remarks and references to Appendices
Vicinity of SAILLY & HEBUTERNE	24/6/16		"U" day. Scheme of active operations commenced. Programme carried out according to Schedule attached to Northern Group Operation Order No 1	Appx No 1 N. Group Opn Order No 1 dated 22/6/16
	24/25	June night	Wire cut by wire cutting group during day kept open at night.	
	25/6/16		"V" day. Programme carried out. Desultory hostile shelling during day – some attention paid to our O.P's. Group HQ at northern end of SAILLY shelled with 4.2 & 5.9 at 2.10 & 2.45 PM	Appx No 2 N. Group Opn Order No 2 dated 23/6/16
	25/26	June night	Hostile Artillery fairly quiet through night, increasing at 5 AM with 4.2 & 5.9 on our front line & above OP's	
	26/6/16		"W" day. Programme carried out. Enemy answered smoke (see Schedule) with heavy bombardment of front line trenches. Also barraged the SAILLY-FONQUEVILLERS road. Also barrage of 4.2 on BAYENCOURT-SAILLY road during morning. Enemy shelled SAILLY 1.5 PM & vicinity of BAYENCOURT 1.20 P.M Enemy shelled HEBUTERNE & front line 8.35 to 9.30 PM, front line & communication trenches 11.30 PM to 12.15 AM & again from 2 to 2.45 AM	
	27/6/16	4.45 AM	in answer to our smoke (see schedule) much heavier shelling by enemy of our old & new front lines.	Appx No 3 N. Group Opn Order No 3 dated 27/6/16
	"		"X" day. Programme again carried out. SAILLY shelled by enemy 8 AM. Heavy hostile shelling 11 AM to 1 PM of front & second line trenches	
		6.30 PM	Very heavy hostile shelling in retaliation for our bombardment. Hostile shelling continuous but not so heavy during remainder of day.	
	27/28	June night	Infantry called for retaliation (1.7 AM). Heavy hostile shelling on Z hedge about 3.50 AM & again at 7 AM in front of NAMELESS FARM	
	28/6/16		"Y" day. Programme proceeded with. Guns of the Group showing signs of the strain & requiring constant attention of artificers. Great demand for inner & outer springs Fairly quiet on front line – moderate hostile fire near battery positions Quiet night	

1875 Wt. W593/826 1,000,000 4/15 J.B.C. & A. A.D.S.S./Forms/C. 2118.

ORIGINAL

56

280 Bde RFA
Appendix 6
Vol 7

WAR DIARIES — JUNE 1916

280/A Battery }
280/D Battery } during periods of detachment (for tactical purposes) from 280th Brigade RFA

280th (City of London) BDE RFA (T.F.)

Army Form C. 2118

Instructions regarding War Diaries and Intelligence Summaries are contained in F. S. Regs., Part II. and the Staff Manual respectively. Title Pages will be prepared in manuscript.

WAR DIARY
or
~~INTELLIGENCE SUMMARY~~

(Erase heading not required.)

Sheet IV

Place	Date	Hour	Summary of Events and Information	Remarks and references to Appendices
Vicinity of SAILLY + HEBUTERNE	29/6/16		Called "Y 1" day – period of operation extended. Fresh programme arranged for Y 1 and Y 2 days. See Northern Group Operation Order No 4 with Schedules.	Appx No. 4 N. Group Opn. Order No. 4 dated 29/6/16
			Hostile Artillery fairly quiet.	
	30/6/16		"Y 2" day. Commenced day with "Y 2" programme, but changed on receipt of information that tomorrow (1st July) will be "Z" day & that the original programme for the original "Y" day is to be carried out today in preparation for "Z" day. Programme carried out accordingly.	
			Guns showing increasing signs of strain & temporarily going out of action. New parts to replace damaged (principally springs, inner rods) in constant demand & fitted as obtained.	
			Desultory hostile shelling of our front & second line increasing at 10 AM, again from 3. PM to 4.30 PM and at 6.30 PM.	
		7 PM	O.C. Group with LIEUT H.V. HUMMEL (280/B Bty) as Group HQ Observing Officer, & 2/LIEUT GOODYER, Orderly Officer (for communications) left for Advanced Group HQ attached to G.O.C. 169th INF BDE, in readiness for "Z" day.	

L. A. C. Southam
Lt Col
Comdg 280th (City of London) Bde R.F.A.

ORIGINAL

280/A BATTERY RFA

Army Form C. 2118

Instructions regarding War Diaries and Intelligence Summaries are contained in F. S. Regs., Part II. and the Staff Manual respectively. Title Pages will be prepared in manuscript.

WAR DIARY
or
~~INTELLIGENCE SUMMARY~~

(Erase heading not required.)

JUNE 1916

Place	Date	Hour	Summary of Events and Information	Remarks and references to Appendices
VICINITY OF HEBUTERNE	19/6/16	3:30 PM	Received orders to vacate position K14C25.50 reconnoitre position for wire cutting. Reconnoitred position & decided to come into action at K8A75.15	REFERENCE 1/10,000 2B HEBUTERNE (TRENCH)
do	20/6/16		Started making gun positions at K8a75.15.	
do	21/6/16		Making gun positions	
do	22/6/16		Making gun positions. Guns in position during night 22/23rd	
do	23/6/16		Making gun positions. Registered wire at K4.d70.20 K4 d 80.10.	
do	24/6/16		Cut wire front line K4d70.20 K4 d 80.10	
do	25/6/16		Cut wire front line and second line K4a10.70 K4d80.10 K4d90.34 K5a10.13. Major H.P.Jones & Lieut F.K. Headington wounded whilst on duty at O.P.	
do	26/6/16		Bty under command of Capt W.E.W. Bird. Cut wire K4d90.34 K5a10.13 K5a30.50 K5a32.42	
do	27/6/16		Cut wire (Quadrilateral) K5a70.15, 73.35 to K5a85.15 87.25. Lieut R.B. Westmacott wounded whilst on duty at O.P.	(REFERENCE GOMMECOURT) 1/5,000
do	28/6/16		Cut lane in wire K5C30.60	
do	29/6/16		Cut wire K4d70.20. K4d80.10 K4d90.34. K5a10.13.	
do	30/6/16	7:30 AM	~~Came under order NORTHERN GROUP~~	

H.P. Jones Major
A/280 (City of London) Bde RFA

1875 Wt. W593/826 1,000,000 4/15 J.B.C. & A. A.D.S.S./Forms/C. 2118.

ORIGINAL

280/D (HOW) BATTERY R.F.A.

Army Form C. 2118

Instructions regarding War Diaries and Intelligence Summaries are contained in F. S. Regs., Part II. and the Staff Manual respectively. Title Pages will be prepared in manuscript.

WAR DIARY
or
INTELLIGENCE SUMMARY
(Erase heading not required.)

JUNE 1916

Place	Date	Hour	Summary of Events and Information	Remarks and references to Appendices
HEBUTERNE	1st		Gun Pits practically completed also a telephonists Dug-out.	
	2nd		One man was slightly wounded by Splinters from a 4.2" H.E. Shell.	
	3rd	Night	No 1 & No 2 Guns were brought into Action	
	4th		Two Shrapnel Proof O.P's constructed in our Support Line and a Shell Proof Tunnel excavated to a distance of 50 feet from one of these O.P's beyond KLEIBER HEDGE, giving an excellent view of the whole of the Sector. A further O.P. was constructed at the Junction of YANKEE STREET and our old Front Line. Wires with metallic circuits were laid out to these and with the exception of a few yards of Trench work, all wires were buried.	
			No 1 & No 2 Guns were registered on their Zero Lines	
	5th	Night	No 3 Gun was brought into action	
	6th		No 3 Gun was registered on Zero Line	
	10th	Night	No 4 Gun was brought into action	
	11th		No 4 Gun was registered on Zero Line	
	15th		The Battery was placed in Wire Cutting Group and one Section was detailed to work under 39th H.A.G. for Counter-Battery Shooting. A great number of Hostile Batteries were registered by Aeroplane by this Section and some 35 important points in the enemy's Trenches registered by the other Section	
	22nd		The whole of the Battery was placed under 39. H.A.G on Counter-Battery work	
	25th		No 2 Gun had a premature 30 feet from the muzzle but fortunately this was only a powder Shell.	

Instructions regarding War Diaries and Intelligence Summaries are contained in F. S. Regs., Part II. and the Staff Manual respectively. Title Pages will be prepared in manuscript.

WAR DIARY or INTELLIGENCE SUMMARY

(Erase heading not required.)

280/D (HOW) BATTERY RFA

JUNE 1916

(Sheet II)

Army Form C. 2118

Place	Date	Hour	Summary of Events and Information	Remarks and references to Appendices
HEBUTERNE	25th.		The Structural work of the Battery was completed, 4 Gun Pits. 4 - 8 ft x 20 ft Dug-outs, a Telephone Exchange + Wireless Ground Station Dug-out constructed together with 2 Ammunition Pits capable of holding, 2000 rounds and also accomodation for Officers. The work has been considerably handicapped by inclement weather and the difficulty of transporting material. 3600 Shells have been dumped in the Battery Positions.	
	29th.	Night	No. 1 Gun was damaged by a 77 mm. Shrapnel Shell. Fortunately, it only put the Gun out of action for 2 or 3 hours.	
	30th.		Since the Battery was placed entirely on Counter Battery work, we have engaged about 30 hostile Battery Targets Considerable difficulty has been experienced on account of the different Ballistic power of N.C.T. + Cordite to Ballistite. It is my experience that N.C.T + Cordite range about 100 yards less than Ballistite but this varies considerably with the different charges and as changes of Barometer + Thermometer affect each charge differently, the question of calibration has become very difficult. I cannot conclude with out paying a very high tribute to the manner in which all Ranks, both in the Battery Position + at the Wagon Line have done their work often under most adverse circumstances and it is entirely due to this hearty cooperation, that we have been able to complete what seems to be a most satisfactory months work.	

[illegible signature]
Captain

1875 Wt. W593/826 1,000,000 4/15 J.B.C. & A. A.D.S.S./Forms/C. 2118.

APP x No (1)   G. 55

SECRET

OPERATION ORDERS No:1. - NORTHERN GROUP

BY LIEUT.COLONEL L.A.C.SOUTHAM.,

COMMANDING NORTHERN GROUP.   22nd June 1916.

1. OPERATIONS

The Operations referred to in these orders will take place on successive days designated "U","V","W","X","Y","Z".

O.C.Batteries are responsible that every Officer under their command knows the exact programme for his Battery so that if communications break, the Battery can still carry on according to time table until communications can be re-established. O.C.Batteries are further responsible that all watches used by Officers, Nos.I and Telephone Operators are regularly synchronised. The importance of keeping these Operation Orders absolutely secret amongst Officers until Z day is to be clearly explained to all concerned. On "Z" day a written copy of time table will be in possession of each No.1.

2. CONSTITUTION

The Northern Group is constituted as follows :-

93rd Battery R.F.A.)
B/280 " ") 18 pdr.
C/280 " ")
D/282 4.5" How.Bty "
A/280 Battery R.F.A. (18 pdr) will come under the orders of Northern Group at zero on Z.day.

Group Headquarters on "Z" day will be at 169th Infantry Brigade Headquarters, HEBUTERNE.

3. TASKS

A Schedule of the tasks of Batteries on U,V,W,X,Y,Z, days is attached.

Times must be adhered to and not number of rounds which latter are a guide and not the controlling factor.

S/CRA/135/25 × Altered for X & Y days

~~From 4 p.m. to 4.30 p.m.~~ daily except "Z" day, all firing will cease to enable photographs to be taken.

× from 5 to 5.30 PM X day (27th)
3 " 3.30 PM Y " (28)

4. Z O N E S

Zones on U,V,W,X,Y, days are allotted to Batteries as under. Those on "Z" day are contained in the Schedule.

Schedule of Zones

93rd Battery — Communication trenches in GOMMECOURT PARK; K.4.a.95.30. to K.4.b.4.2; FIR, EEL, FIBRE, Communication trench to the MAZE, EXE, ERIN; EMS to K.5.a.55.20; ETCH to Junction with EMS.

280/B Battery — K.4.b.4.3. to K.4.d.65.80 to K.5.c.10.95 to K.4.b.95.30. FEUD, FELLOW, FELL, FIST (K.4a.85.35) to FIBRE, the MAZE, ECK, FEAST, FEMALE.

280/C Battery — FIG, FISH, FIRM, FEN, FERRET, FERN, FEVER, FINE, FIGHT, EMDEN, FEED, FEINT.

282/D (Hows) — Trench Junctions of EXE, EMS, ETCH, with 1st, 2nd and 3rd Lines;
The MAZE, CEMETERY CORNER (K.4.d.9.7) Trench Junctions beyond the 3rd Line, viz; EMS with FILLET; ETCH with EMS.

/1.

4. ZONES (CONT)

A list of O.P's is attached. The bombardment of GOMMECOURT PARK and portions of village within the front line trench system will be comparatively light.

5. FRONT LINE SYSTEM

The front line system of Northern Group for these operations is as under :-

Front Line Trench from K.4.c.1.7. to the Junction FEVER - EPTE thence up EPTE to junction with FELL thence to junction FILM - EAE then K.4.b.5.0. to K.4.b.4.2. to K.4.d.10.95. to K.4.a.95.30 to K.4.a.6.4 and all trenches inside this except Trench from K.4.a.40.05. to K.4.a. 6.4. which will not be dealt with. The Term Front Line System also includes:- ETCH from its junction with FELL to its junction with EMS, and EMS from K.5.c.10.85. to K.5.a.55.50.

6. NIGHT LINES

Except when carrying out tasks, Batteries now holding the line will be laid on night lines as at present.

7. LIAISON & OBSERVERS

Officers and details for Liaison and O.P's will be detailed from Batteries by Group Headquarters.

8. NIGHT FIRING

Orders as to times of night firing will be issued by Group Headquarters. The night will normally be reckoned as from 9 p.m. to 3 a.m.

9. CONDUCT OF FIRE

All intervals will be as irregular as possible. By night firing will be by salvoes. Sweeping and searching will be extensively employed and the corrector will be varied with T.S.

In the intense bombardments of selected points Howitzer fire willbe by Battery or Section salvoes.

Rates of fire should be adjusted so as to ensure that guns requiring washing out, etc, are not out of action simultaneously if it can be avoided.

10. RETURNS - AMMUNITION

Returns of ammunition on hand are due at Group Headquarters at 12 noon and 8 p.m. daily during the operations. These returns should be as nearly as possible accurate and to ensure this an intelligent N.C.O. or man should be specially detailed to watch expenditure and prepare the return for the Battery Commander.

The punctual rendering of this return is absolutely necessary as upon it and its approximate accuracy the proper supply of ammunition largely depends.

[signature]

Lieut.,
Adjutant, NORTHERN GROUP.

10 copies taken off.

Copies to - 56 D.A.
O.C. Southern Group
280/A
280/B
280/C
93
282/D
OC

WD

(3)

S C H E D U L E

Day.	Unit.	Objective.	Ammunition. A.	A.X.
U.	All Batteries.	<u>By Day</u> Fire only if required by enemy's attitude.		
		<u>By Night</u>		
	93rd.	Trakks in K.4.b. Railway K.5.a.1.6.to K.5.b.7.9. Indus Trench from K.4.b.60.75 to K.5.b.50.98.	500	
	280/B.	Road K.4.b.9.8.to K.5.b.6.1.	300	
	280/C.	Front Line wire FEN to FEVER inclusive.	200.	

Day.	Unit.	Objective.	A.	A.X.
V.		<u>By Day</u>		
	93rd 280/B. 280/C.	Object Bombardment of Front Line System of Trenches and communication Trenches.		650. 650. 700.
	282/D (Hows)	Trench Junctions and selected points 4 a.m.to 10 p.m. One section constantly in action. 12 noon to 12.30 p.m.co-operative fire on O.P's with 93rd Battery.		~~302~~ 254 B.X.
		7.15.p.m.Bombardment of BUCQUOY in co-operation with H.A.for 5 minutes.		~~48~~ 40 B.X.
	280/B 280/C	12 noon to 12.30.p.m. Bombardment of 2nd Line trenches to allow Mortars to register	50	200 each
	93rd	12 noon to 12.30 p.m.Co-operation bombardment of O.P's with How.Battery (282/D)	300	100.
		<u>By Night</u>		
	93rd	As on U.night.	400	
	280/B	As on U night.	400	
	280/C	Keeping open wire as on U night. Dump at K.4.b.8.7.	600.	

---

(4)

S C H E D U L E (CONT)

W. Day.	Unit.	Objective.	Ammunition A.	Ammunition A.X.
		By Day		
W	280/B.	Bombardment on Front Line System.	~~[illegible]~~	600
	280/C.		~~[illegible]~~	600
	93rd.		~~[illegible]~~	360
	282/D (Hows)	As on ~~X~~ day.		~~100~~ B.X. 75
	All Batteries.	9.45 a.m. to 10.25 a.m. Intense Bombardment in conjunction with H.A. and smoke, bombardment increasing in intensity during last ~~15~~ 10 minutes. Smoke discharge 10.15 am to 10.25 am		
		10.25 a.m. Batteries will lift for 5 minutes on to trenches as under :		
	93rd	EMS, from Junction with FEUD to K.5.a.6.4.	250	300
	280/B.	EAE from Junctions with FILM to Junction with ETCH.	Each Bty.	
	280/C.	EMS from K.5.a.5.2. to junction with EATE.		
	282/D (Hows)	K.5.a.8.1. and K.5.a.9.3. (Trench Junctions)		~~200~~ BX. 150
		10.30 a.m.		
	18 pdr Btys.	On Front Line system for 5 minutes with Shrapnel.		
		By Night		
	93rd	Railway K5 a 1.6 to K 5 b. 7.9 Indus trench from K.4 b 60.75 to K.5 b. 50.98	400.	
	280/B	Road K.4. b. 98 to K.5. b. 6.1 ~~as on V night.~~	800.	
	280/C	Tracks in K.4. b. Dump at K.4.b.8.7	800.	
	282/D (Hows)	K.5.a.7.7. K.6.a.4.8. K.6.a.6.9. E.26.d.2.2.		~~100~~ BX 75

- - - - - - - - - - - - - - - - -

(5)

S C H E D U L E (CONT)

X. DAY.	Unit.	Objective.	Ammunition A.	Ammunition A.X.
		BY DAY		
	280/C)			700
	93rd)			900
	280/B)	AS ON W. DAY.		900
	282/D)			~~150~~ 105 B.X
	(Hows))			
	All Btys.	5.~~5~~15 a.m. to 5.~~45~~55 a.m. Intense bombardment in co-operation with smoke, to increase in intensity during last ~~15~~ 10 minutes. Smoke discharge 5.45 to 5.55 am		
		Ammn. (93rd.	250	
		(280/B & C.		250(each)
		(282/D (Hows)		~~100~~ 70 B.X.
		(6.25 pm - 7.5. pm. (Intense bombardment as above with H.A. no smoke		
		(7.5. pm. (Lift (for 5 minutes) as on W.day without returning to front system.		
		(93rd.	~~250~~	100
		(280/B.	200	~~400~~ (each)
		(280/C	150	~~500~~
		(282/D (Hows) as V.day		~~300~~ 210 B.X.
		BY NIGHT		
	93rd)		370	
	280/B)	AS ON W. NIGHT,	600	
	280/C)		600	
	282/D	On selected points.		~~100~~ 70 B.X.

5

S C H E D U L E (CONT)

Y. DAY.	~~Unit.~~	Objective.	Ammunition A.	A.X.
		BY DAY		
	280/B) 280/C) 93rd)	Bombardment of Front Line System.	~~850~~ 860 ~~850~~ 860 ~~850~~ 860	
	282/D (Hows)	O.P's (Battery Salvoes)	~~302~~ B.X. 233	
	ALL	6.45 - 7.25 a.m. Intense bombardment in co-operation with smoke to increase in intensity during last ~~15~~ 10 minutes. Smoke discharge 7.15 am to 7.25 am		
		280/B.	150	250
		280/C	150	250
		93rd	200	250
		282/D (Hows)		~~185~~ B.X. 96
	282/D (Hows)	8 15.a.m.3 minutes bombardment of BUCQUOY in co-operation with H. A.		~~48~~ B.X. 37
	93rd) 280/B) 280/C) 282/D) (Hows))	4.45 - 5.25 p.m. Intense bombardment and co-operation with H.A. and smoke to increase in intensity during last ~~15~~ 10 minutes. no smoke 5.25 p.m. Lift for 5 minutes as on X. day. 5.30 p.m. Go back to front line system.	300 350 350	300 350 350 ~~300~~ B.X. 231
		BY NIGHT		
	93rd) 280/B) 280/C)	As on X.night	900 800 1000	
	282/D (Hows)	As on W.Night.		~~100~~ B.X. 77

---

(7)

S C H E D U L E (CONT)

"Z" DAY.	Unit.	Objective.	Ammunition.	
		ZONES "Z" DAY	A	AX
		280/C Battery. K.4.c.3.8.-K.4.c.9.4-K.4.d.9.5.- FIR, FEN, FERRET, and 2nd and 3rd Line as far as EMS.		
		280/B Battery FERN, FEVER. 2nd & 3rd Lines between EMS & EPTE.		
		93rd Battery As on other days with EPTE.		
		Before minus 65 minutes		
	93rd	Bombardment of Front Line System, barrage ETCH and EMS.	250	100
	280/B)	Bombard Front Line System.	100	200
	280/C)		100	250
	282/D (Hows)	ditto and O.P's.		~~350~~ BA 301
		Minus 65 minutes to Zero		
	ALL	Intense bombardment of Front Line System. After Zero as per orders attached.	18 prs. 560 / Hows.	1000 each / ~~1150~~ BA 989
		At Zero		
	ALL	Barrage on Front Line. Lifts by 50 yard increases up communication trenches to BLUE BARRAGE arriving there at plus 2, remaining there till plus 4 minutes.		
		Plus 4 minutes — Lift to GREEN BARRAGE, up communication trenches by 50 yard increases.		
	~~93rd~~ 280/C	Plus "Z" minutes — Lift off EMS Trench from junction of EMS and FEUD to K.5.a.60.15.	AS	
	280/A	280/A Lifts off ETCH.		
	All	Plus ~~15~~ 17 minutes — Lift to YELLOW BARRAGE.	REQUIRED.	
		Plus 30 minutes — Lift to RED BARRAGE. Howitzer Battery throughout will deal with trench junctions and selected points in each barrage.		

////////////////

SECRET

Appx No. 2

469

OPERATION ORDER No.2. BY LIEUT.COLONEL.L.A.C.SOUTHAM.,

COMMANDING NORTHERN GROUP

23rd June 1916.

1. The following amendments to Operation Order No.1 of 22nd will be incorporated in all copies. The amendments to barrages are with a view to making them clearer to any officer ~~improperly~~ imperfectly acquainted with the complete scheme.

W. By day 282/D (Hows) Delete "As on U.day" and insert "As on V.Day"

W. NIGHT

Delete

93rd.
280/B } As on V.night.
280/C

Insert

93rd Railway K.5.a.1.6.to K.5.b.7.9.
Indus ~~inland~~ trench from K.4.b.60.75 to K.5.b.50.98.

280/B Road K.4.b.9.8.to K.5.b.6.1.

280/C Tracks in K.4.b.
Dump at K.4.b.8.7.

IN BARRAGES

93rd Battery GREEN. Delete "EMS from 200 yards from junction with 3rd Line trench"
and Insert "Ems,north east of 3rd Line trench but not within 200 yards of 3rd line trench"

280/A Battery GREEN Delete "not within ~~2 00~~ 200 yards ~~from~~ of junction of 3rd line trench"
and Insert "North East of 3rd line trench,but not within 200 yards of 3rd line trench.

[signature]

Lieut.,
Adjutant, NORTHERN GROUP.

C.O.'s copy marked –
Adjt –
W.D. –

SECRET

G 70

O.C.,

Batteries

The following will be attached to Operation Order No.1.for addition:-

Wire cutting will be carried out on U,V,W,X,Y,days. Reconnaissances will be carried out by the Infantry during the nights and during the following hours artillery will only fire in rear of the German Front Line System:-

U/V night ... ...11.0.p.m.to 12 midnight.
V/W night ... ... 1.a.m.to 2.0.a.m.
W/X night. ... ...12 midnight to 1.0.a.m.
X/Y night... ... ... 11 p.m.to 12 midnight.

No instructions have yet been received as to the hours on Y/Z nights.

Lieut.,

Adjutant. NORTHERN GROUP.

23.6.16.

SECRET

5100 Copy No. 8 9.100

App^x No 3

OPERATION ORDER No. [illegible] BY [illegible] COMMANDING [illegible]

[illegible] ARTILLERY GROUP.

27th JUNE 1916.

1. AMENDMENTS

The following amendments to instructions for "Z" day after [illegible] have been issued :-

(i) For "[illegible] minutes" substitute "+[illegible] minutes".

(ii) For "+[illegible] minutes" (Time of lift from [illegible] to [illegible]) substitute "+ 17 minutes".

Certificates will be forwarded by Battery Commanders at the earliest possible moment after all instructions or orders have been amended [illegible] in accordance with above, and all Officers have been informed of and understand the alteration in the scheme.

2. O.P.'s and LIAISON

(a) For "Z" day the following details will be required from Batteries:-

O.P. "[illegible]" ..1 Officer .. [illegible]) All from 8 p.m.
O.P. "R" ..1 Officer and Operators..[illegible]) "Y" Night.

Liaison

Group Headquarters..Lieut.[illegible]..[illegible]/B Battery.

Right Battn. (1/9th London (Queen Victoria's Rifles)..
1 Officer,1 N.C.O.,2 Operators with one instrument..
.....................................[illegible] Battery.

Left Battn. 1/5th London (London Rifle Brigade).......
1 Officer,1 N.C.O.,2 Operators with one instrument..
.....................................[illegible] Battery

Centre Battn.1/16th London (Queens Westminster Rifles)..
1 Officer,1 N.C.O., 2 Operators with one instrument..
.....................................[illegible] Battery.

Time for Liaison detail to report will be notified later.

(b) All personnel of above detail must know where Group and [illegible] Headquarters (former Left Battn.HQ [illegible] ([illegible]).),and [illegible] are situated

(c) In previous active operations most valuable general information has been received through forward artillery Officers who should send back to Group Headquarters all information,positive or negative,and affecting the general situation and progress,as often as possible as well as purely artillery messages.

(d) The general scheme will be carefully explained to above Officers and N.C.O's,but a copy must not be in their possession. Tracings of the Group [illegible] will be sent later for their use.

/1.

OPERATION ORDER No: 8. (continued)

3. COMMUNICATIONS.

The Adjutant will remain at Group Exchange (F.O.R.). Further information as to Divisional and alternative communications will be issued.

4. BARRAGES.

The following instructions as to rate of fire and nature of projectile are intended as a guide and not to hamper the discretion of Battery Commanders nor to indicate that guns are to be fired at a more rapid rate than is compatible with accuracy of laying and fuse setting. The actual proportion of "A" and "H.E" must depend on quantity of each dumped.

300 rounds per gun for 18 prs and 250 rounds per gun for 4.5" Hows will be regarded as the "Iron Ration".

18 prs Zero to end of Blue Barrage: T.S.Maximum rate.
To end of Green Barrage....4/5ths T.S. 1/5th H.E. Maximum rate.
Yellow and Red Barrages 4/5ths T.S., 1/5th H.E., 2 rounds per gun per minute or as situation requires.

4.5" Hows.

As for 18 prs. as far as applicable.

Lifts and barrages should be practised.

Lieut.,
Adjutant, NORTHERN GROUP.

Copy No.1. to 93rd.Battery
2. 280/A Battery
3. 289/B "
4. 280/C "
5. 282/D "
6. } CO
7. } Adjt
8. } Retained. WD
9. }
10. }

SECRET App^x No. 4 Copy No 7. G 118

OPERATION ORDER No.4. BY LIEUT. COLONEL L.A.C. SOUTHAM.,

COMMANDING NORTHERN GROUP.

29th JUNE 1916.

1. Today, 29th inst. will be known as Y.1 Day. The 30th inst will be known as Y.2. day.

2. Programmes for various Batteries and allotment of ammunition are attached.

3. There will be a pause of 30 minutes each day to enable photographs to be taken. This pause will be :-

Y.1 Day... ... ... 3 p.m. to 3.30 p.m.

Y.2. Day... ... ... 3.30 p.m. to 4.0. p.m.

4. Heavy Artillery bombardments will take place each day - but these will be without the co-operation of the Divisional Artillery.

5. There will be an intense bombardment by the Divisional Artillery daily, time to be notified later.

6. O.P's

O.P's will be manned as under :-

O.P. "F" From 8 p.m. 29th inst... ... 280/C Battery
From 8 p.m. 30th inst... ... 282/D Battery

O.P. "H" From 8 p.m. 29th inst... ... 280/B Battery
From 8 p.m. 30th inst... ... 93rd Battery.

Acknowledge

H.P. Manley

Lieut.,
Adjutant, NORTHERN GROUP.

Copies to :

No.1. 93rd Battery.
2. 280/B Battery
3. 280/C "
4. 282/D "
5.) OC Group
6.) Retained. Adjt
7.) W.D. Copy
8.) with C.R.A's orders

SECRET

S C H E D U L E

Unit.		Objective.	Ammunition A.	..
Y. 1.	83rd Battery.	**By Day**		
		Bombardment of FRONT LINE SYSTEM, special attention to C.T's beyond junction with 2nd line.	300	4[illegible]
		From 4.40 p.m. to 5.20 p.m. Intense bombardment of FRONT LINE SYSTEM. Bombardment to increase in intensity during last 10 minutes.		
		At 5.15 p.m. lift for 5 minutes on to [illegible] from junction with [illegible] to junction with [illegible], [illegible] from [illegible].60.15 - [illegible].40.	300	1[illegible]
		At 5.20 p.m. return to FRONT LINE SYSTEM.		
		By Night		
		Salvoes on Railway [illegible] - [illegible] and on communication trenches except during prohibited hours.	400.	
Y. 2.		**By Day**		
		Bombardment of FRONT LINE SYSTEM, special attention to C.T's beyond junction with 2nd Line.	300	[illegible]
		From 8.40 a.m. to 9.20 a.m. Intense bombardment of FRONT LINE SYSTEM. Bombardment to increase in intensity during last 10 minutes.	300	80
		~~[illegible] junction with [illegible] to junction with [illegible] from [illegible].60.15 - [illegible].~~	~~[illegible]~~	~~[illegible]~~
		At 9.20 a.m. return to FRONT LINE SYSTEM.		
		By Night		
		As on Y. 1. Night.	400.	
		At 9.15 a.m. lift for 5 minutes on to [illegible] and [illegible] from the junction with [illegible], [illegible], [illegible] to their junction with [illegible] in [illegible].5.D. and [illegible].	XXX	XXX

SECRET

S C H E D U L E

Unit.		Objective.	Ammunition.	
Y. 1.	280/B.	**By Day**		
		Bombardment of FRONT LINE SYSTEM paying more attention to second and 3rd lines. Occasionally search INDUS trench. Barrage night objectives when hazy.	200.	650.
		From 4.40 p.m. to 5.20 p.m. intense bombardment of FRONT LINE SYSTEM, bombardment to increase in intensity during last 10 minutes. At 5.15 p.m. lift for 5 minutes to EXE from K.5.a.65.~~35~~ 40 to K.5.a.95.20. and EMS from K5 a. 9.1 to K 5 d 45 90 At 5.20 p.m. return to FRONT LINE SYSTEM	~~200~~ 300	300
		By night		
		Salvoes on Road K.4.b.9.8. to K.5.b.6.1. INDUS trench from K.4.b.70.75 - K.5.b.50.98. Occasionally on zone in FRONT LINE SYSTEM.	300	----
Y. 2.		**By day**		
		Bombardment of FRONT LINE SYSTEM paying more attention to 2nd and 3rd lines. Occasionally ~~to search 2nd and third line~~ search INDUS trench. Barrage night objectives when hazy.	200	650
		From 8.40 a.m. to 9.20 a.m. intense bombardment of FRONT LINE SYSTEM, bombardment to increase in intensity during last 10 minutes. At 9.15 a.m. lift on to EXE from K.5.a.65.~~35~~ 40 - K.5.a.95.20 ~~and to EMS from junction with ERGH to junction with AFTE.~~ and from K 5 a. 60 15 to K 5 a 9.1	~~250~~ 300	~~250~~ 300
		By night		
		As on Y. 1. night	300.	---

SECRET

S C H E D U L E.

Unit.		Objective.	Ammunition. [illegible]	[illegible]
Y. 1.	280/C Battery.	**By day**		
		Bombardment of FRONT LINE SYSTEM paying more attention to second and third lines than hazy barrage tracks in K.4. .	~~[illegible]~~ 150	650.
		From 4.40 p.m. to 5.20 p.m. intense bombardment of FRONT LINE SYSTEM, bombardment to increase in intensity during last 10 minutes.		
* K 5 a 9.1 to K 5 a 95.20		At 5.15 p.m. lift on to [illegible] from K.5.a.60.15 to K.5.a.9.1 and also ~~[illegible]~~ from * ~~junction with [illegible] to junction [illegible]~~. At 5.20 p.m. return to FRONT LINE SYSTEM.	150	~~[illegible]~~ 350
		By night		
		Tracks in K.4.b. Dump at K.4.b.8.7. Occasionally on FRONT LINE SYSTEM	300	---
Y. 2.		**By Day**		
		Bombardment of FRONT LINE SYSTEM paying more attention to second and third lines than hazy barrage tracks in K.4.b.	150 ~~[illegible]~~	600
		From 8.40 a.m. to 9.20 a.m. intense bombardment of FRONT LINE SYSTEM, bombardment to increase in intensity during last 10 minutes.		
		At 9.15 a.m. lift to [illegible] between [illegible] and K.5.a.60.15 and from K.5.a.60.15 to K.5.a.65.=40.	150	350 ~~[illegible]~~
		At 9.20 a.m. return to FRONT LINE SYSTEM.		
		By night		
		As on Y. 1. night.	300	---

<u>S C H E D U L E</u>

	Unit.	Objective.	Ammunition.
Y. 1.	282/"D Battery	<u>By Day</u>	
		Bombardment of selected points paying more attention to second and third lines.	100
		From 4.40 p.m. to 5.20 p.m. intense bombardment of FRONT LINE SYSTEM, bombardment increasing in intensity during last 10 minutes. At 5.15 p.m. lift on to trench junctions at X.5.a.60.15, X.5.a.9.1. and junction of EGG and FILLET.	150
		At 5.20 p.m. return to FRONT LINE SYSTEM.	
		<u>By night</u>	
		Selected points.	50.
<u>Y. 2.</u>		As on Y.1. day but time of bombardment at 8.40 a.m. to 9.20 a.m., lift at 9.15 a.m. return to FRONT LINE SYSTEM at 9.20 a.m.	

ORIGINAL

Vol 8

WAR DIARY FOR JULY 1916

OF

280TH (CITY OF LONDON) BDE RFA.

WITH. APPENDIX No 1 – NORTHERN GROUP OPERATION ORDER No 5, 30/6/16

APPENDIX No 2. ARTILLERY NARRATIVE – NORTHERN GROUP 1/7/16

ALSO WAR DIARIES of BATTERIES during periods of detachment; as follows:-

280/A Battery	–	3 – 31	JULY 1916
280/B "	–	4 – 31	" "
280/C "	–	4 – 19	" "
280/D "	–	1 – 31	" "

ORIGINAL

D. Battery. 280th Brigade. RFA **WAR DIARY** or ~~INTELLIGENCE SUMMARY~~ JULY 1916 — 280/D BATTERY RFA

Army Form C. 2118

Instructions regarding War Diaries and Intelligence Summaries are contained in F. S. Regs., Part II. and the Staff Manual respectively. Title Pages will be prepared in manuscript.

(Erase heading not required.)

Place	Date	Hour	Summary of Events and Information	Remarks and references to Appendices
In the Field HEBUTERNE	1st "X Day"	7 30 am	Following Y days bombardment the attack on GOMMECOURT was made at 7.30 am. This Battery was engaged in Counter-Battery work and from 7-20 am to 8.5. am fired 500 rounds of Tear Shell into Hostile Battery Positions. Throughout the remainder of the day 20 Hostile Batteries were engaged. No 840 Corpl Strickland C (Chief of the Battery Staff) received a shrapnel wound about 10.30 pm.	
	3rd	Night	The Guns were withdrawn & the following day handed over to D Battery 125th Brigade RFA. No 897 Gunner Stalks E. was killed by Shrapnel whilst proceeding with the Guns from HEBUTERNE to SAILLY-AU-BOIS. The Battery moved in Sections taking over Guns & position from the 231st D Battery at FONQUEVILLIERS	
FONQUEVILLIERS.	4th		These Guns were registered on their Zero Lines. They were found to be in a very bad condition and owing to the excessive bad weather, the position was thoroughly water-logged and two ammunition recesses built by outgoing Battery caved in, burying several Cartridges and Shells and rendering a quantity of Shrapnel Shells & Cartridges useless.	
	6th	4pm.	No 1 Gun had a premature with an H.E. Shell about 10 feet from the muzzle the Gun Shield was perforated in several places and No 1073 Bomb Baker A.L. & No 1490 Gunner Laker E. J. were both badly wounded, the latter succumbed to these wounds on the 9th inst.	
	12th		The Brigade Wagon Lines were removed from HENU to PAS HUTS taking over much more pleasant Horse Lines and better accomodation for the Men.	

1875 Wt. W593/826 1,000,000 4/15 J.B.C. & A. A.D.S.S./Forms/C. 2118.

ORIGINAL

D. Battery.

280th Brigade RFA

280/D. BATTERY RFA.

Instructions regarding War Diaries and Intelligence Summaries are contained in F. S. Regs., Part II. and the Staff Manual respectively. Title Pages will be prepared in manuscript.

WAR DIARY

or.

~~INTELLIGENCE SUMMARY~~

(Erase heading not required.)

Army Form C. 2118

JULY 1916 (Sheet ii).

Place	Date	Hour	Summary of Events and Information	Remarks and references to Appendices
FONQUEVILLIERS	12th	Night	We supported a Raid by the Infantry, firing 700 rounds on Trench Targets.	
SAILLY-AU-BOIS.	16th	Night	One Section took up new position at "BARKHOW". Capt. I.V. Gray was placed temporarily in Command of this Section.	
	19th 20 21st		The Enemy shelled FONQUEVILLIERS continuously, several shells bursting quite close to the Battery Position	
	21st		News was received that Captain E.R.C. Warrens commanding this Battery had been granted his Majority.	
	22nd		Capt. I.V. Gray left to take up position at Corps Headquarters.	
	23rd		Remainder of Battery moved to "BARKHOW". The Guns taking up a position about 100 yards in front of the other Section.	
	25th		The Brigade Wagon Lines were again moved from PAS HUTS to GAUDIEMPRE	
	26th		Major. E.R.C. Warrens evacuated to Divisional Rest Station.	
	27th		Lt. O.C.W. Johnsen returned to Battery taking over Command.	

31st July/16

L. Johnsen Lt. RFA
for O.C. 280/D. Battery RFA.

1875 Wt. W593/826 1,000,000 4/15 J.B.C. & A. A.D.S.S./Forms/C. 2118.

ORIGINAL.

Instructions regarding War Diaries and Intelligence Summaries are contained in F. S. Regs., Part II. and the Staff Manual respectively. Title Pages will be prepared in manuscript.

WAR DIARY

or

~~INTELLIGENCE SUMMARY~~

(Erase heading not required.)

280TH (CITY OF LONDON) BDE. R.F.A. (T.F.)

Army Form C. 2118

JULY 1916

Place	Date	Hour	Summary of Events and Information	Remarks and references to Appendices
VICINITY OF SAILLY + HEBUTERNE	1/7/16		"Z" day. The night was quiet on our front. About 2 AM. SAILLY heavily shelled near Church. Hostile shelling of our front line + communication trenches commenced later.	
			Programme carried out by Northern Artillery Group according to programme (Zero time = 7.30 A.M.) 280/A Battery rejoined Group at 7.30 AM. – Northern Group then consisting of 280/A 280/B 280/C 93rd and 282/D (How.) Batteries	See N. Group Opn Order No 1 (Appx No 1 JUNE diary) Also – APPx No 1 (N. Group Opn Order No 5)
			The furthest Barrages were maintained + gradually brought back to cover Infantry as they retired from the lines they had taken. Fire died down towards close of day. No of rounds fired during 24 hours to 8 PM "Z" day – 280/A Battery 3432; 280/B " 2682; 280/C " 2453; 93rd " 1797; 282/D (How) Bty 1587	
			See also report by O.C., N. Group (Appx No 2)	APPx No 2 Report by OC Group – Artillery narrative.
	1/2 JULY	NIGHT.	SAILLY shelled with 4.2 at 11.30 PM. Heavy shelling opposite "Z" hedge 12.30 AM.	
			Desultory shelling of positions during night.	
			Opened barrage fire from 2 AM. to 3.15 AM. on enemy's front line. Afterwards quiet.	
	2/7/16		Batteries standing by all day prepared for counter attacks.	
		8 AM. to 11.30 AM.	HEBUTERNE very heavily shelled.	
		12.20 PM	Co-operated with Heavy Artillery by firing on GOMMECOURT VILLAGE in retaliation for shelling of HEBUTERNE.	
			Burying parties out during afternoon.	
		5.6 PM to 5.10 PM.	Batteries fired three salvoes on Front + Second line enemy trenches.	

1875 Wt. W593/826 1,000,000 4/15 J.B.C. & A. A.D.S.S./Forms/C. 2118.

ORIGINAL.

Instructions regarding War Diaries and Intelligence Summaries are contained in F. S. Regs., Part II. and the Staff Manual respectively. Title Pages will be prepared in manuscript.

WAR DIARY

~~or~~

~~INTELLIGENCE SUMMARY~~

(Erase heading not required.)

280TH (CITY OF LONDON) BDE R.F.A. (T.F.)

JULY 1916 (SHEET ii)

Army Form C. 2118

Place	Date	Hour	Summary of Events and Information	Remarks and references to Appendices
VICINITY OF SAILLY & HEBUTERNE	2/7/16 (cont^d)	6 PM	OC GROUP, with Lt HUMMEL (Group Observation Officer) & Lt GOODYER (Orderly Officer) returned from Advanced HQ at 169th INF. BDE. HQ	
		10.30 PM to 10.40 PM	93rd Battery fired four salvoes on EMS trench searching up to GOMMECOURT Cemetery.	
	2nd/3rd	night	93rd & 280/B Batteries fired on selected objectives during the night	
			Hostile shelling of HEBUTERNE & front lines at intervals from 11 PM to 5 AM	
			Desultory hostile shelling of N end of SAILLY with 4.2 from 11.40 PM throughout night.	
			Positions shelled intermittently – lachrymatory shells over 93rd Battery at 10 P.M.	
	3/7/16		Quiet day. Orders received re re-grouping & changing over –	
			93rd & 282/D Batteries taken over by Southern Group 56 Div Arty.	
			280/A Battery takes over 232/B (46 Divn) – one section at 4 P.M. } Guns & Howitzers of these Batteries withdrawn at night to HENU & handed over to 37 Div. Arty.	
			280/D " " " How Bty — " — " " " " "	
SAILLY TO SOUASTRE	4/7/16	12 noon	re-grouping of Divl Artillery – Taking-over by 280/A & 280/D from 46 Div Arty completed. These two Batteries, together with 280/B & 280/C (the remaining Batteries of original group), i.e. all four Batteries of the Brigade, now form part of the new Northern Group, commanded by Lt COL. PRECHTEL.	
			Bde H.Q. left SAILLY for SOUASTRE (in rest).	
HENU TO PAS	12/7/16	12 noon	Bde Wagon Lines changed from HENU to PAS HUTS, arriving 12 noon.	
		6 PM.	Regrouping of Batteries, 56 Div. Arty. 280/A & 280/D Batteries remain in same positions and in N Group under Lt COL. PRECHTEL; 280/B & 280/C Batteries remove to K2d.8.8 & K13.a.9.9 respectively, in Southern Group under Lt COL MACDOWELL. (56 Div Arty Operation Order No. 9)	
SOUASTRE TO PAS	13/7/16	12 noon	Bde H.Q. left SOUASTRE 12 noon. Established in Orchard near PAS (C.16.c.0.8; Sheet 57D 1/40000) at 1 PM. O.C. Bde to exercise general supervision over Wagon Lines of all Batteries of 56 Div. Arty.	

1875 Wt. W593/826 1,000,000 4/15 J.B.C. & A. A.D.S.S./Forms/C. 2118.

ORIGINAL.

Instructions regarding War Diaries and Intelligence Summaries are contained in F. S. Regs., Part II. and the Staff Manual respectively. Title Pages will be prepared in manuscript.

WAR DIARY ~~or INTELLIGENCE SUMMARY~~

(Erase heading not required.)

280TH (CITY OF LONDON) BDE RFA (TF)

Army Form C. 2118

JULY 1916 (Sheet iii)

Place	Date	Hour	Summary of Events and Information	Remarks and references to Appendices
BIENVILLERS	14/7/16		Further re-grouping of 56 Div Arty. 280/B Battery moves to E 8. b. 1. 0. & comes under Northern Group; 280/D Battery comes under Centre Group.	
PAS to SAILLY	19/7/16	5 PM	Bde HQ established at SAILLY. O.C. Bde takes over command from Lt Col. MACDOWELL of Southern Group, consisting of 281 A B C & D Batteries and 280/C Battery. Covering 168TH INF. BDE in Southern Sector of Division, i.e. from SUNKEN ROAD (E. of HEBUTERNE) in South to K.4.d.1.6 (S.E. corner of GOMMECOURT PK) in North.	
VICINITY OF SAILLY & HEBUTERNE	20/7/16		Quiet day. Enemy shelled our trenches at intervals from ROSSIGNOL WOOD. Retaliation on MINENWERFER at K 5 C. 04. 22. Occasional fire on enemy working parties & retaliation at request of Infantry. Registration as necessary.	
	21/7/16		Quiet day. Desultory hostile shelling of trenches. Retaliation on MINENWERFER at K.5.C. 04. 22. Occasional fire on enemy working parties. 280/C Bty registered with Kite Balloon.	
	22/7/16		SAILLY (near GROUP H.Q.) shelled from direction of BIEZ WOOD at 1.40 P.M. Desultory hostile shelling of our trenches during day – heavy from direction of ESSARTS, 4.30 to 5.30 P.M. Retaliation for fire of MINENWERFER at K.17.b.05.80. Occasional fire on enemy working parties & retaliation at request of Infantry.	
	23/7/16	5.30 to 6.30 AM.	Combined co-operation of 281/D (How) Bty & 281/C Bty (18 pdr) with Heavy T.M. Bty (V.56) & Infantry against MINENWERFER & neighbourhood about K.11.d.1.1 (near SUNKEN ROAD). MINENWERFER replied at outset with one round only; then ceased to fire. Our trenches shelled by enemy intermittently during morning; sharp burst from ROSSIGNOL WOOD at 2 P.M. Enemy working parties dispersed during day.	
	24/7/16		Registration of points out of Group Zone for purpose of concentration barrage (for co-operation between Groups). Quiet day.	
		9.20 PM.	Retaliation on ROSSIGNOL WOOD for shelling of SAILLY near Group HQ.	

1875 Wt. W593/826 1,000,000 4/15 J.B.C. & A. A.D.S.S./Forms/C. 2118.

ORIGINAL

Instructions regarding War Diaries and Intelligence Summaries are contained in F. S. Regs., Part II. and the Staff Manual respectively. Title Pages will be prepared in manuscript.

WAR DIARY ~~or INTELLIGENCE SUMMARY~~

(Erase heading not required.)

280TH (CITY OF LONDON) BDE. RFA. (T.F.)

Army Form C. 2118

JULY 1916 (Sheet iv)

Place	Date	Hour	Summary of Events and Information	Remarks and references to Appendices
PAS HUTS to GAUDIEMPRE	25/7/16		Bde Wagon lines moved. Arrived at GAUDIEMPRE 12 noon.	
VICINITY OF SAILLY + HEBUTERNE	– " –		Quiet day. Enemy working parties dispersed. Registration as necessary.	
	26/7/16	3.45 to 4.30 AM	Co-operation of 281/A + 281/C (18 pdr) + 281/D (How) Batteries on ROSSIGNOL WOOD (Dump suspected at K.12 b.1.9) + roads near.	
			Enemy working parties dispersed during day. Retaliation for fire of MINENWERFER at SUNKEN ROAD.	
		3.15 PM	Trenches of sector shelled heavily with 4.2 from direction of PUISIEUX.	
	27/7/16	6.28 to 6.35 AM	Co-operation of 281/C (18 pdr) + 281/D (How) Batteries with Heavy T.M. on MINENWERFER at SUNKEN ROAD + vicinity.	
			Working parties dispersed by our fire during day.	
			Quiet day.	
	28/7/16		Quiet day. Desultory hostile shelling of our trenches 1.50 to 2.50 P.M. Retaliation by 281/D Battery.	
			281/A Bty carried out registration with Kite Balloon + 281/D Bty with aeroplane.	
	29/7/16		281/A + 281/B Batteries registered with Kite Balloon + 281/D Bty with aeroplane.	
			Desultory shelling of our front line in afternoon + heavy shelling of HEBUTERNE + S.W. corner of village at 10 PM	
		11.30 PM	Retaliation by 281/D Bty on ROSSIGNOL WOOD + BIEZ WOOD.	
	30/7/16		Desultory hostile shelling of our Trenches during morning. Also of HEBUTERNE and a few 4.2 on SAILLY in afternoon.	
			Retaliation by 280/C Bty on new enemy Trench (near EPTE) for shelling of our Trenches, and by 281/D on ROSSIGNOL WOOD + FORK WOOD for shelling of SAILLY. Also by 281/C Bty for MINENWERFER in neighbourhood of SUNKEN ROAD	
			Registration during day as necessary.	
	31/7/16		Enemy MINENWERFERS active in early morning. Retaliation by 281/D Bty	
			281/D Bty carried out registration with aeroplane.	
			Quiet day.	

L. A. C. Southam Lt Col
Comdg 280th (City of London) Bde RFA

1875 Wt. W593/826 1,000,000 4/15 J.B.C. & A. A.D.S.S./Forms/C. 2118.

COPY FOR WAR DIARY

APPENDIX No 1
JULY 1916 WAR DIARY.

OPERATION ORDER NO: 5. BY LIEUT.COLONEL.L.A.C.SOUTHAM.,

COMMANDING NORTHERN GROUP.

30th JUNE 1916.

NOT TO BE TAKEN FORWARD OF HEBUTERNE

1. ENEMY'S FORCES
The portion of the enemy's front approximately opposite 56th Division was reported before active operations commenced to consist of One Infantry Regiment (3 Battalions) in first line and local reserve with 5 heavy and 12 field Batteries normally covering the front.

2. OUR FORCES
VIIth Corps has 3 Divisions,37th,46th and 56th,holding the line ~~fmm~~ in above order from North to South.

3. INTENTION
The intention of the VIIth Corps is to establish itself ob a line which runs approximately from our present front line - 250 yards N.E.of 16 POPLARS - East of NAMELESS FARM - along ridge in K.5.a.and E.29c - LITTLE "Z" and thence back to British Line.
46th Division attacks from N.W.and 56th Division from S.W. The two Divisions should meet at about E.29.c.6.0.

4. TASKS
At Zero,NORTHERN GROUP (including 280/A Battery R.F.A) becomes affiliated to 169th Infantry Brigade.
The task of the 169th Infantry Brigade will be carried out in four phases.-
1st Phase To capture from left of 168th Bde along FELL,FELLOW, FEUD, the CEMETERY,ECK,MAZE,EEL,and FIR and establish three strong points viz :-
(1) near CEMETERY.
(2) at the MAZE.
(3) at S.E.Corner of GOMMECOURT PARK.
2nd Phase (to take place immediately after 1st Phase) to clear EMS, ETCH and capture the QUADRILATERAL in K.5.a.
3rd Phase (to commence directly after 2nd Phase)
To secure the cross trenches at K.5.a.7.8.where INDUS crosses FILL and FILLET, to join hands with 46th Divsn.along FILL and to consolidate FILLET facing EAST.
4th Phase (to commence three hours after Zero)
To clear both GOMMECOURT VILLAGE and PARK in a North Westerly directions from the line FIR-EEL-MAZE-ECK-CEMETERY.
The 46th Division will be clearing the village in a South Easterly Direction.

5. ARTILLERY FIRE

Artillery Fire on "Z" day before and after ZERO will be in accordance with the SCHEDULE and table of Barrages issued. A written copy of the time table will be in possession of each Officer and No.1.

The following instructions as to rate of fire and nature of projectile are intended as a guide and are not to hamper the discretion of Battery Commanders nor to indicate that guns are to be fired at a more rapid rate than is compatible with accuracy of laying and fuze setting. After Zero the dump at guns is not to fall below 600 rounds per gun 18pdr and 400 rounds per Howitzer 4.5".

/1.

OPERATION ORDER NO: 5 (continued-

ARTILLERY FIRE (CONT)

18 pdr: ZERO to end of BLUE Barrage..Maximum Rate T.S.
To end of GREEN Barrage......Maximum rate 4/5 T.S.
1/5 H.E.
YELLOW - RED Barrages........2 Rounds per gun per minute
or as situation requires,
4/5 T.S., 1/5 H.E.

6. O.P's and LIAISON

(a) For "Z" day the following details will be required:-

O.P."F" 1 Officer, 282/D, Operators Bde Hd Qrs.) from 8 p.m.
O.P."H" 1 Officer, 2 Operators..93rd Battery.) previous night.

Liaison
Group Hd Qrs Observing Officer Lieut.H.V.HUMMEL, 280/B Battery.

Right Battn.1/9th London (Q.V.R) 1 Officer, 1 N.C.O., 2 telephonists with one instrument...93rd Battery.
Left Battn. 1/5th London (L.R.B) 1 Officer, 1 N.C.O., 2 telephonists with one instrument...280/B Battery.
Centre Battaal/(16th) 6th London (Q.W.R) 1 Officer, 1 N.C.O, 2 telephonists with one instrument...280/C Battery.

Time for liaison detail to report will be notified later.

(b) All personnel of above detail must know whereabouts of Advanced Group Headquarters (K.Y.C) and Advanced Group Exchange (X.O.P)

(c) In previous active operations most valuable general information has been received through forward artillery Officers, who should transmit to Group Headquarters all information, positive or negative, and affecting the general situation and progress, as often as possible, as well as purely artillery messages.

(d) The General scheme will be carefully explained to above Officers and N.C.O's but a copy must not be in their possession.

7. COMMUNICATIONS

Plans of existing communications have been issued to Batteries. In the event of a total breakdown of telephonic communications, Group Headquarters will establish visual signalling posts at about K.8.b.9.0 and K.7.c.50.95. thence by runner to Group Exchange (F.L.A) and batteries.

8. HEADQUARTERS

Advanced Group Headquarters from previous night will be at K.Y.C. The Adjutant will remain at F.L.A.,

(sd) H.J.P.Oakley.,
Lieut.,
Adjutant, NORTHERN GROUP.

Copy No.1..93rd Battery.
2..280/A "
3..280/B "
4..280/C "
5..282/D "
6..56th Div.Arty.
7)
8) retained.

APPENDIX No 2
To
JULY 1916 WAR DIARY
280 (City of London) Bde RFA

ARTILLERY NARRATIVE - NORTHERN GROUP

1st July 1916.

A.M.		Sources of Information.
6.25-7.30.	Intense Bombardment.	
7.30	Lift to BLUE Barrage.	
7.31	Nothing to be seen for smoke, some hostile rifle and machine gun fire.	O.P.H.
7.34	Lift to GREEN Barrage.	
7.39	Partial lift off GREEN Barrage (ETCH and EMS part of)	
7.47	Lift to YELLOW Barrage. Report from GEAGUN "All satisfactory"	
7.50	Cannot now confirm machine gun fire but rifle fire continues.	O.P.H.
8.00	Smoke started from "Z" Hedge. 7.20 and at 7.25 all along the line. Still very thick.	O.P.F.
	Lift to RED Barrage.	
8.30	Our men seem going forward also men further down, judged to be near FELLOW.	O.P.H.
8.35	Enemy's Heavy guns continue shelling reserve line and communication trenches. Unable to see anything of movement of our own infantry.	O.P.F.
8.45	Adjutant (SAILLY) Reports Batteries all firing on RED Barrage, 2 rounds per gun per minute and asks for information. Reply "Everything appears normal" (Being shelled cannot observe.)	O.P.H.
9.00	News has arrived by runner that Q.V.R. and Q.W.R. are held up in K.5.c.1.5. to K.5.c.3.3. by machine gun enfilading from direction of "G" in GOMMECOURT firing down FILM.	R.F.A. Liaison Officer with Q.V.R.
9.10	Infantry checked during establishment of strong point at S. Edge of GOMMECOURT PARK. 93rd Battery in consequence barrage on Trench K.4.c.5.7.- K.4.a.9.1. - 9.20 a.m.	R.F.A. Liaison Officer with L.R.B.
9.20	46th Divisional Infantry Brigade held up in GOMMECOURT WOOD on right.	46th D.A.
9.55.	93rd Battery reports all guns temporarily out of action. 280/A put on above barrage.	
10.10	1 gun 93rd Battery on above barrage.	
10.30	93rd and 280/A Btys off above barrage (G.O.C. 169th Infantry Brigade) 280/B and C. all guns in action.	
	Enemy shelling our front line.	O.P.H.
11.00	Our boards up on all three STRONG POINTS.	O.P.H.
11.15.	No signs of our troops in QUADRILATERAL (280/C back to GREEN Barrage)	Various.
11.20	280/B Barrage EMS from junction with ETCH to junction with EPTE.	
11.30	282/D back to GREEN barrage except one gun on junction of FILLET and FILL. 280/A on to RED Barrage laid down for 280/B. 93rd Bty ditto ditto ditto for 280/C All above approved by G.O.C. "Division will arrange for EPTE". Rate of fire slackened from this time considerably irrespective of necessity in order to keep guns in action.	

2

Time	Event	Source
P.M.		
12.5.	280/C lifts as at plus 9 minutes. 280/A All guns in action. 93rd - 1 gun only in action. Remainder 4 guns in action.	
11.30 - 12.15.	Constant messages as to heavy barrages by enemy's guns apparently firing from direction of ROSSIGNOL WOOD. (R.A.Liaison Officer informed)	O.P.F. O.P.H.
12.23	On account of guns out of action 280/A add to barrage of K.5.b.3.5. - K.5.b.4.3.taking this from 93rd.	
12.35	Enemy now sending over Gas Shells.	R.F.A.Liaison Officer with L.R.B.
1.00 onwards.	Small parties returning to our trenches.	O.P.F.&.O.P.H & other sources.
	S.O.S.various points. 93rd - K.4.central. 280/C - K.4.central to K.4.b.5.0 (concurrence of G.O.C.169th Infantry Brigade)	Various sources.
1.20	Artillery barrage has considerably reduced enemy rifle fire.	R.F.A.Liaison Officer with L.R.B.
1.30	Men returning across No Man's Land from MAZE through FERRET and FEN. Shrapnel barrage on No Mans Land	ditto also O.P.F.&.O.P.H
1.38	Our Infantry are still returning and are showing a red light on the parapet.	O.P.H.
1.45	All batteries BLUE Barrage (G.S.O.2.confirms FELL)	
2.25	Fire on FELL confirmed by G.O.C.169th Infantry Bde after information of an advance towards EPTE. 93rd Battery asked leave to discontinue temporarily on account of state of guns. Told to come off FISH and FIRM but must continue on remainder.	
2.40	280/A to put one gun on K.4.c.6.5.to K.4.d.0.9. 93rd (1 gun only in action in very bad state) remainder of its barrage)	
3.10	Barrage satisfactory, good bursts.	O.P.F. O.P.H.
3.30	At 3.p.m.40 unwounded men of L.R.B.and 1 Lewis Gun in FIR, remainder of Company casualties.	Wounded man to R.F.A. Liaison Ofcr. with L.R.B.
	280/C - K.4.b.5.0 to K.5.a.4.2. 280/B - K.5.a.4.2. to K.5.c.9.6. 282/D - K.5.a.6.2.and Junction EMS & ETCH.	
3.45	Guns in action: 280/A...3 Guns.) 280/C...1 Gun.) Remainder 4.)	Batteries.
4.00	About 100 men in communication trench between FEMALE and FERRET, they appear to be crawling back to our lines on hands and knees.	O.P.F.
	Guns in action : 93rd.. 2. 280/A.. 2. 280/B.. 4. 280/C.. 2. 282/D.. 4.	Batteries.
4.20	Germans massing between FISH and FIRM. 93rd and 282/D on this point. O.P.F.to Observe.	R.F.A.Liaison Ofcr.with L.R.B.
5.00	All guns BLUE Barrage.	
5.20	Enemy massing in K.5.a. 280/B on about K.5.a.3.7.	56th D.A.
5.30	1 Gun of 93rd on further part of its GREEN Barrage (K.4.b.5.0 to K.5.a.2.3.) 280/B return to BLUE	
5.50	Tasks at this time: 93rd No guns in action. 280/A Own Barrage and part of 93rd 280/B ditto ditto	

P.M.
5.50 (cont) 280/C - EXE between FILM - FERRET.
EMS between FEUD and K.5.a.60.15.
282/D - Junction of EMS and FEUD.
6.20 93rd and 280/A on BLUE Barrage.
6.30 Enemy in force in FEUD, FELLOW, FELL. K.Q. Bde Hd Qrs.

6.35 280/B and C on regular BLUE Barrage.
282/D as above and also on junction of ETCH with FELLOW and FELL.
7.25 280/B - Barrage FEINT. Various.
280/C - Barrage FEED

Guns in action:
93rd... 2.
280/A 3.
B.. 4.
C. 1.
282/D 4.

93rd on FIBRE from junction with FEAST to K.4.d.1.9. carefully as only just over heads of our infantry.

7.30 Situation at time :
93rd.. BLUE Barrage less front line trench part and also as above.
280/A.. BLUE Barrage.
280/B FEINT.
280/C FEED.
7.40 282/D K.4.b.5.0.

8.35 Trench Barrage:
280/B FIRM and FIR.
93rd FISH and FIRM
280/C FEN and FERRET
280/A FERN and FEVER
282/D K.4.c.9.4.

8.45 S T O P.

Night lines ordered.

Time from commencement of intense bombardment to STOP:
14 hours 20 minutes.

AMMUNITION EXPENDED DURING "Z" DAY

	"A"	"A.X"	"B.X"	Total
93rd Battery	1001	796		1797
280/A " (up to Zero wire cutting)	1903	1529		3432
280/B...	1966	716		2682
280/C...	1753	700		2453
282/D...			1587	1587
T o t a l... ...	6623.	3741.	1587.	11,951.

To. Officer i/c
A.G's Office
BASE, B.E.F.

A/770

With reference to my S/657 of 6th inst. I now enclose War Diaries of 280/A & 280/D Batteries for June 1916, covering periods of detachment from this Brigade

L. A. C. [illegible]
Lt Col
Comdg 280th (City of London) Bde RFA.

17.7.16

To Officer i/c
A.G.'s Office
BASE, B.E.F.

4/657

I enclose herewith War Diary for this Brigade for the month of June together with four Appendices.

The 280/D Battery was temporarily detached for tactical purposes during the whole of the month and the 280/A Battery for similar purposes during the last week of the month. The Diaries of these Batteries covering the respective periods will follow shortly.

L. A. C. Southam

6. 7. 16

Lt Col
Comdg 280th (City of London) Bde RFA

ORIGINAL

Instructions regarding War Diaries and Intelligence Summaries are contained in F. S. Regs., Part II. and the Staff Manual respectively. Title Pages will be prepared in manuscript.

WAR DIARY
or
~~INTELLIGENCE SUMMARY~~
(Erase heading not required.)

280/A BATTERY RFA

JULY 1916

Army Form C. 2118

Place	Date	Hour	Summary of Events and Information	Remarks and references to Appendices
VICINITY OF FONQUEVILLERS	3.7.16		Orders to move to position E20 c 1 1 & take over one section at 4 PM.	
	4.7.16		Remainder of battery in position during day	
	5.7.16		Registering	
	6.7.16		Registering. Heavy rains	
	7.7.16		Normal. Heavy rains	
	8.7.16		Normal. Heavy rains	
	9.7.16		Bomb attack on enemy fired as ordered by Group	
	10.7.16		Normal	
	11.7.16		Normal	
	12.7.16		Normal	
	13.7.16		Demonstration from 10 PM to 8 AM 1353 rds fired	
	14.7.16		Normal	
	15.7.16		Normal	
	16.7.16		Demonstration 12 midnight - 12.30 AM 191 rds fired	
	17.7.16		Bombardment of front line (hostile) 541 rds fired at 12 midnight	
	18.7.16		Bombardment of front line (hostile) at 12 midnight 154 rds	
	19.7.16		Normal	
	20.7.16		Fired under orders of GROUP Barrage on 2nd line 230 rds.	

1875 Wt. W593/826 1,000,000 4/15 J.B.C. & A. A.D.S.S./Forms/C. 2118.

ORIGINAL

Instructions regarding War Diaries and Intelligence Summaries are contained in F. S. Regs., Part II. and the Staff Manual respectively. Title Pages will be prepared in manuscript.

WAR DIARY
or
~~INTELLIGENCE SUMMARY~~

(Erase heading not required.)

280/A BATTERY RFA

JULY 1916

Army Form C. 2118

(Sheet ii)

Place	Date	Hour	Summary of Events and Information	Remarks and references to Appendices
VICINITY OF FONQUEVILLERS	21.7.16		Hostile shelling of position moved position & occupied position E 20 a 68 93	
	22.7.16		Registering	
	23.7.16		Registering	
	24.7.16		Normal	
	25.7.16		Normal	
	26.7.16		Normal	
	27.7.16		Normal	
	28.7.16		Normal	
	29.7.16		Normal	
	30.7.16		Fired under GROUP orders on communication trenches 58 rds	
	31.7.16		Normal.	

H. P. Jones
Major
"A" Bty
280 Bde RFA.

1875 Wt. W593/826 1,000,000 4/15 J.B.C. & A. A.D.S.S./Forms/C. 2118.

ORIGINAL

280 B BATTERY RFA

Army Form C. 2118

Instructions regarding War Diaries and Intelligence Summaries are contained in F. S. Regs., Part II. and the Staff Manual respectively. Title Pages will be prepared in manuscript.

WAR DIARY
or
~~INTELLIGENCE SUMMARY~~

(Erase heading not required.)

JULY 1916

Place	Date	Hour	Summary of Events and Information	Remarks and references to Appendices
FONQUEVILLERS	1916 July 5.		Fired 50 rds. Shrapnel in bombardment of enemy's front line.	
	" 7.		" 300 rds in Wire Cutting at K.4.8.3.7.	
	" 9.	8.10 to 8.50am	Intense bombardment of Enemy's front line System in conjunction with smoke.	
	" "	4 pm	Wire cutting at K.4.a.12½.	
	" 10	9 a.m.	Destroyed enemy's works & loopholes in FIX & FOCUS trenches.	
	" "	11.21"	Enemy Kite balloon appeared to explode & descend in flames at 122° Mag. Bearing from Battery position	
	" 11.	2.30pm	One of our Aeroplanes (Type B.E.2.C.) observed to come down in German lines at 132½° Mag. Bearing from Battery position	
	12		From 12 Noon on this date Battery vacated position at E26 a 3.2 and handed over to TOMGUN & took over position & Zone of GEAGUN at K.2.b.60.10.	
		2.30pm	Enemy Kite balloon observed to come down rapidly at approx. Mag. Bearing from Battery of 110°.	
	13	3.50pm	Fired on and dispersed enemy working party at L 2 d 4.8	
	"	6 pm	" " " " " " junction of FILLET & INDUS	
	13 & 14	11 pm 8 a.m	Bombardment of Enemy's front line system with 496 rounds Shrapnel and 486 H E by Order of Group	
	14	12 Noon	Vacated position at K 2 b 60.10 and left Southern Group	
BIENVILLERS	15	3 a.m	Took over new Position at BIENVILLERS E 8 d 04.88 from 'B' Battery 123rd Brigade RFA and came under Northern Group. Registered new Zone	
		12 mid night	Fired 100 rounds Shrapnel and 100 rounds H E on tracks and trenches in Zone by order of Group	

1875 Wt. W593/826 1,000,000 4/15 J.B.C. & A. A.D.S.S./Forms/C. 2118.

ORIGINAL

280 B BATTERY RFA

Army Form C. 2118

WAR DIARY
or
~~INTELLIGENCE SUMMARY~~

(Erase heading not required.)

JULY 1916

SHEET 11

Instructions regarding War Diaries and Intelligence Summaries are contained in F. S. Regs., Part II. and the Staff Manual respectively. Title Pages will be prepared in manuscript.

Place	Date	Hour	Summary of Events and Information	Remarks and references to Appendices
BIENVILLERS	16th	5.30 to 6.15	Continued Registration of New Zone	
	16th 17	midnight to 1 a.m.	Bombardment of Enemy's Front line System and tracks in Zone 152 rounds Shrapnel and 128 HE by order of Group	
	17 18	midnight to 12.13 am	Bombardment of Enemy's front and second line trenches between E 24 a 52.92 and E 18 a 24.22. with 85 rounds Shrapnel and 60 H.E. by order of Group	
	"	5.15 pm	Fired 30 rounds Shrapnel on Enemy's front line by request of infantry in retaliation for Enemy shelling our front line.	
	19	9.15 am	Fired and dispersed Enemy working party engaged in laying wires at F 8 c 7.7	
		3.7 pm	Fired 32 rounds Shrapnel on Enemy's front line at request of Infantry in retaliation for shelling our front line.	
		3.20 pm	Fired 82 rounds of H.E. on Enemy's villages in retaliation at request of infantry	
	20	4 to 7	Enemy heavily shelled BIENVILLERS.	
		4.15 pm	Fired 72 rounds HE on Enemy's villages in retaliation for shelling of BIENVILLERS	
		5.20 to 6 pm 6.20 pm	Fired 18 rounds Shrapnel and 18 rds H.E on ESSARTS on order of Group in retaliation	
		7.5 to 8.40 pm		
	21	10 am to 10.30	Fired 24 rounds Shrapnel on ESSARTS by order of Group in retaliation	
		7.58 to 11 pm	Enemy shelled BIENVILLERS with 150 mm and 77 mm shells.	
	22	10.49 am.	Fired 16 rounds Shrapnel on Enemy front line at request of Infantry in retaliation for enemy shelling our front line.	
	25	4.45 pm	Fired 19 rounds HE on enemy's front line at request of Infantry in retaliation for shelling of our front line	
	28	6.40 pm to 7.30 pm	Fired 14 rounds Shrapnel and 42 rounds H E on enemy's works at E 11 d 80.60.	

1875 Wt. W593/826 1,000,000 4/15 J.B.C. & A. A.D.S.S./Forms/C. 2118.

ORIGINAL

Instructions regarding War Diaries and Intelligence Summaries are contained in F. S. Regs., Part II. and the Staff Manual respectively. Title Pages will be prepared in manuscript.

WAR DIARY
or
~~INTELLIGENCE SUMMARY~~
(Erase heading not required.)

280 B BATTERY RFA

Army Form C. 2118.

JULY 1916

SHEET iii

Place	Date	Hour	Summary of Events and Information	Remarks and references to Appendices
BIENVILLERS	1916 July 29	11 am	Fired 40 rounds H.E. on enemy's front line trenches at request of Infantry in retaliation for enemy shelling our front line. Enemy battery ceased firing.	
"	30	4.20 pm	Fired on and dispersed an enemy working party at E 11 d 80.75.	

[illegible] Major
OC B/280 RFA

2449 Wt. W14957/M90 750,000 1/16 J.B.C. & A. Forms/C.2118/12.

ORIGINAL

Instructions regarding War Diaries and Intelligence Summaries are contained in F. S. Regs., Part II. and the Staff Manual respectively. Title Pages will be prepared in manuscript.

WAR DIARY

~~or~~

~~INTELLIGENCE SUMMARY~~

(Erase heading not required.)

"C" Bty 280th Bde RFA

JULY 1916

Army Form C. 2118

Place	Date	Hour	Summary of Events and Information	Remarks and references to Appendices
FONCQUEVILLERS	4 July	Noon	Battery detached from SOUART GROUP – attached to NORTHERN GROUP – Reported to GROUP COMMANDER – allotted Zone – FINE FINFIELD FIX & trenches N.W. Corner of GOMMECOURT PARK.	
	5 "	10am	Registered new Zone from O.P.B. Excellent O.P. well hidden constructed – 500 yds from German trenches – Full direct view of Zone. – Guns showing signs of wear, shooting irregular –	
	6 " 7th "	–	Guns adjusted – sights, recoil system overhauled. Ordinary daily shooting on Zone – Fired on working party in GOMMECOURT PARK + special night shoots by order of GROUP Comdr.	
	8 "	9.30am	Engaged new enemy earthworks – obtained 11 direct HITS with H.E.	
	9 "	9am	Wire cutting at K3 b 9.2 – results good – Fuzes very good. – Guns shooting more evenly.	
	12th "		Battery took over (by Section) new position in SOUTHERN GROUP – at FISHGUN position K13.a 80.95. Reported to GROUP Comdr – allotted Zone. EEL: FEN. FERRET EMS &c Preliminary registration.	
SAILLY	13th	8am	Registered Zone from O.P.H. View from this O.P. limited – not a good O.P. New Gun position sound – Two of pits had been constructed by this Unit early in June last	
		10pm to 8am 14/7/16	Night shoot – by order GROUP Comdr on Front Line System –	
	14th	8am	Ordinary daily shoot on Front Line system. Good shooting obtained on working party behind 3rd Line	
		12 midt to 12.30	Night firing by order of GROUP Comdr	
	15th	9.30	allotted addition to Zone viz: FERN system behind. – Registered new Zone & confirmed old registration.	
		12 Midt to 12.30am	Night firing on Front Line System by order of GROUP Comdr	
	16th	11am	Fired on Enemy working parties – dispersed.	

1875 Wt. W593/826 1,000,000 4/15 J.B.C. & A. A.D.S.S./Forms/C. 2118.

ORIGINAL

280 C Battery RFA

Army Form C. 2118

Instructions regarding War Diaries and Intelligence Summaries are contained in F. S. Regs., Part II. and the Staff Manual respectively. Title Pages will be prepared in manuscript.

WAR DIARY

~~or~~

~~INTELLIGENCE SUMMARY~~

(*Erase heading not required.*)

JULY 1916

SHEET 11

Place	Date	Hour	Summary of Events and Information	Remarks and references to Appendices
SAILLY	17th July	-	Nothing special to report by day - Night firing 150 rds by order of GROUP	
	18th.		Nothing special to report	
	19th			

[illegible]

Major

O.C. C Bty

280th Bde R.F.A.

1875 Wt. W593/826 1,000,000 4/15 J.B.C. & A. A.D.S.S./Forms/C. 2118.

56th Divisional Artillery.

280th BRIGADE

ROYAL FIELD ARTILLERY.

AUGUST 1 9 1 6

Diaries of A,B.C & D Batteries are also attachd

Instructions regarding War Diaries and Intelligence Summaries are contained in F. S. Regs., Part II. and the Staff Manual respectively. Title Pages will be prepared in manuscript.

WAR DIARY
or
~~INTELLIGENCE SUMMARY~~

(Erase heading not required.)

[illegible] 280 - (CITY OF LONDON) BDE RFA (T.F.)

AUGUST 1916

Sheet 1

Place	Date	Hour	Summary of Events and Information	Remarks and references to Appendices
VICINITY OF SAILLY + HEBUTERNE	1/8/16		Quiet day. Minenwerfers fired in early morning from direction of SUNKEN ROAD.	
		6 PM	Co-operation of - 18 pdr Batteries (281/A + 281/C), 4.5 How Bty (281/D), V.56 H.T.M. Bty } on Minenwerfers mentioned above.	
			38th Div. Arty (on right flank) also co-operated.	
			Quiet night.	
SAILLY To BIENVILLERS	2/8/16	10.30 AM	Command of Southern Group handed over to Lt COL. MACDOWELL + H.Q relieved by 281 Bde H.Q.	
		12 noon	Bde H.Q moved from SAILLY to BIENVILLERS.	
		3 P.M.	Lt COL. L.A.C. SOUTHAM took over command of Northern Group from Lt COL PRECHTEL. Bde HQ relieved 282 Bde HQ. Group consists of 280/A, 280/B, 282/A, 282/B (18 pdr. Batteries) and 282/D (4.5 How); all in vicinity of BIENVILLERS + FONQUEVILLERS.	
VICINITY OF BIENVILLERS + FONQUEVILLERS			Batteries fired during day on enemy trenches to keep down hostile rifle + M.G. fire on our aeroplanes. Also retaliated for hostile shelling of our front lines. Registration carried out as necessary. FONQUEVILLERS - SOUASTRE road shelled at night.	
	3/8/16		Considerable shelling of Eastern outskirts of BIENVILLERS in morning; also trenches; apparently directed by hostile aeroplane. Retaliation on ESSARTS, QUESNOY FARM + enemy's front-line made immediately by 280/B + 282/B. Organised retaliation by 280/B + 282/D carried out at 12 noon.	
			Wire cutting by 282/B.	
			Considerable activity in neighbourhood of ADINFER WOOD - Working parties dispersed.	
	4/8/16	3.45 AM.	Bombardment (hostile) of trenches on left flank (Right zone of 46 DIV.) Call received for assistance. Group order given to 280/B + 282/D to assist 46 DIV.	

ORIG

Instructions regarding War Diaries and Intelligence Summaries are contained in F. S. Regs., Part II. and the Staff Manual respectively. Title Pages will be prepared in manuscript.

WAR DIARY or ~~INTELLIGENCE SUMMARY~~

(Erase heading not required.)

1 RFA TF

AUGUST 1916

Sheet ii

Place	Date	Hour	Summary of Events and Information	Remarks and references to Appendices
VICINITY OF BIENVILLERS + FONQUEVILLERS	4/8/16 (cont'd)		Slight shelling of our trenches at intervals during morning. Hostile aeroplanes over BIENVILLERS + FONQUEVILLERS. Enemy active in improving trenches etc – working parties dispersed. Wire cutting by 282/B in afternoon. Hostile Battery located at F.8.b. 15.25. Ceased firing when fired on by 280/B. Quiet night.	
	5/8/16		Hostile Battery again located at F.8.b. 15.25. firing near BIENVILLERS. 280/B fired in return + hostile Battery ceased firing. Another hostile Battery located at F.1.d.35.90 in 46 DIV. area. Right Group 46 DIV. ARTY notified. Registration with Kite Balloon carried out by 282/D + 280/B. Several hostile balloons up during day + hostile aeroplanes active. Quiet night.	
	6/8/16		During morning hostile Batteries from neighbourhood of PIGEON WOOD fired heavily on E 20.c + E 26 a evidently directed by Balloon on Battery positions. Hostile aeroplanes also active. Registration with Kite Balloon carried out by 280/B Hostile Battery previously located at F.1.d. 35.90 again active (on North of our zone). Quiet night.	
	7/8/16		Intermittent shelling of Battery positions in E.20.c. during day + of our trenches during afternoon. Retaliation on Trenches in neighbourhood of "the Z" at request of Infantry. Hostile Balloons up. Quiet night.	

2449 Wt. W14957/M90 750,000 1/16 J.B.C. & A. Forms/C.2118/12.

ORIGIN

Instructions regarding War Diaries and Intelligence Summaries are contained in F. S. Regs., Part II. and the Staff Manual respectively. Title Pages will be prepared in manuscript.

WAR DIARY or ~~INTELLIGENCE SUMMARY~~

(Erase heading not required.)

2nd (City of London) Bde RFA T.F.

AUGUST 1916 Sheet iii

Place	Date	Hour	Summary of Events and Information	Remarks and references to Appendices
VICINITY OF BIENVILLERS & FONQUEVILLERS	8/8/16		Neighbourhood of BIENVILLERS shelled, apparently directed by aeroplane. Hostile aeroplanes active.	
			Working parties of enemy fired on & driven to cover.	
			Retaliation by 280/B Battery, at request of Infantry, for enemy's shelling & Trench Mortar activity on our trenches in left subsector. Enemy fire ceased.	
		10 PM to 10.45 PM	Combined operation by 280/B, 282/B & 282/D on sap heads, Commn Trenches & Trench junctions in E11; also on railway & tracks in rear.	
	9/8/16	9 AM to 11 AM	Hostile shelling in neighbourhood of BIENVILLERS – about 150 rounds (105 & 150 mm.) Hostile aeroplanes active during the firing. Hostile shelling also on HANNESCAMPS & trenches.	
			Hostile kite balloons up & general aerial activity on both sides during morning.	
			Registration as necessary. Enemy working party dispersed.	
			Very hazy later in day.	
			Our Trenches No 72–74 shelled during evening.	
		9.5 to 9.15 PM	Retaliation for above carried out by 280/B Battery in co-operation with Heavy Arty.	
			Quiet night thereafter.	
	10/8/16		Quiet day. Registration as necessary. Wire cutting by 282/B Battery.	
			Misty later in day. Very little activity on either side.	
	11/8/16	1.15 AM to 2.30 AM	Fired on hostile wire cutting party in E17 & hostile patrol in OSIER BED.	
			SNIPER'S SQUARE shelled from 9.20 to 10 AM; otherwise quiet during morning.	
			Hostile aeroplanes active during day.	

2449 Wt. W14957/M90 750,000 1/16 J.B.C. & A. Forms/C.2118/12.

Instructions regarding War Diaries and Intelligence Summaries are contained in F. S. Regs., Part II. and the Staff Manual respectively. Title Pages will be prepared in manuscript.

WAR DIARY or ~~INTELLIGENCE SUMMARY~~

(Erase heading not required.)

RFA TF

AUGUST 1916

Sheet IV

Place	Date	Hour	Summary of Events and Information	Remarks and references to Appendices
VICINITY OF BIENVILLERS + FONQUEVILLERS	11/8/16 (contd)	8.30 PM + 9.15 PM	Combined operation by 282/A + 282/B Batteries. Sharp bursts of fire on enemy's front line + sapheads in neighbourhood of OSIER BED — suspected assembly points of hostile patrols + raiding parties. At 11.40 PM swept OSIER BED on reported enemy patrol.	
			Misty — quiet night.	
	12/8/16		Registration as necessary. Wire cutting by 282/B Battery.	
			Enemy aeroplanes still active. 280/B Battery fired on hostile MG to assist one of our aeroplanes. Hostile planes active also during evening + early night — one plane flying low dropped two bombs on SOUASTRE-FONQUEVILLERS road (E.26.a)	
	13/8/16		Desultory shelling of HANNESCAMPS + our trenches during afternoon.	
			Enemy aeroplanes again active. Several hostile kite balloons up — 19 counted at one time.	
			Quiet night.	
	14/8/16	12.23 AM	Fired on hostile MG reported in OSIER BED	
			Wire cutting by 282/B Battery during morning.	
			Desultory shelling of front line East of FONQUEVILLERS CHURCH during morning. Considerable shelling of HANNESCAMPS + neighbourhood during afternoon.	
		6 PM to 6.20 PM	Combined operation by 280/A 282/B + 282/D Batteries on suspected dugouts &c in F13a in retaliation for shelling of HANNESCAMPS.	
			Enemy working parties fired on during afternoon + evening.	
			Quiet night.	
	15/8/16		Dull morning, observation difficult. Quiet.	
			Considerable shelling of HANNESCAMPS during afternoon with 105 + 77 mm.	
		4.55 PM	Retaliation for above carried out on enemy dugouts in E11d 7.8 by 280/B + 282/D Batteries.	
			282/B Battery fired during afternoon on motor lorries + parties using tracks in F2d + F3.	
		6.30 & 7 PM	Trenches S.E. of FONQUEVILLERS shelled with 150 mm. Quiet night.	

2449 Wt. W14957/M90 750,000 1/16 J.B.C. & A. Forms/C.2118/12.

WAR DIARY or ~~INTELLIGENCE SUMMARY~~

(Erase heading not required.)

280 (CITY OF LONDON) BDE RFA T.F.

AUGUST 1916

Sheet V.

Place	Date	Hour	Summary of Events and Information	Remarks and references to Appendices
	16/8/16		Quiet morning.	
BIENVILLERS		2 PM	Command of Northern Group handed over to L^T COL AF PRECHTEL, and H.Q relieved by 282nd Bde H.Q.	
TO F^ME DE LA HAIE		2.30 to 3.15 PM	Bde H.Q moved from BIENVILLERS to F^ME DE LA HAIE (H.Q of Centre Group)	
		4.30 PM	L^T COL. LAC SOUTHAM took over command of CENTRE GROUP from L^T COL AR. WAINEWRIGHT. Bde H.Q relieved 283rd Bde H.Q. Group consists of 93rd 109th 282/C, 283/C (18 pdr Batteries) + 280/D (4.5 How) situated in plain West of HEBUTERNE + FONQUEVILLERS.	
VICINITY OF HEBUTERNE + FONQUEVILLERS			Batteries fired on hostile M.G to keep down their fire on our aeroplanes. Also fired on new M.G emplacement at K.3.d.75.75.	
			Quiet night.	
	17/8/16		SAILLY shelled with 105 + 150 mm at 1 P.M + 7.30 P.M. Our Trenches – Y56 + Y57 – shelled during afternoon + early evening.	
			Enemy working parties fired on.	
			Quiet night.	
	18/8/16		Considerable shelling of our Trenches Y48, Y49 + Y52-54 with 77 mm. during morning.	
		12.30 PM	SAILLY again shelled with 150 mm coincidently with our retaliation on BUCQUOY for hostile shelling of SAILLY on previous day. 280/D Battery co-operated with Southern Group + Heavy Artillery in this bombardment of BUCQUOY.	
			Trenches Y49-51 shelled during afternoon; also SOUASTRE.	
			Hostile working parties fired on, also M.G emplacement at K3 d 6.7 on which direct hits were obtained by 109th Battery.	
			Quiet night.	
	19/8/16	12.30 PM	SAILLY again shelled with 150 mm but not so heavily as on previous days.	
			Enemy working parties + M.G. fired on; also the M.G emplacement at K.3.d.6.7	
			Quiet night.	

0KM

Instructions regarding War Diaries and Intelligence Summaries are contained in F. S. Regs., Part II. and the Staff Manual respectively. Title Pages will be prepared in manuscript.

WAR DIARY ~~or INTELLIGENCE SUMMARY~~

(Erase heading not required.)

R.F.A. T.F.

AUGUST 1916

Sheet vi

Place	Date	Hour	Summary of Events and Information	Remarks and references to Appendices
VICINITY OF HEBUTERNE & FONQUEVILLERS	20/8/16		Our Trenches Y51 & Y53 shelled during morning with 105 mm & Reserve Trenches in front of FONQUEVILLERS shelled with 150 mm during afternoon. Considerable shelling of HEBUTERNE during evening	
			167TH INF. BDE. (covering this Sector) relieved by 52ND INF. BDE. (17TH DIV.) on the move of 56TH DIV. out of the line.	
			Quiet night.	
	21/8/16		283/C Battery fired on working party at 5 AM; also on other parties in afternoon.	
			SAILLY shelled at 12.30 P.M.	
			Quiet night	
	22/8/16		Misty morning.	
			Enemy trenches shew signs of considerable work	
			Marked increase in number of signals picked up from hostile aeroplanes engaged in ranging Batteries.	
			Quiet day. Enemy working parties fired on during day.	
			Considerable M.G. activity during night.	
	23/8/16		Hostile aeroplanes very active during morning.	
			Considerable shelling during morning of HEBUTERNE & trenches with all calibres up to 150 mm	
			At 11 AM. 280/D & 283/C Batteries fired on DIEZ WOOD & points & roads in vicinity, in co-operation with Southern Group.	
			280/D Battery engaged in Counter Battery work, by order of 39th H.A Group.	
			Working party fired on during evening, at K3 d.77 where considerable work has been done. Work ceased	
			Quiet night on this front.	
	24/8/16		Considerable hostile shelling of Battery positions in SAILLY-HEBUTERNE plain during morning. Also intermittently on Trenches. Hostile aeroplanes active in ranging most of the day.	
			During morning CRA 56 Divn with CRA 17th Divn visited Group H.Q in connection with ensuing relief by 17 Div Arty.	

2449 Wt. W14957/M90 750,000 1/16 J.B.C. & A. Forms/C.2118/12.

OR 14

Instructions regarding War Diaries and Intelligence Summaries are contained in F. S. Regs., Part II. and the Staff Manual respectively. Title Pages will be prepared in manuscript.

WAR DIARY or ~~INTELLIGENCE SUMMARY~~

(Erase heading not required.)

R.F.A. T.F.

AUGUST 1916

Sheet VII

Place	Date	Hour	Summary of Events and Information	Remarks and references to Appendices
VICINITY OF HEBUTERNE + FONQUEVILLERS	24/8/16 (cont.d)		SAILLY heavily shelled during evening.	
			93rd + 280/D Batteries fired on points behind GOMMECOURT, including supposed hostile battery position, suspected of being active.	
			Quiet night in this sector.	
	25/8/16		Brigade + Battery Commanders, 81st Bde R.F.A. (17 DIV ARTY) arrived to discuss preliminary details re taking over.	
			Fairly quiet day on this front, + quiet night.	
	26/8/16		Enemy working parties dispersed during morning. Aeroplanes active on both sides during day.	
			Hostile shelling of our Trenches in afternoon; two sharp bursts of fire on SAILLY in the evening.	
		9 to 12 PM	One section each of 109th 283/C + 93rd Batteries relieved by sections from A B + C Batteries, 81st Bde respectively.	
			Quiet night.	
	27/8/16		Incoming sections of 81st Bde carried out registration.	
			Counter Battery work by 280/D Battery	
			Enemy working parties dispersed.	
			Affiliated Infantry (52nd Inf. Bde) carried out relief of Battn in right Sub Sector.	
			Quiet night.	
	28/8/16		CRA 17th Division + OC 81st Bde called at Group HQ to discuss relief, + obtain particulars regarding this front.	
			Quiet day. Affiliated Infantry (52nd Inf. Bde) carried out relief of Batt.n in left Sub Sector	
			Incoming sections of 81st Bde carried out registration	
			Enemy working party + hostile Machine Guns fired on.	
			Desultory hostile shelling of roads + tracks in rear of line during the evening.	
		9 to 10 PM	One section each of 282/C + 280/D Batteries relieved by sections from B + D Batteries 80th Brigade respectively.	
			Quiet on this front during the night.	

2449 Wt. W14957/M90 750,000 1/16 J.B.C. & A. Forms/C.2118/12.

ORIG...

Instructions regarding War Diaries and Intelligence Summaries are contained in F. S. Regs., Part II. and the Staff Manual respectively. Title Pages will be prepared in manuscript.

WAR DIARY
or
INTELLIGENCE SUMMARY
(Erase heading not required.)

280 (CITY OF LONDON) BDE R.F.A. T.F.

Army Form C. 2118

AUGUST 1916

Sheet viii.

Place	Date	Hour	Summary of Events and Information	Remarks and references to Appendices
VICINITY OF HEBUTERNE + FONQUEVILLERS	29.8.16		Enemy working parties fired on during morning. Hostile shelling between 11 AM. + 12 noon of CHATEAU DE LA HAIE (Inf. Bde. + Group HQ) Organised retaliation at 12 NOON on RETTEMOY FARM. Bad weather. Very heavy thunderstorms during afternoon.	
		9 P.M.	Retaliated at request of Inf. Bde. on point of GOMMECOURT PARK, in co-operation with Stokes Mortars, for hostile Trench mortars firing from that neighbourhood.	
		9 to 10 PM	Remaining Sections of 109th 283/C + 93rd Batteries relieved by Sections from 81/A, 81/B + 81/C Batteries respectively (17 DIV ARTY), Commanders of retiring Batteries (56 Div Arty) remaining in command until the morning.	
			Very heavy firing during the night on right flank	
	30.8.16	7 AM.	Hostile shelling of CHATEAU DE LA HAIE repeated.	
		8 AM.	Organised retaliation carried out by Batteries of Group on RETTEMOY FARM and adjacent sensitive points.	
CHATEAU DE LA HAIE To GAUDIEMPRÉ		10 AM.	Command of Group handed over to Lt COL HARDMAN. 81st Bde RFA. Bde HQ relieved by HQ 81st Bde. Bde HQ arrived at Bde Wagon Line. Battery Commanders 280/A + 280/B Batteries also arrived at Wagon Line on relief of Northern Group by 17 Div. Arty.	
	31.8.16		Preparations made for move to new area (FOURTH ARMY). Billeting party sent in advance to OCCOCHES.	APPx No 1 message to 56th Divn on leaving VII Corps.
		night	Remaining Sections of 280/C + 280/D Batteries relieved by 17 Div Arty from Southern + Centre Groups respectively + proceeded to Bde Wagon Line.	

[signature]
Lt Col
Comdg 280th (CITY OF LONDON) BDE RFA (T.F.)

1875 Wt. W593/826 1,000,000 4/15 J.B.C. & A. A.D.S.S./Forms/C. 2118.

WAR DIARY
or
INTELLIGENCE SUMMARY
(Erase heading not required.)

Army Form C. 2118.

Summary of Events and Information

Remarks and references to Appendices

[illegible] Zone E. 23 [illegible]

[illegible] E 23 A [illegible]

A/Battery

Date	Summary of Events and Information
17th	Fired on machine gun [illegible] about E 23 C 73.58. [illegible]
18th	Normal period.
19th	Infantry [illegible] by [illegible] firing indiscriminately & [illegible] ONCQUEVILLERS
20th	Observed enemy working party [illegible] E 29 B 68 70. Dispersed.
21st	Working party about E 29. [illegible] (Disappeared.)
22nd	Party under an officer seen near [illegible] FARM. Salvos fired. Satisfactory.
23rd	Normal [illegible].
23-24	B.C. of B. 78th Bde went round [illegible] O.P.s & trenches.
24th	Right X relieved by RF X E 78.
25th	Normal [illegible]. Left Zone [illegible] R.X. Commander B/78th Bde.
26th	Brought left X out of action upon completion of relief by B/78.

[illegible signature]

Instructions regarding War Diaries and Intelligence Summaries are contained in F. S. Regs., Part II. and the Staff Manual respectively. Title Pages will be prepared in manuscript.

WAR DIARY
or
INTELLIGENCE SUMMARY
(Erase heading not required.)

AUGUST 1916

Army Form C. 2118

Place	Date	Hour	Summary of Events and Information	Remarks and references to Appendices
E20a6893 NEAR FONQUEVILLERS	16 Aug		Came under orders of NORTHERN GROUP. Covering Zone E. 23 B. 70.70 to E. 29 A 25. 90.	
	17th		Fired on machine from Battle Emplacement about E. 23 C 73.58. Effective.	
	18th		Normal. period	
	19th		Infantry relief by new Division Enemy firing indiscriminately on tracks west of FONQUEVILLERS.	
	20th		Observed Enemy working party at E. 29. B. 68. 70. Dispersed	
	21st		Working party about E 29. B. 65. 73 (Disappeared.)	
	22nd		Party under an officer seen near LA. BRAYELLE FARM. Salvoes fired. Satisfactory.	
	23rd		Normal 24 hours.	
	23-24.		B.C. of B. 75th Bde went round position OPs & trenches.	
	26th		Right X relieved by Rt X B. 78.	
	27th		Normal 24 hours. Shot zone with R. X. Commander B. 78th Bde.	
	29 Aug.		Brought left X out of action upon completion of relief by B. 78.	

[signature illegible]

1875 Wt. W593/826 1,000,000 4/15 J.B.C. & A. A.D.S.S./Forms/C. 2118.

Army Form C. 2118

WAR DIARY

or

INTELLIGENCE SUMMARY

(Erase heading not required.)

Summary of Events and Information

'B' Battery

1875 Wt. W593/826 1,000,000 4/15 J.B.C. & A. A.D.S.S./Forms/C. 2118

Instructions regarding War Diaries and Intelligence Summaries are contained in F. S. Regs., Part II. and the Staff Manual respectively. Title Pages will be prepared in manuscript.

WAR DIARY
or
INTELLIGENCE SUMMARY
(Erase heading not required.)

AUGUST 1916 — Army Form C. 2118 — Sheet 1

Place	Date	Hour	Summary of Events and Information	Remarks and references to Appendices
BIENVILLERS	16/8/16	4 pm	Northern Group was taken over by Brigade Commander 282nd Bde RFA	
		5.42 pm	Fired 4 rounds on enemy transport reported by Aeroplane	
		6.10 pm	Fired 16 rounds on and dispersed working party at E.18 b 1 9.	
	17.8.16	4 pm	Fired 40 rounds into Enemy's Battery at F13 d 7.8 in retaliation for shelling of BIENVILLERS.	
		& 5.45 pm 7.41 pm	Located a locomotive on light railway at E 12 a and E 12 b. Fired 15 rounds at the target with result that a cloud of steam was seen to arise.	
	18.8.16	12.15 pm	Fired 10 rounds on enemy's front line at E 11 c 50 85 where movement was observed	
	19.8.16	3.30 pm	Fired 17 rounds at suspected O.P at F 7 c 35 30	
		3.35 pm	Fired 8 rounds at enemy's gun at F 13 b 9 2.	
		7.40 pm	Fired 6 rounds at F. 7 c. 30.35 where movement observed	
	21.8.16	9.15 am	Fired 7 rds at and silenced hostile Battery at F 17 b. 9 1	
		3 pm	Fired 10 rounds at suspected O.P. at F 13 b 95.50	
	22.8.16	4.18 pm	Fired 2 rounds at request of Infantry at Sect Concentration	
	23.8.16	9.11 am	Fired 9 rounds at Enemy's lone gun at F 13 b 95 80	
	24.8.16	10.7 am	Fired 50 rounds at QUESNOY FARM in retaliation for enemy's shelling our villages	
		2.55 pm	" 52 " " " " " " " "	
	25.8.16	3.50 pm	Fired 14 rounds at enemy working at suspected M.G. emplacement at E 24 d. 7.9. Party dispersed and works damaged	

1875 Wt. W593/826 1,000,000 4/15 J.B.C. & A. A.D.S.S./Forms/C. 2118.

ORIG

Instructions regarding War Diaries and Intelligence Summaries are contained in F. S. Regs., Part II. and the Staff Manual respectively. Title Pages will be prepared in manuscript.

WAR DIARY
or
INTELLIGENCE SUMMARY
(Erase heading not required.)

Army Form C. 2118

AUGUST 1916

Sheet 11

Place	Date	Hour	Summary of Events and Information	Remarks and references to Appendices
BIENVILLERS	26.8.16	6.30 pm	Fired 20 rounds at enemys working party and works at E 24 d 7.9. Party dispersed and works damaged	
		9 pm	Right section was relieved by Section of 17th Divisional Artillery. Right Section proceeded to Wagon Line at GAUDIEMPRE	
	27.8.16	3.36 pm	Fired 20 rounds registering new Section	
		6.30 pm	Enemy fired about 20 rounds of 105 mm and 20 rounds of 77 mm into BIENVILLERS near Battery position	
	28.8.16	1.45 pm	Fired 6 rounds at working party at E 24 d 7.9	
			Fired 20 rounds on tracks in Zone by order of Group as retaliation for Enemy shelling our transport on FONQUEVILLERS Road.	
	29.8.16	6.45 pm	Fired 5 rounds at working party at E 24 d 7 9.	
		9 pm	Fired 10 rounds at order of Group as Test Concentration "Assist Z.2"	
		9.45 pm	Fired 20 rounds on QUESNOY FARM as retaliation on order of Group	
		9.45 pm.	Remaining Section of 17th Divisional Artillery came in and relieved Left Section which proceeded to GAUDIEMPRE	
	30.8.16	10 am	Handed over Zone and command to O.C. B/80 R.F.A and rejoined Brigade at GAUDIEMPRE	

[illegible] Major
O.C. B/240

1875 Wt. W593/826 1,000,000 4/15 J.B.C. & A. A.D.S.S./Forms/C. 2118.

Army Form C. 2118

WAR DIARY
or
INTELLIGENCE SUMMARY

Summary of Events and Information

'C' Battery

ORIG

'C' Bty
38 Bde R.F.A.

WAR DIARY
or
INTELLIGENCE SUMMARY

(Erase heading not required.)

Army Form C. 2118

Instructions regarding War Diaries and Intelligence Summaries are contained in F. S. Regs., Part II. and the Staff Manual respectively. Title Pages will be prepared in manuscript.

AUGUST 1916

Place	Date	Hour	Summary of Events and Information	Remarks and references to Appendices
SAILLY (K.13.a.9.9)	2nd August 1916	-	Shoot on Points with Aeroplane observation – (No 8 Squadron R.F.C.) Satisfactory. Two targets registered.	
			Combined Shoot on enemy Trenches on instruction from GROUP.	
"	3rd Aug			
"	4th "		All quiet – Commenced new bursting layer to Telephone Pit + new Dugout for men.	
"	5th "		Shoot on Points behind Enemy front Line System with Kite Balloon observation. Satisfactory.	
"	6th } 7th }		Shoots on Enemy working parties behind front line system. Results very satisfactory.	
"	8th		All quiet –	
"	9th		Test aeroplane call "LL" – Range 5600 – results not observable.	
"	10th		2 Shoots (Retaliation) by instruction from GROUP. – 40 rds in all. – Results observed from O.P.H. satisfactory –	
"	11th		Retaliation for Minenwerfer fire – Enfilade fire from CENTRAL GROUP apparently more satisfactory than frontal fire in stopping enemy Mortars.	
"	12th		All quiet.	
"	13th		" " during day. "Stand to" received 11-pm – but "Stand easy" received 11.30/pm	
"	14th		Retaliation on orders from GROUP.	
"	15th		Fired on Working Party 2 am	
			Apertures of GUNPITS widened to admit of 26° switch (Left) for special Shoot.	
"	16th		Retaliation	
	17 18 19 20 21		Occasional Shoots on Working parties behind front Line System – otherwise all quiet.	

G. Mead
Major

1875 Wt. W593/826 1,000,000 4/15 J.B.C. & A. A.D.S.S./Forms/C. 2118.

Instructions regarding War Diaries and Intelligence Summaries are contained in F. S. Regs., Part II. and the Staff Manual respectively. Title Pages will be prepared in manuscript.

280 Bde RFA WAR DIARY or INTELLIGENCE SUMMARY

(Erase heading not required.)

AUGUST 1916

Army Form C. 2118

Place	Date	Hour	Summary of Events and Information	Remarks and references to Appendices
SAILLY (K13a9.9)	August 22nd		Retaliation on RETTEMOY FARM.	
"	23rd		Registration of 3 Targets with Aeroplane observation (No 8 Squad R.F.C) – Results very satisfactory, three targets registered in 12 shots.	
"	24th		Registration of new auxiliary Zero Line – the original point being now demolished.	
"	25th		Working parties shelled – good effect.	
"	26th		Battery position shelled with 77 m.m – one man wounded.	
			OC B/79th called was shown over Battery position.	
"	27th		Shoot on EXE – 20 rounds on instns from GROUP.	
			Subaltern from B Bty 79th Bde RFA was shown round Battery & taken to O.P.H. & Zone.	
"	28th	10 pm	Right Section B/79th moved in & relieved No 1+2 guns – which returned to Wagon Line in charge of Section Commdr	
"	29th	12 Noon	Ammunition counted & taken over by B/79th – receipt obtained.	
		3 pm	Registered Nos. 1+2 (B/79) on new Zero Line (X R. th 4°20' R of old Zero Line)	
"	30th		All quiet. Observation almost impossible. No 2 gun re-registered after alteration of sights. Orders recd 9 pm to shoot special 'GAS' Target, but cancelled 9-45 pm	
"	31st	10 pm	Left Section (B/79th) relieved my Left Xn, which returned to Wagon Line under Section Commdr.	

[illegible] Major

1875 Wt. W593/826 1,000,000 4/15 J.B.C. & A. A.D.S.S./Forms/C. 2118.

Army Form C. 2118

WAR DIARY
or
INTELLIGENCE SUMMARY

Place	Date	Hour	Summary of Events and Information	Remarks and references to Appendices
			'D' Battery	

O.C. 280/D. Battery.

Army Form C. 2118

Instructions regarding War Diaries and Intelligence Summaries are contained in F. S. Regs., Part II. and the Staff Manual respectively. Title Pages will be prepared in manuscript.

WAR DIARY or INTELLIGENCE SUMMARY

(Erase heading not required.)

280/D Battery R.F.A. August/16

AUGUST 1916

Place	Date	Hour	Summary of Events and Information	Remarks and references to Appendices
In the Field.	6th		Major E.R.C. Warrens returned to Battery position, from Hospital.	
	8th	1.20.AM	There was an organised Bombardment of the enemy Trench system and of BUCQUOY	
	1st to 16th		From the 1st to the 16th inst during which time the 283rd Brigade R.F.A. controlled the Central Group, very little firing was carried out by this Battery, owing to the fact that the allotment of Ammunition was cut down to a minimum. The time was therefore devoted to clearing up the Battery position, strengthening and camouflaging the Gun Pits etc. A new Telephonists Cabin was built and the old one converted into an Ammunition Pit. A Trench 4 feet deep was also dug between the Rear Section and the Forward section, in which to lay an Armoured Telephone Cable. Two vacated Battery positions, one at K.8 A: 95.30 and the other at J.6.D: 60.40. were also cleared up and camouflaged.	
	31st August 16.			E.R.C. Warrens Major R.F.A. O.C. 280/D. Battery.

1875 Wt. W593/826 1,000,000 4/15 J.B.C. & A. A.D.S.S./Forms/C. 2118.

7th Corps G.S. 1644. 56th Divn.
G.241.

56th Division.

The Lieutenant-General Commanding VIIth Corps in saying good-bye to the 56th Division on their leaving the Corps, desires to record his appreciation of the manner in which the Division has fought and worked while it has been in the VIIth Corps. The gallant manner in which the Division fought at GOMMECOURT will be appreciated in history, but the Corps Commander wishes the Division to know that the less spectacular but more irksome work which the Division has put into the line which they have been holding, has not escaped notice. It is invidious to make distinction when all have worked so well, but he particularly congratulates those units who have so well repaired that part of the line knocked about in the fighting on 1st July.

The Corps Commander wishes all ranks good luck and feels sure that any task committed to the Division in the future will be completed in triumph.

Sgd/ F. LYON, Brigadier-General,
19th August, 1916. General Staff, VIIth Corps.

56th Divisional Artillery,

280th (City of London) BRIGADE R. F. A.

SEPTEMBER 1916.

Diaries of B;C;& D Batteries attached.

ORIGINAL WAR

Instructions regarding War Diaries and Intelligence Summaries are contained in F. S. Regs., Part II. and the Staff Manual respectively. Title Pages will be prepared in manuscript.

WAR DIARY ~~or~~ ~~INTELLIGENCE SUMMARY~~

(Erase heading not required.)

280TH (CITY OF LONDON) BDE RFA

Army Form C. 2118

SEPTEMBER 1916

Sheet 1

Place	Date	Hour	Summary of Events and Information	Remarks and references to Appendices
GAUDIEMPRÉ	1/9/16	12.30 AM	Orders to move cancelled.	
			Brigade standing by during morning ready to move at short notice.	
			Orders to move received in afternoon.	
GAUDIEMPRÉ To OCCOCHES & vicinity		4.15 PM	Brigade moved out of GAUDIEMPRÉ to OCCOCHES & vicinity, arriving about 8.30 P.M.	
			Brigade H.Q. established at MON PLAISIR; A & B Batteries at LE QUESNEL FM; C & D Batteries at OCCOCHES (S. side of River).	
	2/9/16	7.30 PM	Orders received to continue the move on 3rd inst.	
OCCOCHES To COISY	3/9/16		Head of Column moved off from MON PLAISIR at 10 AM. Brigade reached COISY 3.30 P.M.	
		11 PM	Received Orders to move on 4th inst. to DAOURS.	
COISY To DAOURS	4/9/16	10 AM	Brigade left COISY, being clear of village by 10.30 AM. Arrived at DAOURS 3 PM & bivouacked outside village.	
		11.30 PM	Received orders to continue move on 5th inst, two Batteries (280/A & 280/D) to go forward early to relieve Batteries of 55TH DIV.	
DAOURS To vicinity of BRAY-SUR-SOMME	5/9/16	7 AM	280/A & 280/D Batteries moved off } for 55TH DIV. ARTY. wagon lines, N of BRAY-SUR-SOMME.	
		8.30 AM	Bde HQ 250/B + 250/C " " " }	
			One section of 250/A moved into position at night. Reconnaissance made by 280/D Battery.	
	6/9/16	2 AM	C.R.A. called to arrange reconnaissance for advanced positions.	
		5.30 AM	O.C. Bde with 250/B & 250/C Battery Commanders proceeded on reconnaissance.	
	7/9/16	1.30 PM	C.R.A. called & gave orders to O.C. Bde to take over 56 DIV ARTY group of Batteries.	
Vicinity of MARICOURT + HARDECOURT		3 PM	Bde H.Q. left for Group H.Q. situated at A.9.d.2.4 - N.W of MARICOURT (Map 62c N.W)	
		7 PM	Lt COL. SOUTHAM took over command of Group from Lt COL PRECHTEL; 280 BDE HQ relieved 282 BDE HQ. Group consists of 280/A 281/C 283/C & all Batteries of 282 BDE. Information received later that 282/A 282/B & 282/C Batteries are to form a wire cutting Group under Lt. COL. MACDOWELL.	
		About 10 PM	S.O.S. call received. Rapid rate of fire opened, slowing down later.	

1875 Wt. W593/826 1,000,000 4/15 J.B.C. & A. A.D.S.S./Forms/C. 2118.

Instructions regarding War Diaries and Intelligence Summaries are contained in F. S. Regs., Part II. and the Staff Manual respectively. Title Pages will be prepared in manuscript.

WAR DIARY

~~or~~

~~INTELLIGENCE SUMMARY~~

(Erase heading not required.)

280TH (CITY OF LONDON) BDE RFA (T.F.)

Army Form C. 2118

SEPTEMBER 1916

Sheet ii

Place	Date	Hour	Summary of Events and Information	Remarks and references to Appendices
Vicinity of MARICOURT & HARDECOURT	8/9/16	3.15 AM	Barrage opened at request of Infantry Brigade.	
			Enemy shelled valley heavily, in A5d A11b & A6c later in morning.	
			Communications improved & ammunition drawn during the day. One gun of 280/A Battery reported permanently out of action.	
			All guns of 280/D Battery in position – Major E.R.C. WARRENS wounded. This Battery is now definitely included in Lt COL. MACDOWELL'S group.	
			This group (Lt COL SOUTHAM'S) takes the title of "LIFE" Group (being the Code name for Bde H.Q.).	
	9/9/16	1.45 AM	Operation Orders received for ensuing day & Group Operation Orders prepared (attack on GINCHY re – see Appendices)	Appendix No 1 Operation Order No 4 of 8.9.16 (PRECHTEL GROUP) & LIFE GROUP Operⁿ Order No 1 of 9.9.16.
			Bombardment carried out in accordance with programme	
		4.45 PM	Barrages commenced simultaneously with attack. Programme carried out & further Barrage maintained	
		6.23 –	Instructed 282/D Battery to reduce rate of fire by one half.	
		6.35 –	Information received – Everything going satisfactorily. Infantry report our Barrage quite all right.	
		6.45 –	New Barrage ordered – T15.a.0.0 to T15.d.0.0	
		7.30 –	18 pdr Batteries reduce rate by one quarter.	
		7.37 –	282/D Battery report one howitzer damaged by premature. Received another to replace it at midnight.	
		8.0 –	Order received from PRECHTEL Group for "S.O.S" on new Barrage line. Enemy reported to be counter-attacking, but we are believed to be holding good. Batteries increase fire to four rounds per gun per minute.	
		8.27 –	Batteries ordered to slow down to ordinary rate on new Barrage line. Fire gradually slowed down to slow rate.	
		10.50 –	Orders received for LIFE & LUCRE (COL. MACDOWELL'S) groups to fire in two-hours reliefs during night.	
	10.9.16	Dawn	CAPT THOMSON (283/C Battery) sent forward to reconnoitre & report on situation.	
		6.25 AM	Order received to stop firing.	
		11.50 –	Two guns arrived to replace two out of action (283/C). All guns of group now in action.	

1875 Wt. W593/826 1,000,000 4/15 J.B.C. & A. A.D.S.S./Forms/C. 2118.

Instructions regarding War Diaries and Intelligence Summaries are contained in F. S. Regs., Part II. and the Staff Manual respectively. Title Pages will be prepared in manuscript.

WAR DIARY
or
~~INTELLIGENCE SUMMARY~~
(Erase heading not required.)

280th (CITY OF LONDON) BDE. RFA (T.F.) Army Form C. 2118

SEPTEMBER 1916

Sheet iii

Place	Date	Hour	Summary of Events and Information	Remarks and references to Appendices
Vicinity of MARICOURT + HARDECOURT	10.9.16 (cont'd)	2.15 PM	Instructions given to 282/D Battery to reconnoitre for forward position with view to early move – then to come under LUCRE Group. Reconnaissance made during afternoon + evening.	
			Quiet day on our particular front until 5 P.M.	
		5.10 PM	Opened fire on Barrage lines. Information received that enemy is massing for counter-attack.	
		5.15	Changed to Barrage fixed for previous night. Rapid rate at first + then slowed down.	
		6.50 "	Batteries ordered 4 rounds per gun per minute for 5 minutes, then returning to present rate.	
		7.18 "	Information received that enemy is counter-attacking. Batteries ordered 4 rounds per gun per minute for 15 minutes, then present rate.	
		8.33 "	Reduced rate of fire + further reduced it at 9.29 P.M. to one round per Bty per minute.	
		9.45 "	282/D (How) Battery turned on to T20 central where enemy has strong point in the salient wedged in in our new line.	
		10.46 "	Information received from LIAISON Officer (COL. POTTINGER, RFA) that enemy is putting up another Barrage. Batteries ordered three rounds per gun per minute for 10 minutes, then one round per gun per minute.	
		11.5 "	"S.O.S." call received + acted on	
		11.17 "	Reduced fire to one round per gun per minute + at 11.22 to 1 round per Bty per minute.	
	11.9.16	2 AM	Information received from COL. POTTINGER (LIAISON Officer) – request slow rate of Barrage to be maintained.	
		3.15 "	282/D (How) Battery ready to move to new position – permission given. Remainder of Battery moved off at 5.20 A.M.	
		7 "	Stopped firing.	
		8.25 "	Ordered Section salvoes every 10 minutes	
		10.45 "	Stopped firing	
			The Group comes under command of 56 Div Arty H.Q. commanding Right Divl. Artillery XIV Corps	

1875 Wt. W593/826 1,000,000 4/15 J.B.C. & A. A.D.S.S./Forms/C. 2118.

Army Form C. 2118

Instructions regarding War Diaries and Intelligence Summaries are contained in F. S. Regs., Part II. and the Staff Manual respectively. Title Pages will be prepared in manuscript.

WAR DIARY 280TH (CITY OF LONDON) BDE R.F.A (T.F.)

~~or~~

~~INTELLIGENCE SUMMARY~~

(Erase heading not required.)

SEPTEMBER 1916

Sheet IV

Place	Date	Hour	Summary of Events and Information	Remarks and references to Appendices
Vicinity of MARICOURT + HARDECOURT	11.9.16 (cont[d])	12.50 P.M.	New Barrage line allotted to Group.	
			Orders received to reconnoitre for forward positions. Group H.Q. + Batteries to move tonight.	
			Reconnaissance unsuccessful in area mentioned by 56 D.A. owing to nature of ground + congestion of Batteries. Conference of B.C's with Group Commander in afternoon. Further reconnaissance made in other area + arrangements made to move tonight.	
		5.40 PM	Opened fire on new German trench. Operation Order in connection therewith to follow. Batteries not to move tonight until after this operation.	
		6.35 PM	Operation Orders received.	
		6.50 "	Zero time altered from 7.45 P.M. to 12 midnight.	Appendix N° 2 – Left Group Op[n] Order N° 2 of 11.9.16 ~~[illegible]~~
			Operation carried out. See Orders appended.	
	12.9.16	3.30 AM	First information received regarding the Operation – 56 Div partially succeeded, but not yet got all the Quadrilateral + has not yet established touch with Guards Div. Progress being made slowly.	
			Barrage maintained with slight variations throughout the night.	
			Orders received to move one gun only per Battery to new position. Cannot move remainder before daylight; these will go forward on night of 12th/13th.	
		5.10 AM	No further information. Barrage still to be maintained.	
		9.30 "	Barrage maintained until now. Batteries ordered to slow down.	
		9.43 "	Batteries ceased firing.	
		9.51 "	Re-opened fire with slow Barrage.	
		1.10 PM	Stopped firing. New Barrage line given. Brigade Wagon Lines moved nearer positions.	
	12th/13th	9.45 "	Batteries started moving to new positions	
Vicinity of HARDECOURT		night	Batteries got guns into position during night – all complete by 6.30 AM except 2 damaged guns of 281/C under repair at old position.	
	13.9.16	7 AM	Group H.Q. moved to A 5 c 8.8 (N. of BOIS FAVIERE)	
			Light very bad during day + observation difficult. Registration carried out as far as light permitted	

1875 Wt. W593/826 1,000,000 4/15 J.B.C. & A. A.D.S.S./Forms/C. 2118.

Instructions regarding War Diaries and Intelligence Summaries are contained in F. S. Regs., Part II. and the Staff Manual respectively. Title Pages will be prepared in manuscript.

WAR DIARY ~~or INTELLIGENCE SUMMARY~~

(Erase heading not required.)

280TH (CITY OF LONDON) BDE. R.F.A. (T.F.)

Army Form C. 2118

SEPTEMBER 1916

Sheet V.

Place	Date	Hour	Summary of Events and Information	Remarks and references to Appendices
Vicinity of HARDECOURT	13.9.16	6 PM.	Opened fire on Barrage line T15.c.0.9 to T15.d.4.0 dropping to slow rate at 6.30 P.M. Our infantry attacking the quadrilateral in T14 d + T15 c. Barrage maintained until after midnight.	
	14.9.16	12.50 AM.	Stopped firing + guns laid on new Barrage line T15 b 5.4 to T21 d 5.5	
		1.3 AM	S.O.S. call received via 56 Div. Arty. Batteries opened fire on new Barrage at once.	
		1.8	Batteries ordered to slow down. At 1.46 AM. stopped firing.	
			Day spent in preparing for Z day (15th). Orders received from 56 Div. Arty. + Group Orders issued.	See App^x N°3 Left Group O.O. N°3 of 14.9.16 + Div Arty O.O. attached
	15.9.16 (Z day)	6.20 AM (Zero)	Programme carried out in accordance with Operation Orders	
		11.22 AM.	New Barrage ordered + successively changed during the day according to circumstances. Fire maintained throughout the day.	
		4.16 PM.	All Batteries turned on to N.E. end of BOULEAUX WOOD, searching. Enemy counter-attacking. Information received later that the Barrage was excellent + effective. Infantry very pleased with it. Enemy counter attack failed. Rate of fire slowed down during evening.	
		11 PM to	Batteries fired in hourly reliefs.	
	16.9.16	6 AM.		
			Forward O.P. selected by 283/C Battery for close observation of enemy. Slow rate of fire maintained during day on Cross Roads + Railway Track + N.E. end of BOULEAUX WOOD.	
		7 PM.	Fresh Group Barrage received to be fired on from dark to dawn. Batteries fire accordingly at slow rate.	
		midnight to	Batteries fired in reliefs.	
	17.9.16	6 AM.		
			Day spent in registration on line in front of MORVAL + COMBLES + other work preparatory to further operations.	

1875 Wt. W593/826 1,000,000 4/15 J.B.C. & A. A.D.S.S./Forms/C. 2118.

Army Form C. 2118.

Instructions regarding War Diaries and Intelligence Summaries are contained in F. S. Regs., Part II. and the Staff Manual respectively. Title Pages will be prepared in manuscript.

WAR DIARY
~~or~~
~~INTELLIGENCE SUMMARY~~
(Erase heading not required.)

280TH (CITY OF LONDON) BDE RFA (T.F.)

SEPTEMBER 1916

Sheet VI

Place	Date	Hour	Summary of Events and Information	Remarks and references to Appendices
Vicinity of HARDECOURT	18.9.16	12.45 AM	Orders ~~received~~ for forthcoming operations commencing 5.50 AM + Group Orders issued.	See App^x No 4 Left Group O.O. No 4 18/9/16 with Divarty O.O. attached
			Group Programme carried out. Operations hampered by weather. Stopped firing at 11.3 AM	
			Continuous rain throughout the day + ground very difficult.	
			Slow fire during night across + beyond BOULEAUX WOOD.	
	19.9.16		Ground still very difficult.	
			Fired during morning + afternoon on new German trenches in neighbourhood of T1b a + T1b c.	
			Registration on Trenches &c in front of MORVAL carried out by 281/C Battery.	
		6 PM	280/D Battery (How.) comes under control of the Group.	
			Batteries fired during the night (slow rate) on new German trenches in T1b a + T1b c	
	20.9.16		Continued firing on new German trenches as above.	
			Fierce artillery duel from 8 AM onwards between French + Germans. Hostile artillery searched to neighbourhood of Group HQ + included Battery positions.	
			Reconnaissance for forward O.P. made during morning by MAJOR H.P. JONES (280/A Bty) + CAPT. D. THOMSON (283/C Bty) — MAJOR JONES severely wounded.	
		4 PM	Information received as to re-grouping. Group to consist of 280/A, B, C + D Batteries and 283/C Battery and to be engaged in wire cutting. Forward positions to be taken up — reconnaissance made.	
	21.9.16	Morning	Further reconnaissance for new positions. One gun per Battery (280/A 280/C + 283/C) moving to new positions today. Re-grouping carried out.	
			CAPT. W.L.W. BIRD (from B. Echelon 56 D.A.C.) takes over command of 280/A Bty vice MAJOR H.P. JONES (wounded).	
			Communications laid to new positions.	
	21/22	Night	Remaining guns moved during night. Movement made under great difficulties owing to state of ground.	

2449 Wt. W14957/M90 750,000 1/16 J.B.C. & A. Forms/C.2118/12.

Instructions regarding War Diaries and Intelligence Summaries are contained in F. S. Regs., Part II. and the Staff Manual respectively. Title Pages will be prepared in manuscript.

WAR DIARY

or

~~INTELLIGENCE SUMMARY~~

(Erase heading not required.)

250th (CITY OF LONDON) BDE RFA (TF)

SEPTEMBER 1916

Army Form C. 2118.

Sheet VII

Place	Date	Hour	Summary of Events and Information	Remarks and references to Appendices
Vicinity of HARDECOURT & GUILLEMONT & GINCHY	22.9.16		All guns in new positions by early morning & registrations commenced. Difficulties in delivering ammunition still acute.	
		9.30 AM	Lt COL. PRECHTEL commands 56 DIV ARTY Batteries (known as PRECHTEL GROUP) being part of Right Centre Artillery. This Group (LIFE GROUP) remains as a sub-group of PRECHTEL GROUP. Hostile shelling heavy all day.	
			Fired on new German trenches during afternoon & evening. Fired throughout the night on roads in MORVAL (Batteries firing in reliefs).	
	23.9.16	Morning	Continued firing on roads in MORVAL.	
		12 NOON	Started wire cutting on W. & S.W. side of MORVAL. Stopped at 6 P.M. Firing on new German trenches throughout night.	
	24.9.16		Visibility bad owing to fog all the morning. Batteries resumed firing (wire-cutting) at noon. At 1.40 PM zone shortened & re-distribution made to Batteries.	
			Orders received for operations tomorrow & Group orders issued to Batteries.	See Appx No 5. Life Group OO No 5 of 24.9.16 with Right Group R. Centre Arty Opn Orders
			Wire inspected by Battery Officers in conjunction with Infantry. Wire kept open during night.	
	25.9.16		Batteries resumed fire on the wire to ensure that it is completely cut. Special series of shells fired by 250/D Bty (How) prior to zero.	
		12.35 PM (Zero)	Programme carried out & furthest barrage maintained. Infantry found wire well cut & no obstacle to their advance. Operations completely successful.	
		5.15 PM	Rate of fire reduced; further reduced at 6.24 P.M.	
			Batteries of the Group heavily shelled during evening – one gun & detachment of 250/C Bty being completely knocked out.	
			Batteries fired throughout the night on Barrage S.E. of MORVAL, also on hostile battery in that neighbourhood and maintained until 10 AM the following morning.	

2449 Wt. W14957/M90 750,000 1/16 J.B.C. & A. Forms/C.2118/12.

Instructions regarding War Diaries and Intelligence Summaries are contained in F. S. Regs., Part II. and the Staff Manual respectively. Title Pages will be prepared in manuscript.

WAR DIARY ~~or INTELLIGENCE SUMMARY~~

(Erase heading not required.)

280TH (CITY OF LONDON) BDE. RFA (TF)

SEPTEMBER 1916

Army Form C. 2118.

Sheet viii

Place	Date	Hour	Summary of Events and Information	Remarks and references to Appendices
Vicinity of HARDECOURT & GUILLEMONT + GINCHY	26.9.16		Reconnaissance made for forward O.Ps	
			Reconnaissance (called for by XIV Corps) made for approach during daylight to possible forward positions in neighbourhood of west side of MORVAL	
		1.50PM	Slow barrage opened half way between MORVAL and SAILLY-SAILLISEL until 2.30 PM.	
		5PM	280/D Battery warned to move forward tonight.	
		7.17PM	SOS call received - Batteries opened fire	
		7.31PM	Stopped firing.	
			Batteries fired on Barrage lines (in reliefs) throughout the night	
			280/D Battery moved forward during night to new position.	
	27.9.16		Further reconnaissance made by CAPT. D. THOMSON (283/C Bty) early in the day for forward O.P. Information also gained as to movements of the enemy & passed on for action by Heavy Artillery.	
			Reconnaissance made during afternoon & evening for new positions for all Batteries in neighbourhood of MORVAL.	
	27/28th	Night	Batteries fired (in reliefs) throughout the night on Barrage line, & 280/D Bty (Hows) on the roads in that vicinity.	
	28.9.16		Further reconnaissances & arrangements made for 280/B 280/C & 280/D to move to forward positions tonight.	
		11.30AM	283/C Bty fired, by permission of French, on enemy seen in direction of SAILLY-SAILLISEL (in area covered by French)	
		2.55PM	Order to move cancelled.	
		7.5PM	Green rockets reported & Batteries opened fire on their Barrage	
		7.30"	Batteries ordered to slow down. 7.36 PM. Stopped firing.	
			LIFE GROUP is now part of the RIGHT GROUP (consisting of 56 Div. Arty) of Right Artillery of XIV Corps & covers part of the front taken over by 2ND FRENCH DIVN	

2449 Wt. W14957/M90 750,000 1/16 J.B.C. & A. Forms/C.2118/12.

Instructions regarding War Diaries and Intelligence Summaries are contained in F. S. Regs., Part II. and the Staff Manual respectively. Title Pages will be prepared in manuscript.

WAR DIARY

~~or~~

~~INTELLIGENCE SUMMARY~~

(Erase heading not required.)

Army Form C. 2118.

280TH (CITY OF LONDON) BDE R.F.A. (T.F.)

SEPTEMBER 1916

Sheet ix

Place	Date	Hour	Summary of Events and Information	Remarks and references to Appendices
Vicinity of HARDECOURT GUILLEMONT & GINCHY	28.9.16	MIDNIGHT to	Batteries fired until 4.45 AM. and again, in short intense bursts, from 5.15 AM to 7.30 AM, searching & sweeping to catch any of the enemy moving in area from behind MORVAL	
	29.9.16	7.30 AM	in direction of SAILLY-SAILLISEL.	
			Firing as above continued by Batteries in turn throughout the day.	
	29/30	Night	Batteries (18 pdrs) continued firing in turn throughout the night until 4.45 AM.	
	30/9/16	4.45 AM	All 18 pdr Batteries fired short intense bursts on area as above until 7.30 AM.	
		9.45 AM	280/B 280/C & 280/D Batteries warned to move to forward positions tonight.	
			Reconnaissances made accordingly during the morning in direction of MORVAL, to cover front of LESBOEUFS.	
		11.40 AM	283/C Bty fired, with permission of French, on parties of enemy moving in area of the zone covered by French Artillery.	
MORVAL		6 PM	280/D Bty commenced move to new position near MORVAL	
			Other Batteries arranging to move at dawn.	

L. A. C. [illegible]
Lt. Col
Commdg 280TH (CITY OF LONDON) BDE. RFA (TF)

2449 Wt. W14957/M90 750,000 1/16 J.B.C. & A. Forms/C.2118/12.

APPX No 1

SECRET

Copy No 5

OPERATION ORDER No:.1.BY LIEUT.COLONEL.[illegible]OUTRAM.,
COMMANDING LIFE GROUP.

9th SEPTEMBER 1916.

Reference Map
LONGUEVAL 1/10,000.

1. The XIVth Corps intends to attack this day at Zero hour which will be 4.45 p.m.

2. The objectives allotted to 56th Division are as follows :-

<u>1st Objective</u> - T.27.b.10.55 - T.21.d.55.25 - T.21.a.60.25 - T.20.b.45.35.
<u>2nd Objective</u> - T.21.a.60.25 - T.15.c.10.45 - T.14.d.85.40.

3. The lateral boundaries of the zone allotted to Batteries of the LIFE Group for bombardment and barrage are within lines as under :-

A/280	-On the right flank-	A Line drawn through T.21.c.42.92 - T.15.b.85.15.
	On the left.	T.21.a.1.0 - T.15.b.35.35.
C/281	-On the right -	T.21.a.1.0. - T.15.b.35.35.
	On the left -	T.2 0.d.60.82 - T.15.a.70.15.
C/283	On the right -	T.20.d.60.82 - T.15.a.70.15.
	On the left -	T.20 d.22.72 - T.15.a.1.0.

Great care will be taken by all Batteries, including D/282 not to shoot to the W.or N.W.of the line limiting on the left zone of C/283.

Particulars of targets for D/2 82 are given in para 4.

4. A deliberate bombardment will commence at 7 a.m.and will continue until zero time.

Fire of 18 pdr Batteries will be on trenches within the zone. It will be noted that the trench shown on the map as finishing at T.20.b.70.15 now extends through T.21.a.0.2. to T.21.a.2.2.and that in addition to this trench and others shown in the zone of the Group it is certain that the enemy have constructed communication and other trenches.

18 pdr Batteries will fire bursts of 3 rounds gun fire at the rate of five bursts per hour at irregular intervals.

4.5."How.Bty will fire 20 rounds per hour on the front trench T.20.d.30.85 - T.21.a.2.2. until minus 5 minutes. 4.5.How.Bty.will cease firing from 11.20 to 11.50 a.m.to enable photographs to be taken.

5. The Group will fire a "rolling" barrage as under:-

<u>A/280 Bty.</u>
<u>RED BARRAGE</u> - T.21.c.42.92 - T.21.a.1.0.
<u>RED & BLUE BARRAGE</u> - T.21.a.87.60. - T.21.a.43.63.
<u>BLUE BARRAGE</u> - ~~[illegible]~~ T.21.a.95.75. - T.15.c.70.15.
<u>BROWN BARRAGE</u> T.15.b.85.15 - T.15.b.37.37.

<u>C/281 Bty</u>
Red Barrage - T.21.a.1.0. - T.20.d.60.85.
Red & Blue Barrage - T.21.a.43.63 to T.20.b.95.65.
Blue Barrage - T.15.c.70.15 - T.15.c.48.65.
Brown Barrage - T.15.b.37.37 - T.15.a.70.15.

/1.

C/283 Battery
Red Barrage - T.20.d.60.85 - T.20.d.22.72.
Red & Blue Barrage - T.20.b.9[illegible].05 - T.20.b.62.78.
Blue Barrage - T.16.c.45.82.through T.15.c.3.9. to T.15.c.05.87
Brown Barrage - T.15.a.70.15. - T.15.a.1.0.

AT ZERO Batteries as above will fire on Red Barrage and alter Range and line so that an advance of 50 yards per minute is made until the Red & Bl Barrage is reached remaining there until Plus 41 minutes. At Plus 41 minutes they will continue "rolling" as before to Blue Barrage remaining there until plus 61 minutes when they will again roll at same rate to Brown Barrage.

D/282 Battery From minus 5 minutes to Plus 35 minutes - Trench T.21.a.50 65 - T.15.c.25.00.

From Plus 35 minutes onwards - The valley T.15.b.and T.16.a.and c.but not nearer our troops in T.15b.than a curve passing through T.15.b.9.0. T.16.b.50.35 - T.16.b.0.3.

The rate of fire from Zero hour will be as under :-

Zero to Plus 15 - 18 pdrs - 4 rounds per gun per minute.
4.5. Hows., - 2 ditto ditto
Plus 15 to Plus 40 Both natures 1 round per gun per minute
Plus 40 to Plus 55 18 pdrs - 4 rounds per gun per minute.
4.5.Hows., - 2 ditto ditto
Plus 55 onwards Both natures - One round per gun per minute.

The rate of fire is a guide which will be adhered to as far as possible but the greatest care will be taken to maintain at least 3 guns per Battery constantly in action most especially on arrival on final Barrage.

The proportion of "A" and "A.X" up to Gun Range 4000 will be 5 to 1 decreasing at longer ranges.

6. Watches will be synchronised with Group Headquarters and O.C. Batteries will be responsible that the watches of all Officers Nos.1.and signallers are synchronised. The programme of Barrages will be explained to all Officers and Nos.1.

7. Liaison duties will not be found by this Group nor will O.P's be manned.

8. Two orderlies from Group H.Q.will be attached to C/283 Bty as runners to 280/A and 281/C should other communications fail. Visual signalling as an alternative will also be established between these Batteries.

9. This order will be acknowledged by wire.

Lieut.,
Adjutant, [illegible] GROUP.

Copies to:
No.1. A/280 Bty.
2. C/281 "
3. C/283 "
4. D/282 "
5.) Retained.
6.)

SECRET.

Copy No 3.

PRICHTEL'S GROUP Operation Order No. 4.

Reference. Map GUILLEMONT Sheet. 1/20,000, and Secret Trench Map, 1/10,000.

8th September, 1916.

1. The XIV Corps will resume that attack on 9th September at Zero hour, which will be notified later.

2. The objectives allotted to 56th Division are as follows:-

1st Objective. T.27.b.1.5½. - T.21.d.5½.2½.
T.21.a.6.2½. - T.20.b.4½.3½.

2nd Objective. T.21.a.6.2½. - T.15.c.1.4½.
T.14.d.8½.4. -

Flares will be lit on obtaining each objective.

3. The assault will be preceded by deliberate bombardment which will commence at 7-0 a.m. and continue till Zero, except that the 4.5" Howitzers will not fire from 11-20 a.m. to 11-50 a.m. to enable photographs to be taken, nor will they fire on trenches to be assaulted.

4. LIAISON. Lieut-Colonel POTTINGER, R.F.A. will act as Liaison Officer with Left Infantry Brigade (168th Infantry Brigade) whose Headquarters are at A.5.d.25.30. (CHIMPANZEE TRENCH).

5. After the Infantry have started on the attack, if it is essential to turn fire on to any point where the enemy is collecting for a counter-attack, the Artillery Officer with the Brigade concerned may call upon one or more batteries of the stationary barrage to turn on to such a point.

6. Lieut-Colonel POTTINGER will detail an Officer from the 280th Brigade, R.F.A. and one from 283rd Brigade, R.F.A. to act as Liaison Officers.
One with Right Battalion (4th London), H.Q. at T.25.d.9.9.
The other with Left Battalion (12th London), T.25.d.9.4.5.

Liaison Officers will report for duty not later than 6-50 a.m. on the 9th September.

7. RATE OF FIRE.

18-pounders.	Intense.	4 rounds per gun per minute.
	Medium.	2 rounds per gun per minute.
	Ordinary.	1 round per gun per minute.
	Slow.	1 round per battery per minute.
4.5" Howrs.	Intense.	2 rounds per gun per minute.
	Ordinary	1 round per gun per minute.
	Slow.	20 rounds per gun per hour.

From Zero hour Rates of Fire for 18-prs. and 4.5" Hows. will be :-

0 to +15 mins.	Intense.
+15 to +40 mins.	Ordinary.
+40 to +55 mins.	Intense.
+55 onwards.	Ordinary.

8.

8. The greatest care must be exercised by batteries on the Left to keep up with the Time Table accurately, and not to shoot West or North West of the line dividing the Right and Left Divisions (T.20.d.1.5. to T.14.d.8½.4.).

9. BOMBARDMENT. During Bombardment the Rate of Fire of 4.5" Hows. will be Slow throughout, and 18-prs. will fire bursts of Intense fire, sweeping the trenches with Shrapnel and H. E. at odd times.

The wire-cutting Group will continue with their task until Zero hour, and not take part in the bombardment.

10. BARRAGES.

Rolling Barrage. Lt-Colonel SOUTHAM, R.F.A.

Zero. Start Barrage at dotted Red line as shown on Map and keep rolling at 50 yards a minute till they reach the dotted line coloured Red and Blue when they will halt.

+41 mins. Continue rolling as before to Blue line where barrage halts.

Stationary Barrage. Lt-Colonel MACDOWELL, R.F.A.

Zero. Green Barrage.

+2 mins. Lift on to Brown Barrage.

The Rolling Barrage continues rolling at +41 and the Stationary Barrage will lift on to the Blue Barrage as the Rolling Barrage reaches it,and,as the Brown Stationary Barrage will be reached at varying times, the Map has been marked with 50 yards lines, each equalling one minute, so that the exact time when the various parts of the Brown Barrage should be lifted on to the Blue Barrage can be ordered, (e.g., The Rolling Barrage will reach only a small portion of the Brown Barrage where it has to remain until +41 minutes).

Both Barrages.

At +60 minutes, the Infantry will push forward patrols to about 140 contour South of the GINCHY - MORVAL Road to obtain a view of the German line in front of MORVAL.

At +61 minutes, the whole final Barrage will begin to creep forward at 50 yards a minute till it reaches the line T.15.a.1½.0. - T.15.b.0.3., thence 150 yards beyond the 140 contour in T.15.b. & d. and T.21.b. & d.

11. 4.5" Howitzers.

D/280. On sunken Road at Western corner of ORCHARD, T.21.d.8.0. till Zero. Then move 100 yards down Road to S.E., keeping in the ORCHARD and on the Road.

D/282. On the front Trench T.20.d.3.8½. - T.21.a.2½.2½. till Zero -5 minutes.

From Zero -5 minutes to Zero + 35 minutes, trench T.21.a.5.6½. to T.15.c.3.0.

+35 minutes onwards, into the valley T.15.b. and T.16.a. & c.

Fire will be continuous from 7 a.m. till Zero hour, except to enable photographs to be taken.

4.5" Hows. shooting into the Valley in T.15.b. and T.15.a. will not fire nearer our troops than the final

barrage

barrage line 150 yards beyond the 140 contour in T.15.b.& d. and T.21.b. & d. after + 60 minutes.

12. Information should be sent with all possible expedition.

13. Signal Time will be sent as soon as received.

14. Zero hour will be 4-45 p.m.

A Prechtel
Lieut-Colonel,
Commanding PRECHTEL'S GROUP.

Copy No. 1 Right Div. Artys., XIV Corps.
2 Brig-General Commanding 168th Inf. Brigade.
3 Lt-Colonel SOUTHAM.
4 Lt-Colonel MACDOWELL.
5 Lt-Colonel POTTINGER.
6 Filed.

Acknowledge

After Order
Standing Barrage

Zero. One Battery will fire on that portion of the enemy's trenches in T.15.c enclosed in a circle coloured Blue

Rate of Fire

Zero. 3 Rounds per gun per minute
+15 mins. Medium
+35 " Intense
+42 " Lift on to Blue Barrage

Remaining Batteries will carry out Barrages as in Operation Order No 4 para 10. dated today

A Prechtel Lt Col
C/ Prechtels Group

8.9.16

APPX No 2.

SECRET — COPY NO 5

OPERATION ORDER NO.2. BY LIEUT.COLONEL L.A.C.SOUTHAM.,

COMMANDING LIFE GROUP,

11th SEPTEMBER 1916.

~~[illegible]~~

Reference Map
LONGUEVAL 1/10,000.

1. At 12 midnight tonight the 167th Infantry Brigade in conjunction with the Guards Division intends to take Strong Quadrilateral about T.15.c.2.0. - T.14.d.9.4. and seize the line of the road thence to GINCHY.

Two Shallow German Trenches have been dug from :
(a) T.20.b.55.30. - T.20.b.8.8.
(b) T.21.a.10.95 - T.15.c.3.1.

2. Batteries will continue firing salvoes at the rate of 3 per Battery per ~~minute~~ hour at irregular intervals in neighbourhood of these trenches until 11.30.p.m.

3. From 11.30 p.m.onwards Batteries will barrage as under :-

<u>A/280</u>
<u>11.30 p.m.to 12 midnight</u>
Fixed Barrage from T.20.b.72.90 - T.14.d.9.5.
<u>At 12 midnight</u>
From T.15.c.0.9 - T.15.c.35.70.

<u>C/281</u> Not to fire between 11.30 pm. & 11.45 pm.
A rolling barrage commencing from line T.20.b.55.30 - T.15.c.2.0. and rolling to the line T.20.b.55.30 - T.14.d.9.5. will be established at 11.45 p.m.and completed at 12 midnight.
At 12 midnight from T.15.c.68.50. - T.15.d.0.3. (fixed barrage)

<u>C/283</u>
<u>11.30 p.m.to 12 midnight</u>
Fixed barrage from T.20.b.55.30 - T.20.b.72.90.
<u>At 12 midnight</u>
From T.15.c.35.70. - T.15.c.68.50.

The rate of fire during barrages will be:
Up to 12 midnight...1 round per gun per minute
12 midnight to 12.15.a.m....4 rounds per gun per minute.
12.15.a.m.until further orders...2 rounds per gun per minute.
The proportion of "A" and "A.X" will be 5 "A" to 1 "A.X".

4. Ammunition may be moved to new positions provided that dumps are not reduced below 200 rounds per gun in proportion of 5 "A" to 1 "A.X" at 12 midnight.

5. Watches will be synchronised with Group H.Q.and the watches used by all Officers Nos.1 and signallers will be synchronised.

The programme of barrages will be explained to all Officers and Nos.1

6. This order will be acknowledged by wire.

[signature]
Lieut.,
Adjutant, LIFE GROUP.

Copies to: Nos.1. A/280 Bty.
2. C/281 "
3. C/283 "
4.) Retained.

SECRET Copy No: 4

OPERATION ORDER No:3.BY LIEUT.COLONEL.L.A.C.SOUTHAM.,

COMMANDING LEFT GROUP.

14th SEPTEMBER 1916.

Reference Maps
57C 1/40,000
Trench Maps .. 1/10,000.

1. GINCHY and trenches S.E.of LEUZE WOOD have been captured by XIVth Corps and it is anticipated that the situation between LEUZE WOOD and GINCHY will be further improved in the near future.

The Fourth Army intends to take the enemy's defences between the COMBLES RAVINE and MARTINPUICH tomorrow,15th September, (Z day) with the object of breaking through the enemy's ~~defense~~ system of defences. The FRENCH to the South and the Reserve Army on the left are undertaking an offensive simultaneously.

The attack will be pushed with the utmost vigour.

2. The task of the 56th Division will be the clearing of BOULEAUX WOOD and the formation of a protective flank extending as far North-East as the South end of MORVAL and covering the lines of advance from COMBLES and the valley running North-East from COMBLES.

The capture of MORVAL and LESBOEUFS will be undertaken by Sixth and Guards Divisions.

3. The Infantry will be distributed as follows prior to Zero:-

__167th Brigade__ H.Q.at FALFEMONT FARM.
on front T.21.a.6.4. to T.21.d.1.5.and extending in depth back to WEDGE WOOD.

__169th Brigade__ (2 Battalions) H.Q. at CRUCIFIX North of HARDECOURT.
Holding front line from T.21.d.1.5.to South Corner of LEUZE WOOD thence along to trench to about B.3.central.
__N.B.__ A portion of the trench from T.27.a.6.7.to about T.27.b.0.8. will also probably be occupied prior to Zero. Two Battalions 169th Infantry Brigade will be in Divisional Reserve.

__168th Brigade__ H.Q. ANGLE WOOD.
in area South West of WEDGE WOOD - FALFEMONT FARM.

4. The attack will be made on successive objectives. After the capture of each objective,the Infantry will wait until a pre-arranged hour before advancing to the attack of the next objective.

They will establish and consolidate a defensive Right Flank as they advance.

5. The role of the Right Divisional Artillery will be :-
(a) To facilitate the advance of our Infantry.
(b) To establish the defensive right flank barrage. (Details barrages and objectives are appended)

6. Three "Tanks" will be used to assist the advance of the 56th Division.

The greatest care must be taken to follow any instructions issued with the object of preventing damage being done to the "Tanks" by our own Artillery fire.

/2.

7. Gaps through which the Cavalry can be moved forward which must be kept free from shell fire will be notified later.

8. There will be no Liaison Officers with Battalions but F.O.O's will be detailed as under:-

281/C... ...169th Infantry Brigade Front.
283/C... ...167th Infantry Brigade Front.

These Officers will make every effort to keep in close touch with the Battalion and Company Commanders in their neighbourhood and send back intelligence and reports on the effect of artillery fire through their Batteries to Group Headquarters.

One Officer from 280/A Battery will be held available to be sent out as and when ordered by Group Headquarters. F.O.O's will be accompanied by necessary signallers and runners. They will advance to the best positions from which direct observations are possible as soon as these have been reached by our attack.

9. Every effort is being made to fill up the Dumps of Ammunition at Battery Positions but Battery Commanders must, on their own initiative do all they can to expedite its supply during the action and to avoid leaving derelict ammunition in case of a move.

10. In all cases of an advance, ground scouts will be pushed well ahead and every precaution taken to avoid surprise by small parties of the enemy passed over by the infantry.

11. Red flares will be lit:-

(a) On obtaining each objective.,
(b) At 12 noon and 5 p.m., September 15th.
(c) At 6.30 a.m. on September 16th.

The Cavalry are using green flares.

12. Watches will be synchronised soon after 12 noon and 6 p.m. by telephone from Group Headquarters.

13. This order will be acknowledged by wire.

[signature]

Lieut.,
Adjutant, LEFT GROUP.

Copies to:-
No.1. 280/A Battery.
2. 281/C "
3. 283/C "
4.)
5.) Retained.
6.)

B A R R A G E S

J A C K G U N

Zero to Plus 1h.10m. 7-10

Creep 50 yards a minute from line:
T.21.b.25.80 - T.21.b.45.45
to T.15.d.9.5. - T.16.c.15.27.
then return to T.21.b.40.95 - T.21.b.70.75.and remain stationary there.

At plus 1h.10m.to Plus 1h.50m. 8-10

Creep 50 yards a minute to T.16.c.2.8. - T.16.c.5.5. and become stationary.

Plus 1h.50m.to Plus.3.h.30m. 9-50

Stationary barrage from: T.16.d.2.8. - T.16.d.12.50.

Plus 3h.30m.to Plus 4h.20m. 10-40

Creep 50 yards a minute ~~from~~ to: T.16.b.4.5. - T.16.b.65.27. and become stationery.

Plus 4h.20m.

Form DEFENSIVE BARRAGE :- T.22.a.9.9. - T.22.b.35.90.

J O G U N

Zero to Plus 1h.10m.

Creep 50 yards a minute from line:
T.21.b.45.45. - T.21.b.60.18
to T.16.c.15.27 - T.16.c.35.05.
then return to the line T.21.b.70.75 -- T.21.b.92.58.and remain stationary there.

Plus 1h.10m.to Plus 1h.50m.

Creep 50 yards a minute up to T.16.c.5.5. - T.16.c.42.15.

Plus 1h.50m.to Plus.3h.30m.

Stationary Barrage from T.16.d.12.50 - T.16.d.05.23

Plus 3h.30m.to Plus 4h.20m.

Creep 50 yards a minute ~~from~~ to T.16.b.65.27 - T.16.b.85.08. and become stationary.

Plus 4h.20m.

Form DEFENSIVE BARRAGE :- T.22.b.35.90 - T.22.b.75.90.

/1.

B A R R A G E S (CONT)

T O N G U E

Zero to Plus 1h.10m.

Creep 50 yards a minute from line:
T.21.b.45.45. - T.21.b.60.18.
to T.16.c.18.27 - T.16.c.35.05
then return to the line T.21.b.70.75 - T.21.b.92.58 and remain stationery there.

Plus 1h.10.m.to Plus 1h.50m.

Creep 50 yards a minute up to T.16.c.42.15 - T.22.a.3.8. and become stationery.

Plus 1h.50 m.to Plus 3h.30m.

Stationery Barrage from T.16.d.05.25 - T.16.d.0.0.

Plus 3h.30m.to Plus 4h.20m.

Creep 50 yards a minute 15 T.16.b.85.08 - T.17.c.0/9. and become stationery.

Plus 4h.20m.

Form DEFENSIVE BARRAGE T.22.b.75.90 - T.23.a.20.85.

The rate of fire,unless otherwise ordered will be:

12 rounds per Battery per minute while creeping.
6 rounds per Battery per minute for 20 minuts on each stationery barrage and then
3 rounds per Battery per minute and after 1 hour on barrage
1 round per Battery per minute.

On DEFENSIVE BARRAGA 1 round per Battery per minute from commencement.

O B J E C T I V E S

A. (GREEN) - Attack starts at O.
(a) To be taken by 169th Infantry ~~Infantry~~ Brigade - trench T.27.a.65.70 - T.21.d.30.35.
(b) ditto 167th Infantry Brigade - line "MIDDLE COPSE" T.21.b.25.80 - T.21.d.70.95.-T.21.d.30.35

B. (BLUE) - Attack starts from GREEN LINE at Plus 2 hours.
to be taken by 167th Infantry Brigade (who will stay there)
Railway and Road Crossing T.15.d.70.75 - along Railway Line T.16.c.central - along Railway Line to cutting at T.22.a.3.8. - T.21.d.70.95.

C. (RED) - Attack starts from BLUE LINE at Plus 4 hours 30 minutes.
Trench T.16.b.4.5. - T.17.c.0.9. - T.17.d.0.7. - FORK ROAD - T.17.d.2.8. - thence back to T.17.b.0.6. and trench T.17.a.0.6. - T.17.a.3.4. - T.17.a.6.6.
In addition, posts will be established near gun position about T.17.c.0.3. and T.17.c.3.7.

C.O. Off^r No 4

SECRET   Copy No. 4

OPERATION ORDER No.4. by LIEUT.COLONEL.L.A.C.SOUTHAM.,

COMMANDING LIFE GROUP.

18th SEPTEMBER 1916.

Ref.Map.57c.S.W.
1/10,000.

1. The 56th Division will attack this morning with the object of capturing and consolidating the line T.21.d.7.2. - T.21.d.1.5. - along S.E.face of BOULEAUX WOOD to T.21.b.7.3.- MIDDLE COPSE (T.21.b.3.8)

The 6th Division will co-operate on their left and will establish themselves on the line MIDDLE COPSE (exclusive) to T.15.d.5.5 to T.15.a.7.9.

Zero hour will be 5.50 a.m.

2. At Plus 1' 167th Infantry Brigade will attack Eastwards from a line about T.21.a.7.0. - MIDDLE COPSE (T.21.b.3.8);objective - line from T.21.d.1.5.along Eastern end of BOULEAUX WOOD as far as T.21.b.7.3.thence to MIDDLE COPSE.

3. 56th Divisional Artillery will support 167th Infantry Bde.

4. Batteries will barrage as under:-

280/A Bty
From Zero onwards remains on stationary barrage along N.W. Edge of BOULEAUX WOOD T.21.b.75.85.- T.16.c.1.3

281/C Bty
Zero to Plus 4 T.15.d.95.05 - Northern Corner of BOULEAUX WOOD (T.16.c.1.3)
Plus 9 onwards T.15.d.90.32 - T.16.c.0.8.

283/C Bty
Zero to Plus 4 T.21.b.75.85 - T.15.d.95.05.
Plus 9 onwards T.21.b.75.85 - T.15.d.90.32.

Rate of fire from Zero to Plus 4...12 rounds per minute.
Plus 9 till further orders 3 rounds per minute
280/A..Zero to Plus 6..12 rounds per minute; afterwards 3 rounds per minute.

While on the WOOD ... ... 75% H.E.
While firing outside it... 25% H.E.

5. Watches will be synchronised by an Officer with Group Hd Qrs on the latter calling up for the purpose.

6. This order will be acknowledged by wire.

[signature]
Lieut.,
Adjutant, LIFE GROUP.

Copies to:-
No.1. 280/A Bty.
2. 281/C "
3..283/C "
4..) Retained.
5..)

App^x No 5

SECRET Copy No: 6

OPERATION ORDER No:5. BY LIEUT.COLONEL.L.A.C.SOUTHAM.,

COMMANDING LIFE GROUP,

24th SEPTEMBER 1916.

1. The Fourth Army intends to renew the attack on 25th inst in combination with the French to the South and the Reserve Army to the North.

The objective of the XIVth Corps includes the villages of MORVAL and LESBOEUFS.

The attack will be carried out by the 5th Division on the Right, 6th Division in the Centre and the Guards Division on the Left, the 56th Division forming a protective flank facing South.

2. The 56th Divisional Artillery has the task of covering the attack which will be made by the 95th Infantry Brigade on the right of the 5th Division.

3. Schedule of Barrages is attached.

4. Liaison Officers are being provided under Divisional arrangements.

O.P's will be manned by the following Batteries:-

280/C on behalf of 280/A [handwritten: B] and 280/C.
283/C on behalf of 280/B [handwritten: A] and 283/C.
280/D.

All information as to fire of the Group obtained by these Officers, except when affecting the Batteries to which they belong, will be sent to Group Headquarters.

They will furnish intelligence reports at frequent intervals, Nil reports being rendered if necessary hourly.

4. [typed 5., corrected by hand] One Officer from each of the other Batteries will be in readiness to proceed to an O.P. with necessary signallers if called upon to do so by Group.

5. [typed 6., corrected by hand] This order will be acknowledged by wire.

[signature]

Lieut.,
Adjutant, LIFE GROUP.

Copies to:
No.1. 280/A Bty.
2. 280/B "
3. 280/C "
4. 283/C "
5. 280/D "
6. Retained.,

L I F E   G R O U P

SCHEDULE OF BARRAGES

J O G U N

		pm	
Zero:	T.16.a.6.5. to T.16.a.53.15.	12-35	Green
Plus 7 mins:	T.16.b.3.5. to T.16.b.3.2.	12-42	Brown
Plus 2h. ~~20m~~ 2m.	T.16.b.6.4. to T.16.d.7.9.	2-37	Blue
Plus 2h.26m.	T.17.a.1.3. to T.17.a.1.0.	3-1	Sap Green
Plus 3 hours.	T.17.a.6.4. to T.17.a.9.1.	3-35	Yellow
Plus 3h.38m.	T.17.c.2.9. (5) to T.17.b.0.2.	4-13	Red & blue
Plus 4h.	T16d 2-8 to T16d 9-8	4-35	Defensive

B R A G U N

Zero:	T.16.a.53.15 to T.16.c.45.80.
Plus 7 mins.	T.16.b.3.2. to T.16.d.3.9.
Plus 2h.2m.	T.16.d.3.8. to T.16.d.7.9.
Plus 2h.26m.	T.16.d.3.8. to T.17.c.2.9.
Plus 3 hours.	T.16.d.3.8. to T.17.a.9.1.
Plus 3h.38m.	T.16.d.3.8. to T.17.c.2.9. (5)
Plus 4h.	T16d 2-8 to T16d 9-8

B A T G U N

Zero	T.16.a.12.12 to T.16.a.20.25.	12-35	
Plus 3 mins.	Creep to: T.16.d.3.9. to T.16.b.25.18.	12-38	dotted Green
Plus 2h.2m.	Creep to: T.16.d.7.9. to T.16.b.65.18.	2-37	dotted Blue
Plus 2h.38m.	Creep to: T.17.c.15.95 to T.17.a.15.20.	3-13	dotted Red
Plus 3h.12m.	Creep to: T.17.c.52.95 (a.9.1) to T.17.a.50.17. (75.35)	3-47	dotted Sap Green
Plus 3h.46m.	Creep to: T.17.b.0.2. to T.17.b.10.45.	4-21	Yellow
Plus ~~[illegible]~~ 4h.	Lift to T16d 9.8 to T17c 5.9	4-35	Defensive

T O M G U N

Zero:	T.16.a.20.25 to T.16.a.3.4.
Plus 3 mins.	Creep to: T.16.b.25.18 to T.16.b.3.4.
Plus 2h.2m.	Creep to: T.16.b.65.18 to T.16.b.65.40.
Plus 2h.38m.	Creep to: T.17.a.15.20 to T.17.a.15.45.
Plus 3h.12m.	Creep to: T.17a.50.17 (75.35) to T.17.a.50.45. (6.6)
Plus 3h.46m.	Creep to: T.17.b.10.45 to T.17.b.1.7.
Plus 4h.	Lift to T16d 9.8 to T17c 5.9

S C H E D U L E   O F   B A R R A G E S (CONT)

W A R N O W

Minus 3 hours: Area - T.11.c.15.10 - 35.10 - 35.30 - 15.30.

Rate of fire as intense as possible.

All P.S. or WHITE STAR in possession must be used up during this bombardment and no B.S.K. will be fired.

Zero: THE ORCHARD T.16.b.60.35 and Trench T.16.b.45 to T.16.b.70.25.

Plus 2h. 2m. STREET and ORCHARDS T.17.a.3.5. to T.11.c.20.25.

Read Plus 3h.40m. (3.15 P.M) Plus 3h.12m. STREET T.17.a.7.5. to T.17.a.45.85.

Read Plus 3h.12m. (3.47 P.M) Plus 3h.46m. ROAD T.17.d.25.75 to T.17.a.9.1.

Creeping will be at the rate of 50 yards per minute.

Rate of fire from: Zero to Plus 15 mins.
Plus 1 hour to Plus 2h.15m.
Plus 2hours to Plus 2h.15m.
Plus 2h.36m. to Plus 2h.50m.
Plus 3h.10m. to Plus 3h.24m.
Plus 3h.44m. to Plus 3h.59m.

will be 12 rounds per 18 pdr battery, 8 rounds per Howitzer Battery per minute; other times 3 rounds per minute.

18 pdr 3/4ths "A" 1/4 "A.X" but subject to discretion in view of quantity of each in possession.

[To WARNOW - You are said to have 102 B.P.S already in possession. This is NOT Powder Shell. You will be issued with 87 White Star]

SECRET 8/362

The following amendments have been made in the Schedule of Barrages - Please alter your copy.

BATGUN At 3h.12m. Creep to: T.17.a.9.1.to T.17.a.75.35.

TOMGUN At 3h.12m. Creep to: T.17.a.75.35 to T.17.a.6.6.

At Plus 3h.38m.in the case of JOGUN and BRAGUN, for "T.17.c.2.9" read T.17.c.5.9.

Flares will be lit on obtaining each objective and also at 6 p.m.

It should be clearly understood that JOGUN and BRAGUN are standing Barrages and at the specified times "Lift" and do not "Creep".

In the case of BATGUN and TOMGUN the times given are those at which they start the respective "creeps".

Acknowledge

[signature]

Lieut.,

25.9.16. Adjutant, [illegible] GROUP.

OPERATION ORDER No. 2

RIGHT CENTRAL ARTILLERY

SECRET RIGHT GROUP

LIFE

Copy No. 3

Ref. LONGUEVAL & COMBLES Sheet 1/10,000.

24th Sept. 1916.

---

1. With reference to Right Centre Artillery Operation Order No. 1 dated 23/9/16, attached, the following are the tasks allotted.
   ~~LINK~~ LUCRE and two Batteries LIFE will form the Standing Barrage, and ~~LUCRE~~ LINK & other two Batteries LIFE will form the Creeping Barrage.

2. STANDING BARRAGE:-

at ZERO:- ~~LUCRE~~ from T.10.c.55.00 - Cross roads T.16.a.8.0. - T.16.a.6.5.
LIFE - T.16.a.6.5 - T.16.c.45.80.

at + 7 :- Lift to BROWN Line
LUCRE from T.10.c.9.1 - T.16.b.15.90 - T.16.b.3.5.
LIFE - T.16.b.3.5 - T.16.d.3.9.

at + 1 hr. - 2 mins:- 1 Battery LUCRE lifts to dotted BLUE line - T.10.d.2.1 - T.16.b.2.9. Barrage to remaining Batteries on dotted BLUE Line as for BROWN Line.

at + 2 hours - 2 mins:- Lift to continuous BLUE line.
LUCRE - T.10.d.5.1 - T.16.b.6.4
LIFE - T.16.b.6.4 - T.16.d.7.9.
LIFE will form a flank barrage with 1 Battery from T.16.d.3.8 - T.16.d.7.9

at + 2 hours - 26 mins Lift to SAGE GREEN Line.
1 Battery LUCRE will form flank barrage from T.11.c.1.2 - T.11.c.8.4.
3 2 Batteries LUCRE - T.11.c.1.2 - T.17.a.1.4.
1 Battery LIFE - T.17.a.1.4 - T.17.a.1.0.
1 Battery LIFE form flank Barrage. from T.16.d.3.8 - T.17.c.2.9.

(2)

<u>at + 3 hours</u>:- Lift to YELLOW LINE.

~~1 Battery LUCRE flank barrage. - barrage from T.11.a.3.2 to T.11.c.9.4.~~

3 ~~2~~ Batteries LUCRE - T.11.c.3.~~1~~2 - T.17.a.6.~~8~~4.

1 Battery LIFE - T.17.a.6.~~8~~4 - T.17.a.9.1.

1 Battery LIFE - flank barrage from T.16.d.3.8 ~~-~~ - T.17.a.9.1

<u>at + 3 hours 38 mins</u>:- Lift to RED & BLUE line.

LUCRE - T.11.c.9.5 - T.17.b.1.7 - T.17.b.0.2.

LIFE - flank barrage T.16.d.3.8 - T.17.c.5.9 - T.17.b.0.2.

3. <u>CREEPING BARRAGE</u>:-

at <u>ZERO</u>:- Creeping barrage will be put down on line #

LINK. ~~T.16.a.12.12 - T~~

LIFE. T16a1212 & T16a34

4. The dividing line between LINK & LIFE will be T.16.a.34 - T.16.b.3.4 - T.17.a.1.4½ - # T.17.a.5.5 - T.17.b.1.7.

LINK on the North & LIFE on the South.

<u>at + 3 hrs. 51 mins.</u> The creeping barrage joins the Standing Barrage & will thicken it. LINK - T.11.c.9.5 - T.17.b.1.7

LIFE - T.17.b.1.7 - T.17.b.0.2.

<u>at + 4 hours</u>:- The following standing Barrage will be formed:-

LIFE - flank barrage - T.16.d.38 - T.17.c.5.9.

LINK - T.17.c.5.9 - T.17.b.0.2.

LUCRE - T.17.b.0.2 - T.17.b.1.8.

(3)

5. HOWITZERS:-

1 Section LINK, will fire on target in (a)

LIFE & 1 Section LINK on those in (b)
LUCRE on those in (c)

6. Lt. Col. Pottinger will be Liaison Officer with 95th Inf. Brigade. O.C. Wagon Line has been instructed to detail two Subaltern Officers with telephonists to proceed with Lt. Col. Pottinger to 95th Inf. Bde. Hqrs. where they will receive orders.

#

H.G. Fisher
Major, for Lt. Col. RA
Commdg. RIGHT GROUP
Rt. Centre Artillery.

24-9-16

SECRET 24/9/16.

S/G.A/253

O.C. LIFE

Reference Right Group Operation Orders No. 2, please subsitute the following amendments:-

In para (1), for "LINK & two Batteries LIFE will form a Standing Barrage" and "LUCRE & two other Batteries LIFE will form a Creeping Barrage" read

"LUCRE & two Batteries LIFE will form Standing Barrage" and "LINK & two other Batteries LIFE will form Creeping Barrage"

In para (2), for "Cross Roads - T.16.a.8.0" read "Cross Roads - T.16.a.8.6 and

"At + 7 minutes:- Lift to BROWN Line"

At + 2 hours 26 minutes - Barrage will be:-

3 Batteries LUCRE - T.11.c.1.2 - T.17.a.1.3.
1 Battery LIFE - T.17.a.1.3. - T.17.a.1.0.

At + 3 hours:- Barrage will be.-

3 Batteries LUCRE - T.16.c.3.2 - T.17.a.6.4.
1 Battery LIFE - T.17.a.6.4 - T.17.a.9.1.

3. CREEPING BARRAGE:-

At ZERO - Creeping Barrage will be put down on Line:-

LIFE - T.16.a.1½.1½ - T.16.a.3.4.
LINK - T.16.a.3.4 - T.16.a.3.5½ - T.16.a.1½.9.

4. Dividing Line between LINK & LIFE - T.16.a.3.4

Mems. B.M/930/5 attached
Acknowledge.

H. E. Fisher Major for Lt. Col.
Comdg. Right Group. RA Centre Div

SECRET

O.C. LIFE ....

S/GA/259

CONFIRMATION OF

AMENDMENTS TO OPERATION ORDERS NO. 8.

<u>At plus 3 hours 12 minutes</u> Batteries will creep on to the DARK GREEN line, which is amended as follows:-

Two Batteries LIFE - T.17.a.9.1 - T.17.a.[illegible]. ✓

One Battery LINK - T.17.a.6.8 - T.17.a.9.8.

Two Batteries LINK - T.17.a.5.9. - T.11.c.45.20

<u>At plus 3 hours 46 minutes:-</u>

Start creeping again on to YELLOW (Final) Line.

<u>ACKNOWLEDGE.</u>

[signature]

Major for Lt.-Col.R.F.A.
Commanding RIGHT GROUP, Rt. Centre Arty.

LIFE

RIGHT CENTRE DIVISIONAL ARTILLERY + XIV CORPS

R I G H T   G R O U P.

OPERATION ORDER NO. 1....... 23/9/16.

Reference LONGUEVAL and COMBLES Sheets 1/10,000 — Copy O.O. No. 3

1. The XIVth Corps will resume the offensive on 25th September.

2. The Right Centre Division (of which the PRETCHEL GROUP is the Right Group) will cover the attack of the 5th Division on the 25th instant, and assist the preliminary bombardment by the Heavy Artillery on 24th and 25th instant, prior to Zero Hour.

3. Zero Hour will be notified later.

4. A steady bombardment of the hostile positions will commence at 7 a.m. on 24th September, and continue to 6 p.m. that day. It wil be recommenced at 6.30 am. on 25th September, and continue till Zero Hour.

The ground in front of MORVAL, not specially detailed for 4.5" Howitzers will be searched occasionally with 18 pdr. Shrapnel and H.E. Shell.

5. Night firing will be carried on night 24th/25th September between the hours of 6.30 p.m. and 6.30 am.

6. There will be no intensive fire before Zero.

7. The boundaries of the Division will be as follows:-

RIGHT - T.15.d.0.2 to T.18.a.0.5;
LEFT - T.9.d.6.8. to T.11.a.2.3;

8. The boundary line between the Groups will be as follows:-
T.10.c.2.0.- T.10.d.85.15 - T.11.c.50.25 thence due East.

9. 18 pdr.Batteries:-

~~LINK~~ ~~One Battery~~ (LIFE) will continue wire-cutting from T.16.a.7.6 to T.10.c.3.8 and any wire seen in front of New Trench S. and S.W./of MORVAL face

LINK and LUCRE will search occasionally with Shrapnel and H.E. the ground in front and in rear of the German trenches including the roads leading into MORVAL, but not those specially detailed for treatment by 4.5" Hows.

Dividing line - from North of Orchard - T.16.b to Road Junction T.17.a.6.6. LINK - North, LUCRE - South.

10. During the preliminary bombardments the following targets will be kept under fire by 4.5" Howitzers:-

RIGHT GROUP:- One Battery, LUCRE - New Trenches on W. and S.W. edge of MORVAL Village, and the street front T.16.b.4.9 to T.11.c.3.2.

One Battery LINK - The Street T.17.a.6.6. to T.11.c.3.3.and the Road T.11.c.35.05 - T.17.b.80.95.

One Battery LIFE - The Orchard T.16.b.7.4. and trench in its immediate vicinity.

11. RATES OF FIRE:-

	By Day	By Night.
18 pdrs............	As required	200 rds per Batte per night.
4.5" Hows..........	15 rds. per Howitzer per hour.	20 rds. per Batte per hour.

12. Orders for action of Artillery from Zero Hour onwards will be issued later.

H. G. Fisher
Major
for Lieut-Col.R.F.A.,
Commanding RIGHT GROUP ,
Right Centre Divisional Arty.

23-9-16.

PLEASE ACKNOWLEDGE

ORIGINAL

Instructions regarding War Diaries and Intelligence Summaries are contained in F. S. Regs., Part II. and the Staff Manual respectively. Title Pages will be prepared in manuscript.

WAR DIARY ~~or INTELLIGENCE SUMMARY~~

(Erase heading not required.)

280/B BTY RFA

SEPTEMBER 1916

Army Form C. 2118.

Sheet 1

Place	Date	Hour	Summary of Events and Information	Remarks and references to Appendices
SOMME Front	8/9/16		Battery in reserve at wagon lines near BRAY	
	10/9/16		Battery Commander reconnoitred Battery positions in the neighbourhood of ANGLE WOOD	
	11.9.16	4 am	Battery went forward to occupy position allotted at B1d1.2. Morning was very bright and enemy's guns active. Battery remained under cover till late in the afternoon and the guns were finally in position at 6 p.m. Lines laid out by compass and 140 rounds fired on night barrage. The Battery came into Lt Colonel MacDowell's Group. Position heavily shelled Sgt Collinson killed, Bomb. Sadler wounded	
	12.9.16		Observation Station in SAVERNAKE WOOD selected and wired and careful registrations made on COMBLES MORVAL and Enemy's trenches 810 rounds fired on day and night barrage. Enemy heavily shelled our position	
	13.9.16		Fired 1247 rounds on slow night and day barrage with occasional rapid bursts of fire	
	14.9.16		Fired 721 rounds	
	15.9.16		Our Infantry attacked Fired 1662 rounds according to Programme	
	16.9.16		Fired 561 rounds	
	17.9.16		Fired 858 rounds	
	18.9.16		Fired 63 rounds. Battery Commander went forward to reconnoitre Battery positions in WEDGE WOOD Valley. At Northern end of	

2449 Wt. W14957/M90 750,000 1/16 J.B.C. & A. Forms/C.2118/12.

Army Form C. 2118.

Instructions regarding War Diaries and Intelligence Summaries are contained in F. S. Regs., Part II. and the Staff Manual respectively. Title Pages will be prepared in manuscript.

WAR DIARY
or
~~INTELLIGENCE SUMMARY~~
(Erase heading not required.)

280/B BTY RFA

SEPTEMBER 1916

Sheet 11

Place	Date	Hour	Summary of Events and Information	Remarks and references to Appendices
			valley he was fired on by Enemy stick in QUADRILATERAL	
	19.9.16		Fired 48 rounds	
	20.9.16	5am	The Battery moved forward to a position in front of WEDGE WOOD at T 26 D 75 15. Old Battery position was heavily shelled as the Battery was leaving also the WEDGE WOOD VALLEY but the guns were got into new position without casualty. Battery came into Lt Col Southam's Group.	

[illegible] Major
O.C. B/280 Bde RFA

2449 Wt. W14957/M90 750,000 1/16 J.B.C. & A. Forms/C.2118/12.

ORIGINAL

Instructions regarding War Diaries and Intelligence Summaries are contained in F. S. Regs., Part II. and the Staff Manual respectively. Title Pages will be prepared in manuscript.

WAR DIARY or ~~INTELLIGENCE SUMMARY~~

(Erase heading not required.)

280/C BTY RFA T.F.

SEPTEMBER 1916

Army Form C. 2118.

Sheet 1

Place	Date	Hour	Summary of Events and Information	Remarks and references to Appendices
BRAY	8 Sept		In Divisional Reserve at BRAY. Guns &c pooled for supply and replacement of casualties to Batteries of IVth Corps	
	9 Sept		— Ditto —	
	10 Sept		B.C.s reconnaissance on instructions from Divisional Artillery — reported to Div. Arty. upon WEDGE WOOD VALLEY to LEUZE WOOD	
MARIECOURT	11 Sept		Battery moved up to position near MARIECOURT - Teams heavily shelled and Battery position also Shrapnel on position at night - One man wounded. Shrapnel were burst at better height that usual almost 10 degrees above line of sight. Battery in LUCRE group - Registered at 8.30 a.m. 12 Sept. 1916. upon a landmark near COMBLES	
	12 Sept		Reported to Group Commander — Battery fired on Barrage lines under orders from Group — Day & night.	
	13 Sept		Again shelled - but shelling apparently meant for track alongside gun position. Barrage Fire (stationery) under orders from Group.	
	14 Sept		— ditto — Great difficulty experienced in getting ammunition up.	
	15 Sept		Very little firing - opportunity taken to improve Gun position & platforms	
	16 Sept		Firing under orders from Group. F.O.O. observed from LEUZE WOOD	
	17 Sept		—— ditto —— Lt Redfern. wounded at O.P.	
	18 Sept		Came under orders of LINK - reported to Group Commander — observed fire from SAVERNAKE WOOD	
	19 Sept		Fired under orders from GROUP. Fire observed from LEUZE WOOD	

2449 Wt. W14957/M90 750,000 1/16 J.B.C. & A. Forms/C.2118/12.

Instructions regarding War Diaries and Intelligence Summaries are contained in F. S. Regs., Part II. and the Staff Manual respectively. Title Pages will be prepared in manuscript.

Army Form C. 2118.

WAR DIARY
or
~~INTELLIGENCE SUMMARY~~
(Erase heading not required.)

280/C BTY RFA

SEPTEMBER 1916

Sheet ii

Place	Date	Hour	Summary of Events and Information	Remarks and references to Appendices
LEUZE WOOD	20 Sept.		Reconnoitered forward Battery position near LEUZE WOOD — Valley heavily shelled Enemy fire almost nil - Batteries evidently having been moved back	

30/9/16

[illegible signature]
Major
Comdg 280/C Bty RFA

2449 Wt. W14957/M90 750,000 1/16 J.B.C. & A. Forms/C.2118/12.

ORIGINAL

Instructions regarding War Diaries and Intelligence Summaries are contained in F. S. Regs., Part II. and the Staff Manual respectively. Title pages will be prepared in manuscript.

WAR DIARY or INTELLIGENCE SUMMARY.

280/D BTY RFA.

Army Form C. 2118.

SEPTEMBER 1916

280/D Battery RFA (Erase heading not required.) whilst detached from 280th Brigade. RFA.

Sheet 1

Place	Date	Hour	Summary of Events and Information	Remarks and references to Appendices
In the Field	8th	10.AM.	Major E. R. L. Warrens wounded, in Battery position while being prepared.	
		3.pm	Battery came into action on SUNKEN ROAD at A.6.A.6.8 (Map. 62.C.N.W. 1/20.000) Battery attached to "LUCRE" Group.	
	9th		First Battle of GINCHY in which the Battery took part, firing about 1300 rds, including Chemical Shell	
	10th		Two Casualties today.	
	11th	7.45. AM.	Battery shelled out. No 2 Gun blown to pieces. The Gun itself being thrown about 150 yards. One Officer, 2 other ranks casualties. No 1 Gun moved to bottom of the road to the left of No 4 Gun.	
	12th	12 noon	A premature occurred with this Gun. One man killed & 4 wounded. The rifling of the Gun slightly damaged. A party under Lieut Mallett endeavoured to find a new site for Battery position, but were unsuccessful. One other Casualty today. Lieut Priestly joined the Battery.	
	13th		The Artificers having repaired the Gun with which the premature occurred It is now in action again, and placed to the left of the site of No 2. Gun	

1577 Wt. W10791/1773 500,000 1/15 D. D. & L. A.D.S.S./Forms/C. 2118.

Instructions regarding War Diaries and Intelligence Summaries are contained in F. S. Regs., Part II. and the Staff Manual respectively. Title Pages will be prepared in manuscript.

WAR DIARY

~~or~~

~~INTELLIGENCE SUMMARY~~

(Erase heading not required.)

280/D BTY RFA.

SEPTEMBER 1916

Army Form C. 2118

Sheet 11

Place	Date	Hour	Summary of Events and Information	Remarks and references to Appendices
In the Field	14th	3.40 AM.	A premature occurred with C. Subsection Gun. One N.C.O slightly wounded.	
			A Gun was issued to the Battery to replace the one destroyed on the 11th inst and placed in position as No 1 Gun.	
	15th		The second Battle of GINCHY in which the Battery took part firing some 1200 rds including Chemical Shell.	
	16th		A general bombardment continued throughout the day.	
	17th		No 1 Gun fired a premature which damaged the gun considerably. There were no Casualties.	
	19th		Battery was transferred to "LIFE" Group.	

In the Field
30/9/16

W. Johnson Lieut RFA
OC 280/D Battery RFA

1875 W: W593/826 1,000,000 4/15 J.B.C. & A. A.D.S.S./Forms/C. 2118.

DUPLICATE

Instructions regarding War Diaries and Intelligence Summaries are contained in F. S. Regs., Part II. and the Staff Manual respectively. Title Pages will be prepared in manuscript.

WAR DIARY
or
INTELLIGENCE SUMMARY
(Erase heading not required.)

Army Form C. 2118.

[illegible] (London) Bde. R.F.A.

[illegible]

October 1916

Sheet 1

Place	Date	Hour	Summary of Events and Information	Remarks and references to Appendices
[illegible]	1/10/16		[illegible] consisting of 235/A, B [illegible] D Batteries & 283/C Battery moved further forward. 235/A [illegible] Batteries moved [illegible] 283/C Battery [illegible] during the day. [illegible] to position [illegible] 283/C Battery.	
		3.15 PM	Took part in operations in connection with attack by [illegible] Corps & Reserve Army to the north [illegible] LE TRANSLOY.	
		6 PM	[illegible] down [illegible] stopped firing a little later. New positions heavily shelled. Fired throughout the night on allotted area between LESBOEUFS & LE TRANSLOY	
	2/10/16	5–7 AM	[illegible] fire on allotted area.	
		9 AM	Hostile aeroplanes very persistent [illegible] flying low between LESBOEUFS & LE TRANSLOY & firing [illegible] machine guns. Not engaged by our [illegible] aeroplanes. 283/C Battery (CAPT. D. THOMSON) [illegible] gun [illegible] to take advantage of [illegible] opportunity & at third shot brought down one plane. It volplaned rapidly into the German lines between LESBOEUFS & LE TRANSLOY landing behind a ridge.	
			Bad weather. Heavy rain came on in morning & lasted whole day. Barrage firing on allotted area during afternoon & evening & continued with variations throughout the night.	
	3/10/16		Weather still bad. Heavy mist throughout the morning. Observation impossible. Ground very difficult. Fired on allotted area as before during the morning. Considerable improvement in weather in afternoon.	
	3/4th	night	Fired 200 rounds per Battery during the night on allotted area.	
	4/10/16		Fired intermittently throughout the day on allotted area. Operations [illegible] 5th [illegible] postponed [illegible]. Ground still very difficult. [illegible] practically	

2449 Wt. W14957/M90 750,000 1/16 J.B.C. & A. Forms/C.2118/12.

Instructions regarding War Diaries and Intelligence Summaries are contained in F. S. Regs., Part II. and the Staff Manual respectively. Title Pages will be prepared in manuscript.

WAR DIARY
or
INTELLIGENCE SUMMARY
(Erase heading not required.)

250th (City of London) Bde RFA (T.F.)

OCTOBER 1916

Army Form C. 2118.

Sheet II

Place	Date	Hour	Summary of Events and Information	Remarks and references to Appendices
Vicinity of GINCHY and MORVAL (SOMME FRONT)	4/10/16 (cont'd)		impossible. Rations & water unchanged? at positions. Arrangements made for ammunition to be brought up on pack animals.	
		Night	Night firing carried out on allotted area.	
	5/10/16	11 AM to 2 PM	250/D Battery fired in conjunction with other Howitzer Batteries on S^T PIERRE VAAST WOOD with THERMIT Shell.	
			Batteries fired intermittently throughout afternoon & evening on allotted area; also throughout the night.	
	6/10/16		Our Batteries firing on HAZY TRENCH intermittently throughout the day & [illegible] on allotted area.	
		3.15 to 3.45 PM?	D/250 Bty (How) on new trenches etc. in accordance with Operation Orders preparatory to forthcoming offensive.	
			Flashes of hostile Batteries noted & bearings passed to French Heavy Batteries adjacent to Group H.Q. Similar information passed whenever obtained.	
		5 PM	In response to repeated requests for assistance against hostile aircraft who are very persistent, two machine guns from 109th? Bde MG Coy placed at disposal of Group Commander & placed in position near Batteries.	
		Night	Fired 200 rounds per Battery during the night on allotted area. Very heavy hostile shelling in neighbourhood of D/250 Bty. Ammunition delivered with difficulty & casualties sustained in drivers & horses.	
	7/10/16		Heavy [illegible] on HAZY TRENCH during morning.	
		1.45 PM	Zero time. Programme carried out in accordance with orders & various targets engaged as they presented themselves. (See App. No 1) Infantry? [illegible] first objective but not the second. Actual position obscure during afternoon & evening. Infantry back to original line later in evening. Barrages varied in accordance with information received.	App. No 1 [illegible] No 6

2449 Wt. W14957/M90 750,000 1/16 J.B.C. & A. Forms/C.2118/12.

Instructions regarding War Diaries and Intelligence Summaries are contained in F. S. Regs., Part II. and the Staff Manual respectively. Title Pages will be prepared in manuscript.

WAR DIARY
or
INTELLIGENCE SUMMARY
(Erase heading not required.)

Army Form C. 2118.

250th (City of London) BDE R.F.A. (T.F.)

OCTOBER 1916

Sheet iii

Place	Date	Hour	Summary of Events and Information	Remarks and references to Appendices
Vicinity of GINCHY & MORVAL (SOMME FRONT)	7.10.16	8.35 PM	Opened intense barrage fire on HAZY TRENCH & gun pits in vicinity. Slow rate of fire maintained during the night.	
	8.10.16	Dawn	Attack opened on HAZY TRENCH which was taken by our Infantry yesterday & evacuated. Fire on HAZY TRENCH maintained during morning.	
		3.30 PM	Zero hour. Offensive resumed. Artillery programme carried out & further barrage maintained, dropping to very slow rate of fire at 4.50 PM. See App^x N° 2. Infantry advanced on our front to their objective but failed to retain it. Some of our infantry reported in danger of being cut off. Barrage varied during evening.	App^x N° 2 R.A. Arty. O.O. N° 3 & Group instructions.
	8/9th	night	Roads & tracks S. of LE TRANSLOY fired on intermittently throughout the night.	
	9.10.16		Our infantry are back in trenches from which they started with the exception of RAINY TRENCH which they have evacuated. Batteries engaged targets as they appeared during day.	
		night	Fired throughout the night on roads & tracks South of LE TRANSLOY CEMETERY. 75/A (Hun) Bty firing in vicinity of the CEMETERY. Infantry of 56 DIV. relieved during night by 4th DIV.	
	10.10.16	Dawn	One section of 250/D Bty moved to new position & registered during morning. Hostile aircraft very active. Two machine guns from 11th Bde M.G. Coy arrived to replace those from 169th Bde M.G. Coy (which left yesterday) & placed at Group Commanders disposal for anti-aircraft work. Forward O.P. of C/253 Bty knocked in.	
		night	Fired throughout the night on roads & tracks as on previous night.	
	11.10.16	12.45 AM	Warning Order received re Operations on 12th & 13th.	
		Dawn	Remaining Section of D/250 Bty moved to new position & registered in preparation for coming operations. Fired during day in accordance with Operation Orders.	

Instructions regarding War Diaries and Intelligence Summaries are contained in F. S. Regs., Part II. and the Staff Manual respectively. Title Pages will be prepared in manuscript.

WAR DIARY
or
INTELLIGENCE SUMMARY
(Erase heading not required.)

280th (City of London) Bde R F A (TF)

OCTOBER 1916

Army Form C. 2118.

Sheet IV

Place	Date	Hour	Summary of Events and Information	Remarks and references to Appendices
Vicinity of GINCHY & MORVAL (Somme Front)	11.10.16	3.15 PM	Bombardment without Infantry attack commenced	See Appx No 3 – Left Group O.O. No [illegible]
	(contd)	Night	Night firing carried out as on previous nights.	
	12.10.16	2.5 PM	Zero time. Artillery programme carried out & further barrage maintained until 5.30 PM. Information received points to Infantry on our own front having failed.	Appx No 4 See Left Gp O.O. No 8
		5.35 PM	Information received that enemy appears to be preparing for counter attack.	
		5.50 PM	Barrage brought closer in & heavy fire opened, slowing down after a few minutes.	
		6.20 PM	Stopped firing.	
		6.30 PM	Barrage again altered. Night firing ordered on area in rear of Barrage line. Infantry on our front (on right of the [illegible] & on left flank of Division) digging in 200 or 300 yards in front of original line. Brigade on the left achieved first objective. Position still obscure as to where the Right & Left Brigades connect.	
		11 PM	Barrage brought closer in & night firing altered to cover area in rear of this altered Barrage line.	
		Night	Expended 200 rounds per Bty during night on Barrage line & area in rear.	
	13.10.16		Batteries of enemy fired on during day [illegible]	
		5.30 PM	Very heavy bombardment commenced on our North in direction of GUEUDECOURT, also by the French on our South.	
		5.45	Batteries opened fire at slow rate, increasing it on report by Infantry of a general attack then slowed down & stopped firing at 6.10 PM.	
		6.30	Barrage line slightly altered. Batteries firing 200 rounds per Bty from evening until morning on Barrage & area in rear.	
	14.10.16	Morning	Enemy aeroplanes active over trenches & Battery positions.	

2449 Wt. W14957/M90 750,000 1/16 J.B.C. & A. Forms/C.2118/12.

Instructions regarding War Diaries and Intelligence Summaries are contained in F. S. Regs., Part II. and the Staff Manual respectively. Title Pages will be prepared in manuscript.

WAR DIARY
or
INTELLIGENCE SUMMARY

(Erase heading not required.)

250th (City of London) BDE RFA (TF)

OCTOBER 1916

Army Form C. 2118.

Sheet V

Place	Date	Hour	Summary of Events and Information	Remarks and references to Appendices
Vicinity of GINCHY & MORVAL (SOMME FRONT)	14.10.16 (Cont'd)	6.30 PM	Attack made by Infantry without bombardment to secure Trenches & gun pits not secured in previous operation. Batteries standing by in case of S.O.S.	App. No 5 See LIFE 51 O.O. No 9
		6.51 PM	Heavy hostile shelling started on our front.	
		7.7 PM	Fire on Barrage line opened. Stopped firing at 7.30 PM.	
			Our infantry attack apparently unsuccessful	
		Night	Night firing carried out as on previous nights – 150 rounds per Bty.	
	15.10.16	5.35 AM	Operation by 18th INF. BDE. on our left. Artillery programme carried out by this Group. Hostile aeroplane activity maintained.	App. No 6 See LIFE 59 O.O. No 1
			Orders issued to Batteries as to co-operation with Heavy Artillery in preparation for next attack.	App. No 7 See LIFE 6[illegible] O.O. No 11
		Night	Night firing as on previous nights.	
	16.10.16		Batteries co-operating in accordance with Operation Order No 11 of yesterday. Heavy Artillery firing on gun pits, strong points &c. Batteries of this group firing on portions drawn out by Heavies & on area of trenches bombarded by them	
		Night	Night firing carried out. 150 rounds per Bty (18 pdr). 2 S/D Hows Btys on special points.	
	17.10.16		Very misty until 10 AM. Night firing continued. Batteries fired during day in accordance with Opn Order No 11 & in preparation for next attack. Orders received for tomorrow's offensive & Group Orders issued. 16th INF. BDE. relieved by 71st INF. BDE. in our sector of front. Night firing carried out until zero – 200 rds per 18 pdr Bty; 2 S/D (How) Btys on special points.	

2449 Wt. W14957/M90 750,000 1/16 J.B.C. & A. Forms/C.2118/12.

Instructions regarding War Diaries and Intelligence Summaries are contained in F. S. Regs., Part II. and the Staff Manual respectively. Title Pages will be prepared in manuscript.

WAR DIARY
or
INTELLIGENCE SUMMARY
(Erase heading not required.)

Army Form C. 2118.

[illegible] (City of London) Bde R.F.A. (T.F.)

OCTOBER 1916

Sheet VI

Place	Date	Hour	Summary of Events and Information	Remarks and references to Appendices
Trenches of GINCHY & MORVAL (forward area)	18.10.16	3.40 AM (Zero)	Artillery preparation carried out & further barrage maintained until 7.40 AM. Resumed at 8.35 AM until 9.15 AM	App. No 8 See Lire Group Op. Order No 12 [illegible]
			Infantry & infantry [illegible], conflicting information as to exact points reached & consolidated.	
			Very bad weather conditions.	
			Orders received for further operations & Group Orders issued to Batteries.	
"		11.45 AM (Zero)	Artillery preparation carried out in accordance with Operation Order	App. No 9 See Lire Group Op. Order No 13 [illegible]
		3.55 PM	Firing reduced to very slow.	
		5.35 PM	Stopped firing.	
		Night	Batteries fired 100 rounds per Battery in relief throughout the night on barrage line & area to depth of 500 yards in rear.	
			Information received that SAILLY-SAILLISEL has been completely taken by the French.	
	19.10.16		Definitely ascertained that we hold [illegible] Trench as result of yesterday's operations. Ground very difficult - wheeled traffic practically impossible in forward area.	
		5 PM	Heavy firing on flanks. Batteries opened fire on their Range lines at 5.7 PM & slowed down & stopped at 5.30 PM. Information received the French were meeting a diversion.	
		Night	Batteries fired 200 rounds each during the night in relief, on last night's & on LE TRANSLOY Trench Line	
	20.10.16		Bombardment of Trenches & Strong Points carried out by D/250 (How) Battery during morning. C/283 Battery co-operating to catch enemy on the run.	App. No 10 See Lire Group Op. Order No [illegible]
		4.30 PM	Batteries put down flank Barrage in co-operation with French, until 5.25 PM. Considerable amount of lachrymatory gas during afternoon & evening in neighbourhood of C's Battery positions & area in their rear.	
		Night	Batteries fired 200 rounds per Battery during night in relief. At 10.30 PM D/250 (How) Battery fired 100 rounds BSK intensively on enemy dump.	

2449 Wt. W14957/M90 750,000 1/16 J.B.C. & A. Forms/C.2118/12.

Military Cross awarded to LIEUT. G. MALLETT (250/D Battery)

Instructions regarding War Diaries and Intelligence Summaries are contained in F. S. Regs., Part II. and the Staff Manual respectively. Title Pages will be prepared in manuscript.

WAR DIARY
or
INTELLIGENCE SUMMARY
(Erase heading not required.)

Army Form C. 2118.

286th (City of London) Bde R.F.A. (T.F.)

OCTOBER 1916

Sheet VII

Place	Date	Hour	Summary of Events and Information	Remarks and references to Appendices
Vicinity of [illegible] & NICKEL [illegible]	21.10.16		Barrages put down at various times during day in accordance with programme.	Appx No 11 See LIFE Group Op. Order No 15
			Batteries registered for wire cutting on points in front of LE TRANSLOY Trench Line.	
			Battery positions subjected to very heavy hostile shelling – more so than average.	
		Evening &	Barrages put down in accordance with programme, in addition to firing throughout	Appx No 12 See LIFE Group Op Order No 16
	22.10.16	5 AM	the night on allotted areas by Batteries in relief.	
			Warning order received & issued to Batteries for operations on 23rd inst.	
			Batteries carried out wire cutting during day, in front of LE TRANSLOY Trench Line, but long distance & low visibility prevented good observation of actual effect.	
			Rehearsal of one of the Barrages ordered for 23rd inst, carried out in afternoon.	
		Night	300 rounds per Battery fired by Batteries in relief during the night on allotted areas.	
	23.10.16		Offensive resumed. Owing to very heavy mist Zero postponed from 11.30 AM to 2.30 PM. Firing on allotted areas by Batteries in relief maintained until Zero hour.	
		2.30 PM (Zero)	Barrages carried out in accordance with the programme in support of attack by 4th Division. Slowed down from Ordinary rate at 5 PM & stopped firing at 6.15 PM. Infantry took part of first objective but actual situation obscure for some hours. Later definitely established that the gun pits attacked in previous operations have been taken.	Appx No 13 See LIFE Group Op Order No 17
		6.30 PM	New Barrage line ordered. Barrage line altered & brought nearer in at various times during evening as position became less obscure.	
		Night	Batteries fired in relief throughout the night on specified areas.	
	24.10.16		Very heavy mist & rain throughout the day, except for short period in afternoon. Firing [illegible] carried during the day by Batteries in relief as per night firing. 286/D (How) Bty fired on LE TRANSLOY during afternoon.	

LIEUT W O C JOHNSEN, Commanding 286/D Bty proceeded to Hospital today, having been wounded on 22nd inst & command of Battery taken over by LIEUT. G. MALLETT.

Instructions regarding War Diaries and Intelligence Summaries are contained in F. S. Regs., Part II. and the Staff Manual respectively. Title Pages will be prepared in manuscript.

WAR DIARY
or
INTELLIGENCE SUMMARY

(Erase heading not required.)

280th (CITY OF LONDON) BDE RFA (T.F.)

OCTOBER 1916

Army Form C. 2118.

Sheet viii

Place	Date	Hour	Summary of Events and Information	Remarks and references to Appendices
Vicinity of GINCHY & MORVAL (SOMME FRONT)	24.10.16	Night	Infantry of 4th Div relieved by 33rd Division. Barrage line brought further in. Batteries fire 200 rounds each on Barrage line & area in rear in reliefs.	
	25.10.16		Continuation of bad weather. Instructions received to support operations by French, but cancelled later, the weather continuing unfavourable. Bombardment carried out by Heavy Artillery during day. Batteries of Group on lookout to co-operate.	
		Evening	Instructions received, Group placed in readiness for cooperation with French. Cancelled morning	
		Night	Batteries fired until daylight on Barrage line & area in rear. 200 rounds per Bty.	
	26.10.16		Bombardment by Heavy Artillery during day on the German enemy trenches, 2 8x/D (How) Bty taking part. Other Batteries on lookout. Operation orders in support of French postponed indefinitely.	
		Night	Night firing carried out as on previous night – 200 rounds per Battery.	
	27.10.16		Bombardment by Heavy Artillery continued during day, 28x/D (How) Bty again cooperating.	
		2 PM.	CRA 56 Div. and CRA 5th Div called to discuss arrangements for relief of Group by 5th Div [illegible]	
		2.30 PM	Operation carried out by 251/A and 2x3/C Batteries on old German gun positions in [illegible] square N36c (between LES BOEUFS & LE TRANSLOY).	
		7.30 PM	Operation Order issued for proposed attack, in cooperation with French, but cancelled later.	
		Night	Batteries fired in reliefs throughout the night as before – 200 rounds per Battery.	
	28.10.16	1.30 AM	Orders received to cover Infantry (33rd Division having relieved 4th Div) in early morning attack & barrage during issued to Batteries.	App[x] No. 14 [illegible]
		6 AM	Programme carried out in support of 95th Inf Bde (33rd Div) in barrage [illegible] at slow rate until 10.30 AM. Operations [illegible] [illegible] barrage line [illegible] [illegible] Officer & two telephonists [illegible] Batteries relieving Group (15th Bde RFA 5th Div [illegible]) [illegible] positions.	

2449 Wt. W14957/M90 750,000 1/16 J.B.C. & A. Forms/C.2118/12.

Instructions regarding War Diaries and Intelligence Summaries are contained in F. S. Regs., Part II. and the Staff Manual respectively. Title Pages will be prepared in manuscript.

WAR DIARY
or
INTELLIGENCE SUMMARY
(Erase heading not required.)

Army Form C. 2118.

280th (City of London) Bde. R.F.A. (T.F.)

OCTOBER 1916.

Sheet [illegible]

Place	Date	Hour	Summary of Events and Information	Remarks and references to Appendices
Vicinity of GINCHY / MORVAL (Somme Front)	28.10.16	10 PM	Orders received for further operations early tomorrow morning.	
		Night	Batteries fired throughout the night on enemy [illegible] in rear, [illegible] rounds per Battery.	
	29.10.16	5.45 AM	Programme carried out in support of attack by 19th Inf. Bde. [illegible] attack apparently failed but operations continued. Barrage [illegible] until 11 AM. [illegible] [illegible] line of objective.	App. No. 1 [illegible]
			Arrangements made to co-operate with French attack on our right.	
		11.45 AM	Group Commander and Battery Commanders ([illegible] Bde. R.F.A.) arrived in connection with ensuing relief [illegible] conducted to Battery positions.	
			Operations in conjunction with French postponed to tomorrow. Relief postponed 24 hours. Weather conditions [illegible] same [illegible].	
		Night	Batteries fired throughout the night on [illegible] 200 rds per Bty.	
	30.10.16		Batteries warned as to operations in conjunction with French; postponed later in day. Very heavy rain during day.	
		11 AM / 12.30 PM	Batteries [illegible] wagon lines in BEAULENCOURT [illegible] LE TRANSLOY.	
			[illegible] 8th Div. Arty. called [illegible] in connection with ensuing relief.	
			Military Cross awarded to CAPT. D. THOMSON (C/[illegible] Battery).	
			Sections of 1st 3rd 5th & 37th (How) Batteries relieved sections of 280/A [illegible] [illegible] (How) Batteries. Reports [illegible] [illegible] sections. Sections relieved proceeded to Wagon Lines.	
		Night	Batteries fired throughout the night as before. Heavy rains continue.	
	31.10.16		Further sections of Batteries of 8th Div. Arty. arrived at positions. Operation orders issued. Battery Commanders handed over. Command of Group handed over to C.R.A. [illegible] [illegible]	
		From 2 PM onwards	HQ remainder of Batteries [illegible] [illegible] Wagon Lines.	

[illegible] Comdg. 280th (City of London) Bde. R.F.A.

2449 Wt. W14957/M90 750,000 1/16 J.B.C. & A. Forms/C.2118/12.

ORIGINAL

Vol 12

WAR DIARY

FOR

NOVEMBER 1916

280TH (CITY OF LONDON) BDE RFA (T.F.)

ORIGINAL

Instructions regarding War Diaries and Intelligence Summaries are contained in F. S. Regs., Part II. and the Staff Manual respectively. Title Pages will be prepared in manuscript.

WAR DIARY ~~or~~ ~~INTELLIGENCE SUMMARY~~

(Erase heading not required.)

280TH (CITY OF LONDON) BDE RFA (TF)

NOVEMBER 1916

Army Form C. 2118.

Place	Date	Hour	Summary of Events and Information	Remarks and references to Appendices
SOMME FRONT TO DAOURS	1/11/16		Relief by 8th Div Arty complete except for one Section of A/280 Bty. The relief by incoming section was delayed & the attempt overnight to remove guns in the darkness resulted in them getting stuck in bad ground near position between MORVAL & LESBŒUFS.	
		6.45AM	The Brigade less one section of A/280 Bty above mentioned, moved off from Wagon lines near MAMETZ on the way to join First Army.	
		3 PM	Arrived at DAOURS.	
		10 P.M	Orders received to continue move tomorrow & succeeding days, to relieve 60th Div Arty.	
DAOURS TO TALMAS	2/11/16	7.15AM	Brigade moved off & marched to TALMAS, arriving there at 12 noon.	
TALMAS TO AMPLIER	3/11/16	9.45AM	" " " " AMPLIER " " 2 PM.	
AMPLIER TO REBREUVE & REBREUVIETTE	4/11/16	9.15AM	" " " " REBREUVE & REBREUVIETTE, arriving at 2 P.M	
REBREUVE TO NEUVILLE ST VAAST FRONT.	5/11/16	7.30 AM	Brigade moved off to effect relief of 60TH DIV ARTY, & marched to Wagon lines of 302ND BDE RFA. Bde HQ, D/280, C/280 & one section A/280 Batteries arrived at LARESSET at 1 PM. D/280 Bty proceeded to ACQ. Corresponding Wagon lines taken over at these places from 302nd Bde. The Brigade, augmented by 93rd Battery (made up to 6 guns) to form CENTRE GROUP of 5th DIV ARTY, attached to and covering 3rd Canadian Division in the line E & S.E. of NEUVILLE ST VAAST.	See appendix Warning Order 5th DA Opn Order No 37 of 4.11.16
		4 P.M.	Guns started from Wagon lines for Battery positions of 302ND BDE between MAREUIL & NEUVILLE ST VAAST.	
		4.30 PM	Bde HQ moved up to Advanced Group HQ near Bty positions " " " preparatory to taking over from HQ 302nd Bde.	
	6/11/16	7.30 AM.	Officers & gun detachments started from Wagon lines for Bty positions. Relief carried out during day. Lt Col L A C SOUTHAM & Bde HQ relieved Lt Col DRAKE & HQ 302nd Bde. A/280 with one Section B/280 relieved D/302; C/280 with one Section B/280 relieved A/302; 93rd Battery relieved C/302, and D/280 (How) Bty relieved D/302.	
		4 PM	Relief completed.	

2449 Wt. W14957/M90 750,000 1/16 J.B.C. & A. Forms/C.2118/12.

Instructions regarding War Diaries and Intelligence Summaries are contained in F. S. Regs., Part II. and the Staff Manual respectively. Title Pages will be prepared in manuscript.

WAR DIARY
~~or~~
~~INTELLIGENCE SUMMARY~~

(Erase heading not required.)

Army Form C. 2118.

280th (CITY OF LONDON) BDE R.F.A. (T.F.)

NOVEMBER 1916

Sheet ii

Place	Date	Hour	Summary of Events and Information	Remarks and references to Appendices
VICINITY OF NEUVILLE - ST VAAST	6/11/16 (Cont'd)		Registration of incoming guns during day, in connection with the relief. Short counter offensive by A/280 Bty at request of Infantry on account of hostile T.M. activity.	
	7/11/16	2.35 to 3.15 PM	Counter offensive by A/280 Bty for hostile TM which ceased fire. Poor visibility during day – weather conditions unfavourable.	
	8/11/16	3.15 to 4 PM	D/280 (How) Bty fired as counter offensive in vicinity of hostile TM which ceased firing. Visibility again poor all day.	
	9/11/16		Batteries carried out registration of many points during afternoon, taking advantage of good visibility. Considerable aeroplane activity during day. 93rd Battery, R.F.A. (made up to 6 guns from Section of C/283 Bty) commanded by CAPT. D. THOMSON, becomes part of the establishment on reorganisation of the Brigade into three 6-gun Batteries (18 pdr) and one 4-gun Battery (4.5 How). The Group in the line consequently consists of the Batteries of the Brigade.	
		8.45 + 10 PM	D/280 (How) Bty fired on suspected T.M. and Communication Trenches as counter offensive for hostile T.M. activity.	
	10/11/16		Registration & minor targets during day.	
		Night	From dusk to dawn Batteries fired in short bursts on Trench junctions & rear Communication Trenches in connection with suspected German relief.	
	11/11/16		C/280 Bty fired on enemy working party. A/280 Bty fired in vicinity of hostile T.M as counter-offensive; hostile T.M. ceased firing. Visibility poor.	
	12/11/16		Observation indifferent – hazy at times. D/280 (How) Bty fired a few rounds in vicinity of hostile T.M. Enemy working parties fired on just before dark.	
	13/11/16		Visibility again poor.	
		10 P.M.	D/280 (How) Bty fired 12 rds on two suspected T.M's which ceased firing.	

2449 Wt. W14957/M90 750,000 1/16 J.B.C. & A. Forms/C.2118/12.

Instructions regarding War Diaries and Intelligence Summaries are contained in F. S. Regs., Part II. and the Staff Manual respectively. Title Pages will be prepared in manuscript.

WAR DIARY ~~or~~ INTELLIGENCE ~~SUMMARY~~

(Erase heading not required.)

280th (CITY OF LONDON) BDE R.F.A. (T.F.)

NOVEMBER 1916

Army Form C. 2118.

Sheet iii

Place	Date	Hour	Summary of Events and Information	Remarks and references to Appendices
VICINITY OF NEUVILLE-ST VAAST	14/11/16	8.25 AM	"Gas Alert" on.	
			Registration as necessary. D/280 (How) Bty fired as counter offensive to hostile T.M.	
			93rd Battery enfiladed Communication Trench where enemy were seen to be moving.	
			Inspection by M.G.R.A First Army – Battery positions in morning; Wagon lines in afternoon.	
	15/11/16		Visibility poor.	
			D/280 (How) Bty fired on suspected T.M. emplacement as counter offensive. Hostile T.M. ceased fire on each occasion.	
			Remaining Section of A/280 Bty (which was unable to move with the Brigade on 1st inst. owing to late relief by 8th Div. Arty) arrived at Brigade Wagon lines LARESSET at 2 P.M., having marched from the SOMME FRONT with 6th Div. Arty.	
			B/280 Bty divided; A/280 & C/280 each taking one section on reorganisation into 6-gun Batteries. MAJOR W.E. BATT who commanded B/280 Bty posted to command of D/280 (How) Bty.	
			Lt COL. L.A.C. SOUTHAM proceeded to 56 Div. Arty HQ as Acting C.R.A. during absence on leave of BRIG. GENl ELKINGTON. MAJOR W.E. BATT assumes command of Brigade while Lt COL. SOUTHAM is so acting.	
	16/11/16		Considerable aeroplane activity on both sides.	
			Short counter offensive at intervals during day against hostile T.M's.	
			Inspection of Battery positions by G.O.C. R.A. Canadian Corps.	
	17/11/16		A/280 Bty fired on Sniper's Post on information given by Infantry. C/280 fired on enemy working party & dispersed it.	
			Registration carried out in preparation for afternoon shoot.	
		1.30 PM	Batteries co-operated with bursts of fire; Hows on suspected T.M's; 18pdr Batteries enfilading main Communication Trenches. Medium T.M's also cooperated.	
		2.10 PM	Operation repeated. Very material damage observed to trenches &c.	
		3.15 PM	A/280 Bty carried out registration by aeroplane.	
			Aeroplanes active on both sides.	

2449 Wt. W14957/M90 750,000 1/16 J.B.C. & A. Forms/C.2118/12.

Instructions regarding War Diaries and Intelligence Summaries are contained in F. S. Regs., Part II. and the Staff Manual respectively. Title Pages will be prepared in manuscript.

WAR DIARY
or
~~INTELLIGENCE SUMMARY~~

(Erase heading not required.)

Army Form C. 2118.

280th (CITY OF LONDON) BDE R.F.A. (T.F.)

NOVEMBER 1916

Sheet iv

Place	Date	Hour	Summary of Events and Information	Remarks and references to Appendices
VICINITY OF NEUVILLE - ST. VAAST.	18/11/16		Shot counter-offensive by D/280 (How) Bty in vicinity of hostile T.M's which ceased firing.	
			Observation difficult during day, owing to weather conditions.	
	19/11/16	5.45 AM	"Gas alert" off.	
			Registration carried out.	
			93rd Bty fired on & dispersed enemy working party.	
			C/280 Bty carried out registration with aeroplane observation.	
	20/11/16		C/280 Bty stood by during morning for registration by aeroplane, which however had to return. Wind high all day.	
			Heavy Artillery carried out shoot on suspected TM observing from Group O.P. with assistance of Group F.O.O.	
	21/11/16		Very quiet day. Observation impossible beyond 50 – 100 yards the whole day.	
		1 PM	Hostile aeroplanes (unseen but heard flying very low) passed over Battery positions & Group HQ during the fog & dropped bombs in neighbourhood of adjoining Group on left flank.	
		10.30 PM	"Gas Alert" on.	
	22/11/16	12 NOON	"Gas Alert" off.	
			Misty in morning. Batteries carried out registration later in day, C/280 Bty registering by aeroplane.	
			A/280 Bty carried out successful shoot on hostile M.G. emplacement.	
			Usual T.M. activity. Aeroplane activity in afternoon.	
	23/11/16		C/280 & 93rd Batteries carried out registration by aeroplane.	
		2.30 to 2.55 PM	A/280 & 93rd Batteries fired three short bursts of fire synchronising with three rounds fired by Heavy TM in registration on supposed hostile TM emplacement. Considerable TM activity in afternoon, especially about time of this shoot. Hostile fire ceased first.	
	24/11/16		Visibility indifferent. D/280 (How) Bty fired as counter-offensive to hostile TM. C/280 Bty fired on & dispersed enemy working party.	

2449 Wt. W14957/M90 750,000 1/16 J.B.C. & A. Forms/C.2118/12.

Instructions regarding War Diaries and Intelligence Summaries are contained in F. S. Regs., Part II. and the Staff Manual respectively. Title Pages will be prepared in manuscript.

WAR DIARY
~~or~~
~~INTELLIGENCE SUMMARY~~

(Erase heading not required.)

Army Form C. 2118.

280th (CITY OF LONDON) BDE RFA (T.F.)

NOVEMBER 1916

Sheet V.

Place	Date	Hour	Summary of Events and Information	Remarks and references to Appendices
VICINITY OF NEUVILLE - ST. VAAST	25/11/16		Constant rain throughout day. Visibility bad. Slight clearance about 3 PM. & TM's then became active for a short time. D/280 (How) Bty fired on vicinity of hostile TM which ceased firing.	
	26/11/16		D/280 (How) Battery fired on vicinity of hostile TM as counter offensive; C/280 Battery fired on enemy dug-out from which smoke was seen to issue. Visibility very good & Batteries carried out various registrations in the course of the day. Enemy observation balloons were up.	
	27/11/16	6 AM to 6.25 AM	Batteries co-operated with sharp bursts of fire — 18 pdr Batteries enfilading & sweeping enemy support trenches; 4.5 Hows firing on enemy canteen & kitchens & suspected TM emplacements. Heavy Artillery cooperated with a few rounds. Fire appeared to be effective & enemy retaliation was very slight.	
		Aftn	Batteries registered on front of Group on right flank	
		4.30 PM	O.C. 10th Canadian F A Bde. with Adjutant & 2 Officers per Battery arrived in connection with ensuing relief by 3rd Canadian Div. Arty.	
		10 PM.	Short burst of fire by 18 pdr Batteries on same targets as in early morning operations. Salvoes fired at irregular intervals until 1 A.M.	
	28/11/16		C.R.A. 56 D.A. & C.R.A. 3rd Can. Div. Arty. visited Group H.Q. & Batteries in connection with ensuing relief. Visibility very good after sunrise but heavy mist came down later in morning. Quiet during morning — TM activity in afternoon. In the late afternoon D/280 (How) Battery fired 20 rds in vicinity of hostile TM which ceased firing.	
	29/11/16		Visibility poor throughout the day owing to mist. D/280 (How) Bty fired in morning as counter offensive to hostile T.M.	

Instructions regarding War Diaries and Intelligence Summaries are contained in F. S. Regs., Part II. and the Staff Manual respectively. Title Pages will be prepared in manuscript.

WAR DIARY

~~or~~

~~INTELLIGENCE SUMMARY~~

(Erase heading not required.)

280TH (CITY OF LONDON) BDE RFA (TF)

Army Form C. 2118.

NOVEMBER 1916

Sheet VI.

Place	Date	Hour	Summary of Events and Information	Remarks and references to Appendices
VICINITY OF NEUVILLE - ST VAAST	29/11/16 (Cont'd)	2.30PM	All Batteries of Group co-operated in burst of fire on hostile T.M. at A5.c.5.4 in accordance with orders received from 56 Div. Arty.	
		Evening	First part of relief by 10th CAN. F.A. BDE carried out by 7.45 PM. One section of each Battery of 280th BDE remains in action until tomorrow night. Reliefs by Batteries are as follows: 93rd Bty to be relieved by 30th CAN. F.A. Bty A/280 " " " 38th " C/280 " " " 39th " D/280 (How) " " " 43rd "	
	30/11/16		Visibility indifferent. Day spent in showing line to relieving artillery & in registrations.	
		6.30PM	Final Sections relieved by Sections of incoming Batteries. OC Bde, Adjutant & one officer per Battery, with details, remain overnight, pending final handing-over due at 8 AM tomorrow.	

[signature] Major

Commanding 280TH (CITY OF LONDON) BDE RFA

APPENDIX 6 WAR DIARY
for November
280 Bde RFA.

SECRET

S/CRA/338/43

4.11.16

280th Brigade R.F.A.
281st Brigade R.F.A.
282nd Brigade R.F.A.
283rd Brigade R.F.A.
56th Divl. Ammn. Col. ✓

WARNING ORDER

The 56th Divisional Artillery will probably commence to relieve the 60th Divisional Artillery on the night of the 5/6th November.

The guns will be taken up by teams provided by the 60th Divisional Artillery and will be manned by 60th Divisional Artillery on that night.

56th Divisional Artillery will register on the 6th instant and the relief will be completed on the night of the 6th/7th instant.

60th Divisional Artillery will, if possible, leave one officer per Battery to help the 56th Divisional Artillery till the afternoon of the 7th instant.

There will probably be a shortage of room in the wagon lines until the 60th Divisional Artillery have left.

Bruce Macm[illegible]

Captain,
for Brigade Major, R.A.,
56th Division.

4.11.16.

Copy No. 1

O P E R A T I O N   O R D E R No.37

BY BRIGADIER GENERAL R.J.G.ELKINGTON, C.M.G.

COMMANDING 56th DIVNL. ARTILLERY:

November 4th 1916.

Reference 1/100,000 LENS Map.

1. 56th Divisional Artillery will continue the march tomorrow November 5th to Wagon Lines at ACQ, CAPELLE-FERMONT, LARESSET and FREVIN-CAPELLE.

2. For the purposes of relief of 60th Divisional Artillery the 56th Divisional Artillery will be formed into three groups and the 18-pdr Batteries will consist of 6 guns.

Groups as follows:-

RIGHT GROUP:

Commanding - Lieut-Colonel E.C.POTTINGER

282nd Brigade H.Q.	2, 18-pdr Btties. (6-gun Btties.)
282nd Brigade R.F.A.	1, 4.5" How. Bty.

CENTRE GROUP:

Commanding - Lieut-Colonel L.A.C.SOUTHAM.

280th Brigade H.Q.	3, 18-pdr Bties. (6-gun Bties)
280th Brigade R.F.A.	1, 4.5" How. Bty.
and 93rd Battery R.F.A. made up to 6 guns.	

LEFT GROUP:

Commanding - Lieut-Colonel C.C.MACDOWELL.

281st Brigade H.Q.	3, 18-pdr Bties. (6-gun Bties.)
281st Brigade R.F.A.	
and 109th Battery R.F.A. made up to 6 guns.	1, 4.5" How. Bty.

3. The 282nd Brigade complete will march to Wagon Lines to the North of LARESSET, via LE CAUROY - AVESNES-LE-COMTE - HABARCQ.

H.Q. and the present 18-pdr Batteries of 280th Brigade R.F.A. to Wagon Lines North of LARESSET, route as above.

93rd Battery made up to 6 guns, to Wagon Lines at ACQ, via LE CAUROY - AVESNES-LE-COMTE - TILLOY-LES-HERMAVILLE.

D/280 Battery to Wagon Lines at ACQ, route as for 93rd Battery.

109th Battery made up to 6-guns to ACQ, route as for 93rd Battery.

The 281st Brigade R.F.A. complete less Brigade H.Q. will march to Wagon Lines at CAPELLE-FERMONT via LE CAUROY - AVESNES-LE -COMTE - TILLOY-LES-HERMAVILLE.

56th D.A.C. will march to FREVIN-CAPELLE via LE CAUROY - AVESNES-LE -COMTE - TILLOY-LES-HERMAVILLE.

Hdqrs.Coy., 56th Divnl.Train, A.S.C., will march to HAUTE-AVESNES via LE CAUROY - AVESNES-LE-COMTE and TILLOY-LES-HERMAVILLE.

3. (continued)

The 93rd and 109th Batteries will be clear of the Cross Roads at ETREE-WAMIN Station by 7-45 am.

The 281st Brigade R.F.A. will pass this point at 8-0 am.

The 280th	"	"	"	"	"	"	at 8-30 am.
the 282nd	"	"	"	"	"	"	at 9-0 am.
The 56th Divnl.Ammn.Col.		"	"	"	"	"	at 9-30 am.

H.Q.Coy.56th Divnl.Train will be clear of ETREE-WAMIN by 7-15 am or will march in rear of the Divisional Artillery as preferred by the O.C., H.Q.Company.

4. H.Q. 283rd Brigade R.F.A. will for the present be attached to the RIGHT GROUP.

5. Advanced parties of Batteries going to LARESSET should be at the Wagon Lines at 9-30 am.

Advanced parties of remaining Batteries and D.A.C. to be at 60th Divisional Artillery Headquarters at AUBIGNY at 9-0 am.

Advanced party from H.Q. Coy. 56th Divnl. Train should be at HAUTE-AVESNES by 10-0 am to take over billets from H.Q.Coy., 60th Divnl. Train.

6. Group Headquarters will march to-morrow morning as follows:-

RIGHT GROUP - to Wagon Lines at LARESSET.
CENTRE GROUP- " " " " "
LEFT GROUP - to Wagon Lines at ACQ,

and will proceed to Forward Headquarters (positions to be notified later) at night.

7. 56th Div.R.A.,H.Q. will close at REBREUVE at 9-30 am 5th Nov. & be established at AUBIGNY at 10-30 am same day.

BRUCE MACMIN,

Captain,
for Brigade Major,R.A.,
56th Division.

4-11-16.

Copy No.1,to 280th Brigade R.F.A.
2,to 281st Brigade R.F.A.
3,to 282nd Brigade R.F.A.
4,to 283rd Brigade R.F.A.
5,to 56th Divnl.Ammn.Col.
6,to H.Q.Coy.56th.Div.Train.A.S.C.
7,to 56th Division.
8)
9)
10)to 60th Division.
11)
12,to 60th Divisional Artillery.
13,to Canadian Corps.
14,to IVth Corps.
15,to First Army.
16,to Third Army.
17,to Fifth Army.

ORIGINAL

Vol 13

WAR DIARY

DECEMBER 1916

280TH (CITY OF LONDON) BRIGADE R.F.A. (T.F.)

(Diaries of Batteries during period of detachment in other Groups, attached)

PB

Army Form C. 2118.

Instructions regarding War Diaries and Intelligence Summaries are contained in F. S. Regs., Part II. and the Staff Manual respectively. Title Pages will be prepared in manuscript.

WAR DIARY
~~or~~
~~INTELLIGENCE SUMMARY~~
(Erase heading not required.)

250TH (CITY OF LONDON) BDE RFA (T.F.)

DECEMBER 1916

Sheet 1

Place	Date	Hour	Summary of Events and Information	Remarks and references to Appendices
VICINITY OF NEUVILLE ST VAAST	1/12/16	8 AM.	Relief of Group by 10th Canadian F.A. Bde. completed. OC Group, Adjutant + remaining personnel returned to Wagon Lines at LARESSET + ACQ preparatory to moving on the morrow. One Officer each left by 93rd + A/250 Batteries to assist corresponding incoming Batteries with their registration.	
LARESSET + ACQ To RAIMBERT	2/12/16	8 AM.	Brigade moved off on march to XITH Corps area for purpose of relieving 6th Div Arty, covering the 5th Division in the line. Arrived at RAIMBERT at 4 PM.	See App x N° 1. 5b Div Arty Warning Order + March Order of 1/12/16.
RAIMBERT To ST FLORIS	3/12/16	8 AM.	Move continued. Brigade arrived ST FLORIS at 11.30 AM. Orders received from 56 Div Arty + issued to Batteries as to relieving 6 Div Arty	
VICINITY OF VIEILLE CHAPELLE + RICHEBOURG-ST VAAST	4/12/16	9 AM.	O.C. Brigade, Battery Commanders, with Adjutant, Orderly Officer and one other Officer per Battery proceeded by 'bus to neighbourhood of VIELLE CHAPELLE. Arrived at Group HQ at 10.15 AM. Battery Commanders proceeded to respective positions. (24TH BDE RFA. – 6TH DIV ARTY). Guns arrived at 3.30 PM. to replace guns of outgoing Batteries in one Section in each main position + enfilading position. First relief reported complete at 7.15 PM.	See App x N° 2. 5b Div Arty Op Order N° 40 ~~[illegible]~~ of 3/12/16.
	5/12/16		During the morning Batteries carried out registration of incoming guns.	
		3.15 PM.	250TH BDE HQ. relieved 24TH BDE HQ. in command of Left Group 5TH DIV. ARTY.	
		5 P.M.	Relief of last Section of Batteries complete – 93rd Batty RFA. relieved 112TH BATTY RFA A/250 – – 111TH C/250 – – 42ND D/250 – – 43RD	
	6/12/16		Batteries carried out registration. Wagon Lines moved up in accordance with 56 Div Arty. March Order of 4/12/16	See App x N° 3 56 DA. March Order of 4.12.16.
		10.8 PM.	Test carried out. Batteries fired on receipt of call.	

2449 Wt. W14957/M90 750,000 1/16 J.B.C. & A. Forms/C.2118/12.

Instructions regarding War Diaries and Intelligence Summaries are contained in F. S. Regs., Part II. and the Staff Manual respectively. Title Pages will be prepared in manuscript.

WAR DIARY
~~or~~
~~INTELLIGENCE SUMMARY~~
(Erase heading not required.)

Army Form C. 2118.

280TH (CITY OF LONDON) BDE R.F.A. (T.F.)

DECEMBER 1916

Sheet ii.

Place	Date	Hour	Summary of Events and Information	Remarks and references to Appendices
VICINITY OF VIEILLE CHAPELLE & RICHEBOURG-ST. VAAST.	7/12/16		C.R.A. 5th DIV. ARTY. called during morning. Various points in connection with past & ensuing relief discussed.	
			Very heavy mist throughout the day. Observation impossible. Quiet on both sides.	
	8/12/16	10.36 AM	C/280 Batty. fired on & dispersed enemy working party.	
			Further registrations carried out during day.	
	9/12/16		Registration as necessary.	
			D/280 (How) Batty fired on hostile T.M. reported by Infantry.	
		5.15 PM	First part of relief completed by Batteries of 27TH BDE RFA (5TH DIV. ARTY) as under –	
			93rd Batty RFA by 121st BATTY. RFA.	
			A/280 " 120TH "	
			C/280 " 119TH "	
			D/280 " 37TH "	
	10/12/16		Registration of guns of incoming Batteries	
		5 PM	Final relief of Batteries completed.	
		8 PM	Command of Group handed over to COL. HARDING NEWMAN. H.Q. 280TH BDE. relieved by H.Q. 28TH BDE RFA.	
LAVENTIE			Lt. COL. L.A.C. SOUTHAM having returned from leave on night of 9/12/16 resumes command of the Brigade.	
			Brigade H.Q. established in LAVENTIE. Batteries remain at present Wagon lines.	
	11/12/16		Battery Commanders of C/280 & D/280 report to Left Group Commander, 56 DIV ARTY; Batty Comr. 93rd Battery to Right Group Commander – for purpose of reconnaissance preparatory to forming part of those respective Groups.	
	12/12/16		O.C. Brigade visited positions of Right Group with C.R.A. 56 DIV ARTY preparatory to taking over	

2449 Wt. W14957/M90 750,000 1/16 J.B.C. & A. Forms/C.2118/12.

Instructions regarding War Diaries and Intelligence Summaries are contained in F. S. Regs., Part II. and the Staff Manual respectively. Title Pages will be prepared in manuscript.

WAR DIARY ~~or INTELLIGENCE SUMMARY~~

(Erase heading not required.)

280TH (CITY OF LONDON) BDE RFA (T.F.)

Army Form C. 2118.

DECEMBER 1916

Sheet iii

Place	Date	Hour	Summary of Events and Information	Remarks and references to Appendices
LAVENTIE	15/12/16		Preparations made for taking over control of Right Group.	
	16/12/16	10 AM	Command of Right Group 56 Div. Arty. formally taken over by Lt COL LAC. SOUTHAM from Lt COL. POTTINGER	
			280TH BDE H.Q. relieves 282ND BDE H.Q. A/280 Batty (personnel only) relieves B/282 Batty (personnel only)	
			Group now consists of 93rd Batty RFA 109th Batty RFA A/280 A/282 (How) C/282 & D/282 (How).	
		11.30 AM to 1.45 PM	Combined operation by 18 pdr. 4.5 Hows & T.M's on the "ROTUNDA" & front line system.	
			Considerable damage apparent. Small amount of retaliation by enemy on our front line.	
	17/12/16		Visibility poor owing to mist.	
		2 to 6 PM	18 pdr Batteries fired on Roads & Road junctions likely to be used when not observed.	
			Fired during afternoon as counter-offensive to hostile T.M's which ceased firing.	
	18/12/16	11.30 AM to 12.30 PM	Bombardment by 18 pdr & 4.5 How in co-operation with M.T.M's & Stokes on Trenches in	
			M 30 & M 36. Considerable damage done. Very little retaliation by enemy.	
			93rd Battery carried out registration.	
			Batteries fired in afternoon as counter offensive to hostile T.M's	
	19/12/16	11.25 AM	D/282 (How) Batty co-operated with Stokes TM in bombardment of Trench junctions.	
			Batteries carried out registration during the day as necessary.	
		5 PM to midnight	Batteries fired at irregular intervals on Roads & Road junctions & on MOULIN DE PIETRE.	
	20/12/16		Several enemy working parties dispersed during the day.	
			Registration carried out as necessary.	
			Hostile T.M's active in afternoon. Our Batteries fired in retaliation on known & suspected emplacements	
			Our Medium T.M's fired during evening & night, supported by 93rd Batty & D/282 (How) Batty.	

2449 Wt. W14957/M90 750,000 1/16 J.B.C. & A. Forms/C.2118/12.

Army Form C. 2118.

Instructions regarding War Diaries and Intelligence Summaries are contained in F. S. Regs., Part II. and the Staff Manual respectively. Title Pages will be prepared in manuscript.

WAR DIARY
~~or~~
~~INTELLIGENCE SUMMARY~~
(Erase heading not required.)

280TH (CITY OF LONDON) BDE R.F.A. (T.F.)

DECEMBER 1916

Sheet iv.

Place	Date	Hour	Summary of Events and Information	Remarks and references to Appendices
LAVENTIE	21/12/16		Several enemy working parties dispersed during the day. Registration carried out as necessary. During afternoon fired on hostile T.M. believed to have been located.	
		11 P.M. to midnight	D/282 (How) Battery fired on hostile T.M's.	
	22/12/16		109TH & D/282 (How) Batteries temporarily placed under command of Lt COL. POTTINGER commdg. Left Group of 37TH DIV. (composite) artillery, the 109TH Battery covering the same zone as before, (on Right flank). Group zone reduced accordingly.	
			Working parties dispersed by our fire during morning.	
			Hostile T.M's very active during afternoon & evening. Batteries fired on front line & T.M. emplacements as counter offensive.	
		9 PM to 2 AM	Hostile T.M's again active. Our Batteries fired on known emplacements.	
	23/12/16		Hostile raid carried out on our Trenches as soon as their T.M. fire lifted. Our Batteries were immediately turned on to NO MANS LAND to catch the raiding party as they returned to their own line.	
			Three different parties of enemy fired on during day with good effect. Several casualties seen. Quiet day.	
	24/12/16		Quiet morning. Batteries registered in preparation for the Xmas shoot. Hostile T.M's active during afternoon & evening. Batteries bombarded their emplacements in return.	
		7 PM	Xmas shoot opens. See Group Operation Order No. 4 with Schedules.	
	25/12/16		Xmas shoot continued. Enemy quiet except for certain amount of shelling on our back country & some T.M. activity which was rather persistent during evening, but finally silenced about 8 PM.	
	26/12/16		Visibility poor. Xmas shoot concluded – fire distributed over enemy's front-line system, road junctions & frequented spots. Enemy abnormally inactive.	

Instructions regarding War Diaries and Intelligence Summaries are contained in F. S. Regs., Part II. and the Staff Manual respectively. Title Pages will be prepared in manuscript.

WAR DIARY
or
INTELLIGENCE SUMMARY
(Erase heading not required.)

Army Form C. 2118.

280th (City of London) BDE R.F.A. (T.F.)

December 1916 Sheet V.

Place	Date	Hour	Summary of Events and Information	Remarks and references to Appendices
LAVENTIE	27/12/16		Quiet day. Registration carried out. A/280. Batty registered in co-operation with aeroplane.	
"	28/12/16		Visibility very poor. A programme shoot by our 18 pdrs & 4.5s in conjunction with T.M's on enemy C.T's M.G's and T.M. emplacements, during the afternoon, resulting in much damage to enemy trenches etc.	
"	29/12/16		Quiet morning. Five different hostile parties fired on and dispersed. Hostile T.M's somewhat troublesome as our H.T.M's and M.T.M's had successfully bombarded enemy front system etc. Three specific hostile T.M's were singled out and eventually silenced by our Hows.	
"	30/12/16		Most unusually good visibility. Many enemy parties seen & fired upon. Enemy burst very high shrapnel over our trenches frequently during the day, and also made a pretty good target of Battery position of C/282 with their 4.2's. Hostile T.M's again troublesome during afternoon, & were fired upon by A/282 on three occasions.	
"	31/12/16	10.0 am to 4.0 Pm	A busy day was spent in annoying the enemy. Combined shoots were carried out by our 18 pdrs 4.5s, H.T.M's and M.T.M's on enemy front system. During the day 93rd Bty cut wire in M.30.C. Enemy T.M's responded to a small extent, and were specially treated by fire from A/282 and 93rd Battery.	
		4-30 Pm to 4-35.	Short sharp bursts of fire directed upon support, reserve, & C T's by all batteries with a view to catching working parties.	
		10.55 (German time) 11.55.	All batteries fired rapid bursts on frequented spots in enemy's rear, and also on support and reserve trenches. Enemy did not respond.	

L. A. C. [illegible]

SECRET

Copy No 10.

OPERATION ORDER No.4.BY LIEUT.COLONEL.L.A.C.SOUTHAM.,

COMMANDING RIGHT GROUP.

23rd DECEMBER 1916.

1. In accordance with Corps and Divisional Orders a bombardment of the enemy's front system will be carried out from 7 p.m.December 24th to the morning of December 27th in co-operation with H.A.,T.M's and Infantry.

The object of the bombardment is to prevent the enemy from leaving his trenches and to prevent our troops from going out to join him.

2. So far as is compatible with this,loss and damage will be inflicted on him.

Fire will be directed on the front and support trenches except when otherwise ordered,or if the enemy exposes himself,and will be so far as possible controlled by observation.

A schedule up to 4.30 p.m.on 25th inst is attached.

3. O.P's will be manned from 7 a.m.to 5 p.m. 24th onwards and by day every portion of the front line should be kept under close observation.

Batteries will be ready to open rapid fire immediately on any of the enemy attempting to leave their trenches or otherwise exposing themselves, and F.O.O's will act accordingly within or outside their battery zones, irrespective of allotment of ammunition.

4. Batteries will adhere strictly to schedule attached as to times of firing,and distribute widely over zones allotted.

The following extra ammunition is at disposal of batteries for counter offensives on T.M's:-

93rd Battery... ... 50 "A".
C/282 " ... ... 30 "A"
A/282 " ... ... 50 "B.X"

Up to this amount above Batteries may fire without reference to Group, but circumstances and expenditure will be reported at once on each occasion,so that,if desirable,co-operation of 6" may be asked for and so as to keep Group informed of situation. A special report of quantity unexpended under this heading will be made at 12noon, 25th.

5. Fire will usually be frontal on C.T's and by enfilade sections on first and support lines,but the points in attached schedule allotted to STOKES T.M.will not be fired on. During bombardment by M.T.M's fire will be specially directed on trenches in vicinity. Co-operation with H.T.M.is arranged for in schedule.

4.5" Hows.will fire on trench junctions,suspected strong points, and especially on trenches facing M.29.1.

6. There will be as little other firing as possible on 24th,subject to retaliation requirements. Any rounds necessary for corrector verification will be fired before 1 p.m.

7. Watches will be carefully synchronised twice daily. O's.C.Batteries are responsible that those of Officers,Nos.1.and signallers are synchronised.

8. Acknowledge by wire.

[signature] 2/Lieut.,
Adjutant, RIGHT GROUP.

Copies to:
No.1..93rd Bty.
2..A/280 "
3..A/282 "
4..C/282 "
5..D.O.T.M.) for information.
6..169 Inf.Bde)
7..)
8...)
9..) Retained.
10..)

SECRET   G/533

O.C.,

Batteries.

Owing to information as to likely German festivities, the following alteration will be made to schedule :-

Delete all firing from 7.45 - 11.5.p.m. and insert :

7.45pm.- 9.0.p.m.) 9.35 - 10.p.m.)	GEAGUN - Front Line in Group Zone)		30 A.X
9.30 - 9.35.p.m.	JOGUN - MOULIN de PIETRE and radius of 100 yards)	20.A.	30.A.X.
	COOGUN. Trenches in zone leading from front system to JOGUN's target.)	10.A.	20 A.X.
	GEAGUN. ditto.	10.A.	20.A.X.
	HUHOW. As for JOGUN.		20.B.X.
10.0. - 10.5.p.m.	COOGUN) GEAGUN) As above. HUHOW)	10.A. 10.A.	10.A.X. 10.A.X. 20.BX.
10.57 - 11.3.p.m.	JOGUN) COOGUN) C.T's and enfilade fire on front and support GEAGUN) lines, own zones.	10.A. 10.A. 10.A.	20.A.X. 20.A.X. 20.A.X.
	HUHOW. MOULIN DE PIETRE.		10.B.X.

Acknowledge by wire.

[signature] 2/Lieut.,
Adjutant, RIGHT GROUP.

24.12.16.

SECRET.

OPERATION ORDER No.4. - SCHEDULE

Time.	Battery.	Target.	Ammunition A.	A.X.	B.X.	Remarks
Decr.24th.						
7 p.m.	JOGUN	C.T's and enfilade fire on front line, own zones.	24.	12.	-	Duration not to exceed 2 minutes.
	COOGUN		24.	12.	-	
	GEAGUN		24.	12.	-	
	HUHOW.		-	-	12.	
7.30 - 7.35.p.m.	JOGUN	C.T's and enfilade fire on support line, own zones.	-	12.	-	
	COOGUN		-	12.	-	
	GEAGUN		-	12.	-	
7.45 - 9.45 p.m.	GEAGUN.	C.T's and enfilade fire on front and support line in Group zone.	-	30	-	
10.53 - 11.5.p.m.	JOGUN	C.T's and enfilade fire on front and support trenches, own zones.	30	50	-	JOGUN to enfilade COOGUN's front as well as own.
	COOGUN		30	50	-	
	GEAGUN		30	50	-	
	HUHOW.		-	-	30	
11.5.p.m. - Decr.25th 1.0.am.	COOGUN	Front system within Group zone.	-	50	-	Infantry patrols out between 1 a.m. & 3 a.m.
	GEAGUN	ditto (enfilade only)	-	30	-	
3.0.a.m. - 6.0.am.	JOGUN.	Front System within Group zone.	-	50	-	
6.0.a.m.	JOGUN	Own zone and each to take half COOGUN's zone.	-	20	-	To be fired within 3 minutes.
	GEAGUN		-	20	-	
6.0. - 7.0.a.m.	COOGUN	Front system within Group zone.	-	20	-	
8.0. - 8.3.a.m.	JOGUN.	Front and support lines, own zones. JOGUN & GEAGUN enfilade only.	10	10	-	
	GEAGUN		10	10	-	
	COOGUN		10	30	-	
	HUHOW.		-	-	36.	

OPERATION ORDER No.4. - S C H E D U L E (CONT)

Time.	Battery.	Target.	Ammunition A.	A.X.	B.X.	Remarks
Decr.25th(cont)						
8.18 - 8.21.am.	J O G U N)	C. T's., - own zones.	-	30.	-	
	G E A G U N)		-	30	-	
	C O O G U N)		-	30.	-	
	H U H O W.		-	-	36.	
8.30.-11.a.m.	G E A G U N.	C.T's and enfilade fire in Group zone.	-	80.	-	
10.52.-11.30.a.m.	J O G U N.)	Support Line near M.30.c.62.75 (JOGUN enfilade)	40	20	-)	Support of H.T.M.
	H U H O W)		-	-	30)	
11.30.am.-1.10.pm.	J O G U N.	Trenches in Group zone.	-	40	-	
1.5. - 1.45.p.m.	J O G U N)	Trenches near M.30.c.62.75.	30	40	-)	Support of H.T.M.
	H U H O W)		-	-	40)	
2.0. - 4.30 p.m.	C O O G U N	Front system within Group zone.	-	70	-	

TRENCH MORTAR PROGRAMME

Time.	Target.	Total Rounds. Medium.	Heavy.	Remarks
7 p.m.Dec.24th - to- 8 a.m.Dec.25th	Front line trenches within zones of fire.	40	--	At irregular intervals during night. No firing between the hours of 10 and 11 p.m. and 1 and 3 a.m. Start promptly on conclusion of these pauses.
8.a.m.Dec.25th. ~~XXXX~~ to 8.21.a.m.25th.,	2" Mortars will be moved to any of their positions according to circumstances.	12 12	-- --	In co-operation with organised shoot.
10.5.a.m.Dec.25th. 10.55.am. " 25th	M.30.c.62.75 do Front line trenches as above.	10 ~~40~~ 10	-- 7	~~TARGET~~ HEAVY T.M. Artillery support for 30 minutes. Bursts of fire every 5 minutes beginning 10.55 am.
12-20 p.m 1.10 p.m." 25th	M.30.c.62.75.	20	7	~~TARGET~~ HEAVY T.M. Artillery support for 30 minutes. Bursts of fire every 5 minutes beginning 1.10.p.m.
6 p.m.Dec.25th -to- 6 a.m. Dec.26th.	Front line trenches as above	20	-	At irregular intervals during the night

STOKES TARGETS

M.24.d.5.0.   M.30.a.9.5.   M.30.a.40.15.   M.30.c.5.6.   M.36.a.3.4. M.36.c.0.5.

SECRET G/5 4 4

O.C.,

Batteries.

Herewith schedule of firing 4.30 p.m.25th to 5.p.m.25th insts.

In the event of Hostile T.M's firing,the 18 pdr Battery called on will fire 10.A. 30.A.X., A/282 will fire 50 D.X.,fire being directed on supposed hostile emplacement or emplacements and trenches in vicinity. On the second occasion,the same amount will be expended.

It is of great importance that such counter-offensives should be prompt and intense. A report will be made at once to Group Headquarters,and,after second burst of fire is called for, further instructions will be given.

After opening fire,as much information as possible should be obtained from the infantry (or by day from the F.O.O) as to precision of identification and volume of fire.

Acknowledge.

2/Lieut.,

25.12.16. Adjutant, RIGHT GROUP.

SECRET

OPERATION ORDER No.4. SCHEDULE (CONT)

Time.	Battery.	Target.	Ammunition. A.	A.X.	B.X
Decr.25th					
4.45 -4.46p.m.)	G E A G U N.	MIN DE PIETRE.	4.	4.	
4.49 -4.50p.m.)		Cross Roads,N.25.b.35.20.	4.	4.	
4.45 -4.46.p.m)	C O O G U N	Cross roads N.25.c.60.15.	4.	4.	
4.49 -4.50 p.m)		Cross roads PIETRE.	4.	4.	
5.0.- 8.15.pm.)	G E A G U N	Front system within Group zone.	-	30.	
8. 0. p. m.)		M.de PIETRE and Cross Roads as above.	6.	6.	
8.15.-11.45.p.m.)	C O O G U N	Front system within Group zone	-	30.	
8.30.p.m.)		Cross roads as above.	6	6.	
2 -5 a.m.	J O G U N.	Front system within Group zone	-	30	
5 - 8 a.m.)	G E A G U N	ditto		20	
5.45.30 a.m.)		In Bursts of fire over ~~above~~ same.)	24.	24.	
6.15.-7 a.m.)					
8.0. - 11.a.m.)	C O O G U N	Front system within Group zone	-	20.	
9.20 ~~9.20~~ a.m.&)		ditto)	10.	20.	
10.30 a.m.)		Co-operation with M.T.M.)			
11.a.m. - 1.p.m.	J O G U N.	Front system within Group zone.	-	20.	
11.10 - 11.50 am.	do:)	Co-operation with H.and M.T.M	20	30.	
	H U H O W.)	support line near M.30.c.62.75 (JOGUN enfilade.)	-	-	25.
1 p.m.-3 p.m.	G E A G U N.	Front system within Group zone.	-	20.	
2.5. - 2.35 p.m.	G E A G U N)	Support line near M.30.c.62.75	20.	30.	
	H U H O W)	Co-operation with H.&.M.T.M.	-	-	25.
3. - 5 p.m.	C O O G U N.	Front system within Group zone	-	30.	-

S E C R E T

OPERATION ORDER No.4. - SCHEDULE (cont)

Time.	Battery.	Target	Ammunition. A.	AX.	BX.
Decr.26th 5 - 8 p.m.	J O G U N.	Front system within Group area.	-	50.	-
8 - 10.50 p.m.	G E A G U N.	- ditto -	-	40.	-
Decr.27th 1 a.m. - 4.am.	C O O G U N.	- ditto -	-	40.	-
5 - 7 a.m.	J O G U N.	- ditto -	-	50.	-

In addition C O O G U N and G E A G U N will fire short sharp bursts of fire on targets behind front system as on night of 25/26th. — not between hours of 11-0 pm & 1-0 am Allotment for each battery for the purpose - 10.A.30.A.X. In the event of fire being called for on T.M's 18 pdrs will fire 10 A.X., 4.5" Hows - 10 B.X, rapidly, then call for report, and if latter is not satisfactory or if same T.M's re-open within one hour, may fire up to 18 pdrs 40 A.X., 4.5" Hows 50.B.X, reporting to Group.

acknowledge by wire

V G Goodwin

ORIGINAL

Vol 14

War Diary

JANUARY 1917

280th (City of London) Bde R.F.A.

Army Form C. 2118.

Instructions regarding War Diaries and Intelligence Summaries are contained in F. S. Regs., Part II. and the Staff Manual respectively. Title Pages will be prepared in manuscript.

WAR DIARY
or
~~INTELLIGENCE SUMMARY~~
(Erase heading not required.)

280th Bde R.F.A (City of London)

JANUARY 1917

Place	Date	Hour	Summary of Events and Information	Remarks and references to Appendices
LAVENTIE.	1/1/17		Enemy artillery very active. Our trenches and O.P's heavily bombarded, and also the position of C/280. We responded to the extent of 350 Rds.	
"	2/1/17	10-0am 12-0 6-30Pm	All batteries took part in a systematic bombardment of enemy support & reserve trenches also his suspected O.P's. In all 1100 Rds of BX. and AX. used. The 93rd Battery carried on a small amount of wire cutting in N.30.C.	
"	3/1/17		Enemy very quiet during the morning. Infantry relief in progress. Work in connection with reconstruction of O.P's initiated.	
		3.30Pm	Command of Group handed over to Lt. Col. C.C. Macdowell. Lt. Col. L.A.C Southam ~~taking~~ taking up quarters in rest billets in Laventie. Bde. H.Q. office transferred to 56th D.A School annexe.	
"	4/1/17	2-0Pm	Lt Col L.A.C Southam took over as Commandant 56th Div Arty School for Officers.	
"	5/1/17	5-15Pm	a Lecture at D.A. School by Major Thompson (93rd Batty) on the 18pdr gun in trench warfare. Lt Col L.A.C Southam in the chair. Major Brady (280/C battery), Capt [illegible] (of A/282 battery) and others took part in the discussion.	
"	15/1/17	10-0am.	Lt. Col. L.A.C Southam with H.Q. staff relieved Lt. Col. E.C Pottinger in command of "Left Group" — Group consisting of D/280. A/281. B/281, D/281 and B/282 batteries. A very quiet day. Few rounds only being fired on enemy trenches by A/281.	
"	16/1/17		A quiet morning. D/280, A/281 and B/281 fired on new enemy works in the vicinity of Rue Delevas during the afternoon and early evening. Enemy very quiet, and made no response.	
"	17/1/17		Small shoots all day with a view to annoying enemy. Many working parties fired on. In the evening the Roving Gun and B/281 & B/282 fired on Rue Delevas & back area	

2449 Wt. W14957/M90 750,000 1/16 J.B.C. & A. Forms/C.2118/12.

Army Form C. 2118.

Instructions regarding War Diaries and Intelligence Summaries are contained in F. S. Regs., Part II. and the Staff Manual respectively. Title Pages will be prepared in manuscript.

WAR DIARY
or
~~INTELLIGENCE SUMMARY~~

(Erase heading not required.)

280th Bde (City of London) R.F.A.

JANUARY. 1916.

Place	Date	Hour	Summary of Events and Information	Remarks and references to Appendices
LAVENTIE	18/1/17		Various programme shoots carried out by D/280, A/281, B/282 & V/56 T.M. on Rue Deleval etc & observed working parties on suspected new enemy defences. Early in the evening an alarm received from infantry that "BERTHA" Post was being attacked was promptly responded to by D/280 and A/281 (within 3 minutes). Infantry highly elated at the promptness & vigour of our fire.	
"	19/1/17	8-0 am to 12-15	Seven different working parties seen and fired on. At about 1-0 pm the enemy C.T. "Clara" and junctions, up to Rue Deleval, bombarded by A/281, B/281 & V/56 T.M. Enemy M.T.M. in this C.T. replied, and was silenced by D/281.	
"	20/1/17	8.15 pm	Many enemy parties fired on. From 2.25 to 7-0 pm various spots on and around Rue Deleval were fired on by all batteries, about 200 Rds used of 4.5 and 18 pdr being used. A/281 fired on hostile T.M. in CLARA" which was troubling our advanced post "ENFIELD". The day generally was quiet, and a relief was suspected to be in progress.	
"	21/1/17		During the day many working parties fired upon. "BERTHA" and "FLAME" posts were attacked at about 5.48 pm. Fire was immediately opened by A/281 & B/282. At 7.34 alarm that "IRMA", "BARNET & ENFIELD" posts were in danger and B/281 A/282 & B/282 were soon in action. This proved to be a false alarm. Continuous fire was kept up till 8.53 pm. At about 9-0 pm it was definitely established that BERTHA had been taken	
"	22/1/17	5.0 am	Intense fire brought to bear on "BERTHA" preparatory to an infantry assault to regain this post. Our attack was successful and at 6-0 am this post was in our hands. Remainder of day quiet	
"	23/1/17	1.20 am	"BERTHA" post again reported in enemy hands and at about 2-0 am a short & intensive bombardment was directed upon this post by A/281. At 5.30 am a further bombardment by A/281 preceded an infantry attack, followed by a lift of our fire to the rear. At 6-0 am our infantry reported that post was again in our hands. Careful registration of the Post was made before our bombardment, so that infantry might lie down in no man's land at a spot 70 yards in front of BERTHA". During remainder of the day enemy fairly quiet & we fired on back areas, C.T.s and enemy T.M's. In the early evening a barrage was put up in rear of our advanced posts to protect our relief parties. The Right section of A/282 (How) battery was transferred to 280th Bde and embodied in D/280 battery. D/280 battery transferred to Right Group. Left Group now consisting of A/281 B/281 D/281 B/282, and 1 Section of A/282.	
"	24/1/17	6-15 pm	In the afternoon many of the enemy seen coming towards "IRMA" C.T. (apparently a relief). A rapid fire was put upon tracks in vicinity of this C.T. by B/281 & D/281 for about 30 minutes. An alarm received that all our advanced posts were being attacked. Fire by all batteries immediately brought to bear. The position was one of considerable uncertainty for some hours, but was cleared up about 9-0 pm. The posts were still ours. During our bombardment position of B/282 was shelled and we shelled enemy back country. At about 10-10 pm it was reported that enemy after unsuccessfully attacking "Enfield" post were falling back over the River LAIES. We opened out for a few minutes on river crossings with shrapnel.	

2449 Wt. W14957/M90 750,000 1/16 J.B.C. & A. Forms/C.2118/12.

Army Form C. 2118.

Instructions regarding War Diaries and Intelligence Summaries are contained in F. S. Regs., Part II. and the Staff Manual respectively. Title Pages will be prepared in manuscript.

WAR DIARY
or
~~INTELLIGENCE~~ SUMMARY

(Erase heading not required.)

280th BDE R.F.A. (City of London)

JANUARY 1917.

Place	Date	Hour	Summary of Events and Information	Remarks and references to Appendices
LAVENTIE	25/1/17		A quiet morning – very cold. At noon V/56 H.T.M. fired on portions of enemy front line & their fire was covered by fire from B/282 and also a few 4.5s. At 6.30 P.m. the usual alarm came through "Help BERTHA". A/281 and B/281 opened fire but stopped within 5 minutes – a false alarm. This day otherwise comparatively quiet.	
"	26/1/17		Very cold weather continues (Temperature down to 15 F.) Our H.T.M. V/56 again busy during the morning on enemy front line. Hostile shelling spasmodically all day of our advanced posts. Our batteries spent the day re-registering various points and tracks used by enemy – tracks revealed by recent air photographs taken since the snow-fall.	
"	27/1/17		A special counter-offensive programme was prepared for today in case the enemy displayed extra activity on the Kaiser's birthday. At 9.40 am "IRMA" post was rather heavily shelled and A/281 & B/281 replied vigorously up and around this C.T. for about 30 minutes. At 11.40 am a further 150 A.X. and 50 B.X. were fired by these batteries as counter offensive. At 7.50 P.m this was repeated by us. At 8.10 P.m. BERTHA and IRMA reported threatened and at 8.33 batteries were in full swing. Posts reported safe at about 9–10 P.m. Infantry highly pleased at our efforts. At 11.0 P.m. enemy reported to be in "IRMA" Post, which post we shelled at various intervals during the night	
"	28/1/17	5.30 am	A very rapid rate of fire brought to bear on "IRMA" to cover attack of our infantry. Post once again occupied by us at 6.0 am. Remainder of day quiet. All our posts evacuated permanently during the night.	
"	29/1/17		A quiet day. Still very cold – 14 degrees of frost. At 8.30 P.m, and also to a lesser degree at 8.54 P.m. intense bombardment by all batteries on "BERTHA" C.T. with a view to catching working parties repairing damage effected by our H.T.M. and M.T.M. batteries on the trench during the afternoon. Stokes mortars and machine guns joined in.	
	30/1/17	10.0 am 10.30.	The command of LEFT GROUP handed over to Major ~~[illegible]~~ Aschwanden by Lt. Col. L.A.C. Southam. Lt. Col. Southam with H.Q. staff took over from Major Aschwanden command of RIGHT GROUP consisting of 280th BDE batteries, plus C/282 and D/282. Temperature still very low, and some snow.	
	31/1/17		Cold weather still intense. Enemy rather more active. A few enemy parties seen and fired on. Considerable care has been necessitated lately in the effective camouflaging of gun positions due to the recent snow-falls. A re-arrangement of group took place. Batteries of 282nd BDE departing on night of 31st/Feb 1st to form a new group on our right. Group now commanded by Lt Col. L.A.C. Southam consists of 280th BDE Batteries only.	

L. A. C. Southam Lt Col
Commanding 280th (City of London) Bde R.F.A.

2449 Wt. W14957/M90 750,000 1/16 J.B.C. & A. Forms/C.2118/12.

Original

Vol 15

War Diary

280th (City of London) Bde

R.F.A.

February 1917

Instructions regarding War Diaries and Intelligence Summaries are contained in F. S. Regs., Part II. and the Staff Manual respectively. Title Pages will be prepared in manuscript.

WAR DIARY
or
INTELLIGENCE SUMMARY
(Erase heading not required.)

Army Form C. 2118.

280th. (CITY OF LONDON) BRIGADE. R.F. A.

Place	Date	Hour	Summary of Events and Information F E B R U A R Y . 1 9 1 7 .	Remarks and references to Appendices
LAVENTIE.	1-2-17.		Comparatively quiet day. Very low temperature still.	
	2-2-17.		Visibility poor. Enemy retaliated for the fire on their front line C.T's and tramway by D/280. This Battery fired 300.BX.in all. During this shoot one How.had a bore premature which destroyed entirely piece and carriage, with but 2.casualties in the gun pit.	
	3-2-17.		Enemy T.M's troublesome. The definate counter-offensive programme was put in motion and D/280. appeared to silence them very quickly. Working parties dispersed with apparent casualties by 93rd.	
	4-2-17.		Programme shoot carried out by D/280.and V/56.H.T.M. in preparation for coming raids. A/280.and D/280.also fired as counter-offensive for enemy T.M.activity.Again working parties scattered during the day.	
	5-2-17.		A busy day again spent by Y/56.T.M. and D/280.in further preparation for raid.Suspected hostile T.M.emplacements were treated by 93rd.Battery whilst this was on. The application of a definate anti-hostile T.M.programme seemed highly successful in keeping the enemy quiet. A section of D/280. was withdrawn during the night to help form a composite battery for temporary/ /loan to the 5th.D.A.	
	6-2-17.		Further preparation for raid by D/280.,V/56.,H.T.M.,and Y/56.M.T.M.Batteries. The 93rd.and A/280. carried out the standard retaliation programme for enemy L.T.M.fire in the afternoon. Enemy was on a whole quiet during the day. A section from 93rd.,was withdrawn during the night to form a composite 18.pdr.Battery from the 56th.Div.to aid 5th.Div.who have a daylight raid in contemplation.	
	7-2-17.		The M.T.M.battery at wire cutting etc in preparation for raid. 71.medium bombs being fired. A/280.and D/280.fired standard retaliation programmes for enemy offensive fire on their battery zone. 93rd.dispersed working parties twice during the day.	
	8-2-17.		Much movement seen during day. Y/56.,X/56.and V/56.T.M.Batteries fired on points where raids are to take place. D/280.D/280.likewise, and assisted in the control of the fire of a 6"How.battery with the same objective. 93rd and A/280.fired on hostile parties. In the early evening 93rd and C/280.carried out a dummy raid programme on a portion of enemy front where a raid will not take place. Some 200.Rds.AX.were fired. Enemy brought down his S.O.S.barrage 12.minutes late.	
	9-2-17.		A comprehensive programme prepared for this day. Two Medium T.M.batteries,3. 18.pdr.batteries 1. 4-5"How.,and also 6"How.battery and Stokes T.M.engaged at various parts of the day on cutting wire, damaging front and support lines etc in further preparation for raid. In the evening, 18.pdrs.used on tracks and rendez-vous of the enemy who presumably would come down to make good damage during the day.	
	10-2-17.		A small amount of fire directed on to enemy front line by D/280. The Y/56.M.T.M. put record number (130 Rds)on to wire at raiding point. Two raids at 7-0.p.m. An elaborate scheme of barrages was worked out, necessitating the assistance of the greater portion of the Divn.Artillery.	

/continued.

2449 Wt. W14957/M90 750,000 1/16 J.B.C. & A. Forms/C.2118/12.

/continued.

Instructions regarding War Diaries and Intelligence Summaries are contained in F. S. Regs., Part II. and the Staff Manual respectively. Title Pages will be prepared in manuscript.

WAR DIARY
or
~~INTELLIGENCE SUMMARY~~
(Erase heading not required.)

Army Form C. 2118.

280th.(CITY OF LONDON) BRIGADE. R. F. A.

Place	Date	Hour	Summary of Events and Information --FEBRUARY.1917.--	Remarks and references to Appendices
LAVENTIE.	10-2-17. (Continued)		The raid on S.end of our zone was carried out under fire and was over by 7-35.p.m. The other raid was by stealth and only in case of attack by enemy was it intended to make use of our Artillery. A dummy raid was carried out at another point, and this seemed to deceive the enemy as his barrage was put down at that point at first. All batteries of 280th.Brigade plus A/281., D/281., A/282.,and D/282.,Stokes mortars and machine guns were employed in close cohesion. Our Infantry expressed great satisfaction at the Artillery fire. A great deal was learnt by these minor operations,particularly was the problem of conveying messages by Rockets and other means found difficult. (see appendices No 1. and 2. for details of the operation.)	
	11-2-17.		Markedly quiet day. Working parties seen and fired on. Small amount of hostile T.M.fire. A break in the weather,and but a few degrees of frost. Section of 4-5"Hows lent by D/280. to 5th. Div. returned to the Group during the night.	
	~~12-2-17.~~		~~Visibility very poor. H.T.M. (V/56.) fired 10.Rds.~~	
"	12-2-17.		Visibility very poor. H.T.M.(V.56.) fired 10. rds. in preparation for another raid. Visibility so very poor that a shoot with Aeroplane registration and also one on enemy front line by D/280 was postponed.	
"	13-2-17.		Infantry relief. The 93rd alone fired during the day on two different working parties. Enemy very quiet.	
"	14-2-17.		The H.T.M. & M.T.M. on the wire and trenches near point of entry of next Raid. D/280 also on enemy front line and M.G. emplacements. This Battery also registered points behind front line with an Aeroplane Observer whose corrections were checked from one of our O.P.'s. The impression gained was that this R.F.C. Observer knew his work.	
"	15-2-17.		Owing to the usual poor visibility during the morning V/56, Y/56, and D/280 were compelled to carry on in the afternoon their preparations for the next raid. The 93rd and A/280 annoyed the enemy in rear. Each 18 pdr. battery fired a small amount of A., part of which had been exposed for two months and part of which had been kept in boxes. Evidence pointed to the highly satisfactory nature of the water-proofing of those which had been exposed in this humid country. A small "spoof" attack at 10.0 p.m. in connection with the firing by our Infantry of a Bangalore torpedo in enemy's wire was carried out by A. and D/280 Batteries.	
"	16-2-17.		The usual persistent bombardment of various spots on the enemy front by all batteries and two T.M. batteries. H.Q. very busy in perfecting arrangements for raid on our front on this night- See Appendix No.3., the diversion put up by this Group in support of the raid by Group on the right early on the morning of the 17th.,-See Appendix No.4., another raid on our front on the 18th.,-See Appendix No.5., plus the usual programme shoots.	

2449 Wt. W14957/M90 750,000 1/16 J.B.C. & A. Forms/C.2118/12.

/Continued.

Instructions regarding War Diaries and Intelligence Summaries are contained in F. S. Regs., Part II. and the Staff Manual respectively. Title Pages will be prepared in manuscript.

WAR DIARY
or
INTELLIGENCE SUMMARY

(Erase heading not required.)

Army Form C. 2118.

280th.(City of London) BRIGADE. R. F. A.

Place	Date	Hour	Summary of Events and Information	Remarks and references to Appendices
LAVENTIE.	17-2-17.		12.20 a.m. The raid- See Appendix No.3.- was unsuccessful in consequence of enemy machine guns not having been dealt with prior to our Infantry going over. During the day, furthur preparation for next raid-See Appendix No.5.- M.T.M's put over again a record number of rounds on to enemy wire. D/280 fired on enemy front line and all 18. pdr. batteries at various parts of the day searched MOULIN DU PIETRE with a view to annoying the enemy. This drew enemy's fire and again revealed that this spot was a "tender" one of the enemy.	
"	18-2-17.		All batteries very active annoying the enemy during the day, who was undoubtedly annoyed as he returned fire on our tracks and roads. Evidence pointed to the fact that he had recently taken air photographs of our back country and tracks, as his fire, remarkably accurate, was directed on a new track only used whilst snow was down. Raid for to-night at 7.20 p.m. was postponed.	
"	19.2.17.		An infantry relief in progress. V/56. and D/280 fired in the morning on front line. 93rd. and D/280 fired in retaliation by request of Infantry during the afternoon.	
"	20.2.17.		Visibility very low. D/280 on German new trench, V/56. and Y/56. on front line carried out Programme shoots. A/280, C/280, and 93rd. did a certain amount of spasmodic shooting whenever opportunity presented on the lifting of ground fog.	
"	21.2.17.		11. a.m. to 2.p.m. An effort was made to breach the banks of the River des LAIES so as to flood enemy reserve trenches near MIN DU PIETRE. D/280 expended 100 rds. on this work and also put 150 rds. into BAS POMMEREAU whilst the 93rd. sprayed C.T.'s between both places. A/280 and C/280 at dusk endeavoured to at least annoy the enemy by expending 50 rds. of AX. on spots near Reserve trenches where the enemy might foregather.	
"	22.2.17.		Visibility so very poor that all batteries merely fired on tracks and roads at irregular intervals during the day and evening. Hostile T.M.'s dealt with by D/280 on three occasions. Enemy otherwise quiet.	
"	23.2.17.		A single gun of D/280 and of 93rd. moved to a spot nearer front line with the object of firing on new targets outside our zone to deceive enemy in believing that we had re-inforced our Artillery on this front. It was too foggy for registration however. Y/56. T.M. fired as	

2449 Wt. W14957/M90 750,000 1/16 J.B.C. & A. Forms/C.2118/12.

/Continued.

Instructions regarding War Diaries and Intelligence Summaries are contained in F. S. Regs., Part II. and the Staff Manual respectively. Title Pages will be prepared in manuscript.

WAR DIARY
or
INTELLIGENCE SUMMARY
(Erase heading not required.)

2 80th. (City of London) BRIGADE. R.F.A.

Army Form C. 2118.

Place	Date	Hour	Summary of Events and Information	Remarks and references to Appendices
LAVENTIE.	23.2.17.		(Continued) usual on enemy front line in the morning and all other Batteries of the Group spasmodically searched during the day, tracks and roads frequented by enemy.	
"	24.2.17.		9.15 a.m. to 9.30. a.m.- A combined shoot on an important C.T. in conjunction with Stokes Mortars undertaken by D/280 and 93rd. Hostile Minnies called for frequent counter-offensive shoots by D/2 80 during the day. 93rd and D/280 carried out registration of their lone guns with the idea of deceiving enemy. Tracks and roads treated by all 18. pdr. Batteries at dusk.	
"	25.2.17.		Roads and tracks fired on at irregular intervals all day and in the early evening. Hostile T.M.'s very offensive, though no more so than we had been with our own. T.M.'s practically every day for ~~xxmonth~~ over a month.	
"	26.2.17.		Visibility very good. Infantry relief in progress. Hostile T.M.'s alone fired on.	
"	27.2.17.		The Group took over about another 1000 yards of front on the right and relinquished about the same amount on the north. C/280 Battery left the Group and joined the Left Group. A/282 joined this- Centre- Group; both Batteries remaining in the same positions.	
"	28.2.17.		The lone guns of 93rd. and D/280 carried out registrations of new targets, etc. A/280 and 93rd. co-operated with Heavy Artillery, firing bursts of shrapnel on the Heavy target. Y/56 carried out a bombardment of Hostile T.M. Emplacement. D/280 spent 30 rounds BX. on one of the tramlines known to serve an offensive T.M. Weather exceptionally mild- Temperature 41, Barometer 30.11.	

[signature]
Major,
Commanding, 280th Brigade, R. F. A.

2449 Wt. W14957/M90 750,000 1/16 J.B.C. & A. Forms/C.2118/12.

Original

SECRET

Vol 16

War Diary

March 1917

280th (City of London) Bde R.F.A.

Army Form C. 2118.

Instructions regarding War Diaries and Intelligence Summaries are contained in F. S. Regs., Part II. and the Staff Manual respectively. Title Pages will be prepared in manuscript.

WAR DIARY or ~~INTELLIGENCE SUMMARY~~ 280th (City of London) BRIGADE, R.F.A.

(Erase heading not required.)

Place	Date	Hour	Summary of Events and Information ~~February~~ March 1917.	Remarks and references to Appendices
LAVENTIE	1.3.17.		Very little fire all day. 93rd and A/280 Batteries co-operated with 6" and 8" Hows. on targets well in the rear of the enemy. Lone guns of 93rd and D/280 carried out more registrations. Enemy fired on our back area.	
"	2.3.17.		D/280 carried out shoots at long ranges on enemy strong points. Enemy quiet, no hostile T.M. activity, our method of blowing up his tram lines apparently being the surest way of curtailing this offensiveness.	
"	3.3.17.		A sharp drop in Temperature. Relieving Group Commander (Lt.-Col. Whitley. C.M.G.) and Battery Commanders of the 246th Brigade, R.F.A. arrived at 11.30 a.m. as a preliminary to taking over the Group. This Brigade relieves A/280 (B/246), 93rd (C/246), D/280 (D/246), of Centre Group. A/246 relieved C/280 who are for tactical purposes under the Left Group., Mirgun, A/282 remains in this Group. ~~(See Appendix 12)~~	
"	4.3.17.		The personnel of two sections of each Battery relieved by those of 246th Brigade.	
"	5.3.17.		Personnel of remaining sections relieved and command of Batteries handed over. Brigade and Battery Officers and staffs travelled to and concentrated at CALONNE-sur-LYS.	
CALONNE.	6.3.17.		At CALONNE, repacking vehicles for coming march.	
ESTREE BLANCHE	7.3.17.		March to ESTREE BLANCHE, near AIRE.	
ANVIN.	8.3.17.		" " ANVIN. Very cold.	
LIGNY-sur-CANCHE.	9.3.17.		" " LIGNY-sur-CANCHE. A trying journey.	
LUCHEUX	10.3.17.		" " LUCHEUX into the Vll Corps.	
"	11.3.17.		Batteries carried out various minor Field Operations in training.	
"	12.3.17.		ditto.	
"	13.3.17.		ditto.	

2449 Wt. W14957/M90 750,000 1/16 J.B.C. & A. Forms/C.2118/12.

Army Form C. 2118.

WAR. DIARY
or
INTELLIGENCE SUMMARY

28th (City of London) Brigade, R.F.A.

(Erase heading not required.)

Instructions regarding War Diaries and Intelligence Summaries are contained in F. S. Regs., Part II. and the Staff Manual respectively. Title Pages will be prepared in manuscript.

Place	Date	Hour	Summary of Events and Information March 1917.	Remarks and references to Appendices
LUCHEUX.	14.3.17.		Marched to SIMENCOURT by a long route owing to "Thaw" conditions on most of the roads in this area.	
SIMENCOURT	15.3.17.		O.C. Brigade and Battery Commanders visited ACHICOURT & reconnoitred wire cutting positions.	
SIMENCOURT & ACHICOURT	16.3.17.		The whole Brigade engaged in taking up ammunition and making preparations for the occupation of the new positions. Parties from each Battery were also sent to work on positions eventually to be occupied by Batteries of another Division.	
"	17.3.17.		O.C. Brigade again visited ACHICOURT. All batteries at work on new positions.	
ACHICOURT	18.3.17.		The Brigade suddenly received orders to get into position and worked feverishly at the position to the South of the village. It was then definitely established that the enemy had fallen back some miles and work was suspended on these positions.	
"	19.3.17.		At 6 a.m. O.C. Brigade and Battery Commanders went forward and fixed positions in former front line of enemy at about M.16.a.4.8. (Sheet 51.b.S.W.1) and work proceeded during the day on these positions. Teams were kept saddled up for a good part of the day in view of eventualities. At 11 a.m. G.O.C., R.A., 56th Division and O.C. Brigade furthur examined the ground forward with a view to putting another 4 Brigades in about the same position.	
ACHICOURT & AGNY.	20.3.17.		Great uncertainty prevailed all day. In the evening 93rd, A/280 and C/280 put all their guns in the new position and D/280 1 Section only, keeping the other two sections parked down at ACHICOURT. Brigade Headquarters moved up to AGNY at 2.30 p.m.	

2449 Wt. W14957/M90 750,000 1/16 J.B.C. & A. Forms/C.2118/12.

Army Form C. 2118.

Instructions regarding War Diaries and Intelligence Summaries are contained in F. S. Regs., Part II. and the Staff Manual respectively. Title pages will be prepared in manuscript.

WAR DIARY
or
INTELLIGENCE SUMMARY.
(Erase heading not required.)

280th.(CITY OF LONDON) BRIGADE., ROYAL FIELD ARTILLERY.

Place	Date	Hour	Summary of Events and Information — MARCH.1917.	Remarks and references to Appendices
AGNY.	21-3-17.		Great activity all day in further preparation of positions and getting up of ammunition. D/280.put in position its two other sections. A/280 and 93rd.,took over a portion of Divisional front from 281st Batteries.	
	22-3-17.		The task of getting up 12,000 rounds per battery was persisted in vigorously. Horses show signs of the effort already and some died with exhaustion. The Wagon Lines of the Brigade removed from SIMENCOURT to WAILLY today. The C.O.Brigade reconnitred positions with other Brigade Commanders for other batteries loaned to the 56th.Divn.Arty.	
	23-3-17.		Ammunition transportation chief item of interest. Reconnitring for other possible positions near MERCATEL undertaken. The enemyholding his commanding position "Telegraph Hill"makes this an impossibility. C/280.during the night fired 800.Rounds on a road well in the rear of the enemy.	M
	24-3-17.		A reconnaisance of positions in the devastated village of MERCATEL was made during the day. No cover for batteries has been left by the enemy.	
	25-3-17.		Definately decided that 93rd and C/280 must go up to MERCATEL. Roads were reconnoitred and found to have been blown up by enemy in many places.	
AGNY & MERCATEL.	26-3-17.		O.C.Brigade and B.C's of 93rd and C/280 reconnoitred and fixed definately positions at MERCATEL -positions such as one would not dream of,but for very special reasons or necessity.	
	27-3-17.		Positions even nearer NEUVILLE VITASSE were searched for in vain during the morning by O.C. Brigade. D/280 carried on desultory fire during the night on enemy roads. A/280 wire cutting all day. The Brigade spent an appreciable amount of time and labour in assisting Officers of 280th and 251st Brigades who are coming into our positions eventually or just alongside. The commanding advantage of the enemy's position on this particular front fascinates all even though it represents a maximum of disadvantages to us.	
	28.3.17.		A day of preparation. The defence of the Southern portion of Divisional Front taken over from this Brigade by 281st & 293rd A.F. Brigades to enable work on the advanced positions to proceed without interruption.	
	29.3.17.		O.C.Brigade inspected Wagon Lines at WAILLY. 93rd & C/280 engaged on taking up ammunition & constructional material to new position. Pack transport was chiefly employed for getting up of ammunition. A/280 carried on wire cutting.	
MERCATEL & BEAURAINS	30.3.17.		Brigade H.Q. moved to new H.Q. in German Front Line just South of BEAURAINS. A/280 carried on wire cutting all day. 93rd & C/280 put guns in new positions at MERCATEL during the night	

2353 Wt. W2544/1454 700,000 5/15 D. D. & L. A.D.S.S./Forms/C. 2118.

Army Form C. 2118.

Instructions regarding War Diaries and Intelligence Summaries are contained in F. S. Regs., Part II. and the Staff Manual respectively. Title Pages will be prepared in manuscript.

WAR DIARY

~~or INTELLIGENCE SUMMARY~~

(Erase heading not required.)

280th (City of London) Brigade, R.F.A.

Place	Date	Hour	Summary of Events and Information — M A R C H - 1 9 1 7-	Remarks and references to Appendices
MERCATEL & BEAURAINS.	30.3.17.		(Continued) after overcoming huge difficulties.	
"	31.3.17.		All 18.pdr. Batteries carried on wire cutting and at night the keeping open of gaps. Ammunition during the night was taken up by pack animals to MERCATEL.	

[illegible signature]
Commdg 280 Bde R.F.A.

Original

Vol 17 56 Divn

War Diary

280th Bde RFA.

April 1917

Army Form C. 2118.

Instructions regarding War Diaries and Intelligence Summaries are contained in F. S. Regs., Part II. and the Staff Manual respectively. Title Pages will be prepared in manuscript.

WAR DIARY
or
INTELLIGENCE SUMMARY

(Erase heading not required.)

280th (City of London) BRIGADE, R.F.A.

Place	Date	Hour	Summary of Events and Information — APRIL, 1917.	Remarks and references to Appendices
BEAURAINS & MERCATEL.	1.4.17.		Wire-cutting by 93rd, A/280 & C/280. Owing to there being no flash over at MERCATEL positions, A/280 kept gaps open during the night. O.C. Brigade attended Conferance on coming operations in the morning.	
"	2.4.17.		A small amount of wire cut, but strong wind interfered with this work greatly.	
"	3.4.17.		Wire-cutting and preparations for Bombardment. Battery Commanders attended Conferance at H.Q.	
"	4.4.17.		"V" Day of the Bombardment. 18.pdr. Batteries cut wire and also practised barrages on various parts of enemy line. (See Appendix No.1) D/280 experimented with 101 Fuse on wire cutting. A lane was cut, but apparently ground was too much broken.	
"	5.4.17.		"W" Day. At 6.20 a.m. Batteries took part in a practise barrage on their "Z" Day tasks. Owing to dense Ground fog it was impossible to determine effectiveness. Wire cutting proceeded all day and at night it was kept open by A/280 whose flashes are not visible like those of C/280 & 93rd.	
"	6.4.17.		"X" Day. Practise barrage at 8.30 a.m. with 18.pdr. Batteries. D/280 fired nearly all day on many Objectives. 18.pdr. Batteries on wire cutting.	
"	7.4.17.		This was named "Q" Day of the Bombardment. 93rd & C/280 having cut their allotted wire took on the cutting of a large stretch of wire which the Heavies had not been able to cut. D/280 assisted. A/280 completed its task and kept open at night wire of forward Batteries. At 8.5. p.m. 93rd covered a small Infantry attack on M.G. Emplacement in NEUVILLE MILL. This attack succeeded but the Mill eventually had to be evacuated.	
"	8.4.17.		"Y" Day of Bombardment. Wire cutting all day. A/280 working night and day, and now cutting wire allotted to 293rd Brigade originally. D/280 fired B.S.K. and B.C.B.R. shells on enemy gun positions all night.	
"	9.4.17.		"Z" Day. Zero hour on our front 7.45 a.m. (See Copies of Operation Orders issued). All Batteries firing practically all day. Our "BLUE" Objective was gained very quickly and our "BROWN" would appear to have been captured on Schedule time, but for the fact that the 30th	

2449 Wt. W14957/M90 750,000 1/16 J.B.C. & A. Forms/C.2118/12.

Army Form C. 2118.

Instructions regarding War Diaries and Intelligence Summaries are contained in F. S. Regs., Part II. and the Staff Manual respectively. Title Pages will be prepared in manuscript.

WAR DIARY or INTELLIGENCE SUMMARY

(Erase heading not required.)

280th (City of London) BRIGADE, R.F.A.

Place	Date	Hour	Summary of Events and Information — A P R I L, 1917.	Remarks and references to Appendices
BEAURAINS & MERCATEL	9.4.17.		(Continued) Division on our right were held up on their left by wire. The situation was one of great uncertainty and during the night our front was not definite. C/280 & 93rd put down a barrage well beyond points believed to be in our hands. Evidence was conclusive that the wire on our front was entirely demolished and that our Infantry met no obstacles.	
"	10.4.17.		At 5.30 a.m. C/280 & 93rd joined in an attack on a portion of 30th Div. Front which the 56th Division were compelled to take on. The whole front seemed held in patches by the enemy and C/280 carried out a small shoot at urgent request of Infantry on one of the points during the early afternoon.	
"	11.4.17.		At 5.30 a.m. a furthur effort was made to "clear up" some of the small pockets of the enemy.- C/280 and 93rd once again joining in. At 9.45 a.m. Fire from these Batteries was again opened with the same object. The enemy apparently was holding on with small parties tenaciously. The process of "mopping up" was slow, but yielded quite a lot of prisoners.	
MERCATEL & NEUVILLE VITASSE			A/280 & D/280 moved forward during the day as soon as ever it was definitely established that they were too far behind for effective shooting. 93rd & C/280 also moved forward from MERCATEL to a position East of NEUVILLE VITASSE and registered their guns, alongside C/280 & D/280	
"	12.4.17.		Brigade H.Q. moved forward to MERCATEL. All Batteries directed a little fire at a very long range well in front of our Infantry. Close shooting impossible owing to uncertainty of our Infantry posts. At night the Brigade was responsible for the front whilst other Brigades were advancing. Every moment permission to move our guns forward was expected.	
"	13.4.17.		Country East of ST.MARTIN-sur-COJEUL was reconnoitred and positions provisionally fixed for all Batteries. The Brigade did no shooting all day as no target presented itself.	
"	14.4.17.		At 5.30 a.m. another attack was launched, which only partially succeeded. Many small "pockets" of the enemy putting up strong resistance from small posts which were situated very skilfully. Our gun teams were standing by at the guns all day, expecting to advance to positions which were, early in the morning, still in enemy hands. The night was very quiet indeed and all obtained a well-needed rest.	

2449 Wt. W14957/M90 750,000 1/16 J.B.C. & A. Forms/C.2118/12.

Army Form C. 2118.

Instructions regarding War Diaries and Intelligence Summaries are contained in F. S. Regs., Part II. and the Staff Manual respectively. Title pages will be prepared in manuscript.

WAR DIARY
~~or~~
INTELLIGENCE SUMMARY.
(Erase heading not required.)

28Oth (City of London) BRIGADE, R.F.A.

Place	Date	Hour	Summary of Events and Information — A P R I L, 1917.	Remarks and references to Appendices
MERCATEL & NEUVILLE VITASSE.	15.4.17.		The whole situation very uncertain and our Batteries remained quiescent all day. C/280 and 93rd moved wagon lines to MERCATEL and BOIRY respectively. A/280 and D/280 moved wagon lines to AGNY.	
"	16.4.17.		A small amount of fire from D/280 and C/280 on a new enemy trench.	
NEUVILLE VITASSE & ST.MARTIN sur COJEUL	17.4.17.		All 18-pdr.Batteries reconnoitred for positions and got in before 1.0 p.m. The advance was but 1,000 yards owing to the indefinite situation ahead. Each Battery took forward at least 1000 rounds which was no mean undertaking owing to the bad roads. D/280 moved half the Battery. Headquarters remained at MERCATEL.	
"	18.4.17.		D/280 took forward remainder of Battery. All 18.pdr. Batteries carried out small Programme shoot in rear of enemy lines as an attack once again was expected on WANCOURT TOWER. a vantage point which commanded a large tract of country and for which the enemy had made many efforts since we originally took it.	
"	19.4.17.		Batteries still busy "digging in" and getting up their 3,000 rounds. Weather very bad. Some shooting at night on rear of enemy lines.	
"	20.4.17.		All Batteries spent about 500 rounds during the day and night in annoying enemy and interfering with his transport. Battery positions were shelled by hostile 8" shells and gas shells all night, but had ~~but~~ 8 casualties only.	
"	21.4.17.		A similar programme as previous day, in preparation for a furthur "Z" Day on the 23rd. Batteries again heavily shelled with 8" shells but with no casualties.	
"	22.4.17.		Heavy bombardment all day and night of enemy defences and some little wire that enemy had put up. D/280 fired 900 "Lethal" shells on and about Village of CHERISY.	
"	23.4.17		Another "Z" day, providing many exciting periods. Zero hour 4.45 a.m. when our Batteries commenced their "creeping" barrages. This effort was unsuccessful. At 5.20 p.m. orders given to repeat programme at 6.0 p.m. same as at 4.45 a.m. (with slight variations) This effort again partly failed as the enemy seemed to have planned to counter attack at about the same moment. His attack was directed on the front of the Division on our right and caused us a great deal of	

2353 Wt. W2544/1454 700,000 5/15 D. D. & L. A.D.S.S./Forms/C. 2118.

Instructions regarding War Diaries and Intelligence Summaries are contained in F. S. Regs., Part II. and the Staff Manual respectively. Title pages will be prepared in manuscript.

WAR DIARY
or
INTELLIGENCE SUMMARY.
(Erase heading not required.)

Army Form C. 2118.

280th (City of London) BRIGADE, R.F.A.

Place	Date	Hour	Summary of Events and Information APRIL, 1917.	Remarks and references to Appendices
NEUVILLE VITASSE & St. MARTIN sur COJEUL	23.4.17.		(Cont) anxiety for some hours. Continuous fire was maintained for nearly 24 hours. All were exhausted by the long strain.	
"	24.4.17.		An uneventful day. Enemy more or less quiescent A little sniping by 18-pdr. Batteries. Only.	
HENINEL & ST.MARTIN sur COJEUL.	25.4.17.		All Batteries moved forward again. Very few suitable positions obtainable that were not under direct vision of enemy. A/280 took over a position out of which a Battery of the 14th Division had been shelled but 24 hours previously and C/280 and 93rd went alongside. Bde. H.Q. moved to vicinity of ST. MARTIN. Weather dry but extremely cold.	
"	26.4.17.		Owing to exposed positions of 18-pdr. Batteries, no firing was done other than mere registration. D/280 who are in a good covered position spent some 300 rounds on Cross Roads in rear of enemy's lines during the day and night.	
"	27.4.17.		Howitzer Battery shelled roads in rear of CHERISY. Weather very unusual for April- hazy and yet very cold. N. Wind-visibility very poor	
"	28.4.17.		At 4.25 a.m. all Batteries joined in a feint attack which was designed to assist Corps on left who were attacking. A creeping barrage was put down on enemy front line, crept forward for some 16 minutes and then returned to front line for 2 minutes. This process was repeated 32 minutes later. Enemy put up, apparently in alarm, all types of coloured rockets but was very late indeed- about 20 minutes- with his own defensive barrage which was quite insignificant.	
"	29.4.17.		During last night D/280 expended about 450 Gas shells on a certain small wood that was believed to shelter guns and also a H.Q. of the enemy. The wind was very favourable and good results were counted on. Batteries remained quiescent all day. Weather at last fine and warm. Roads excellent for transport. Brigade Commander attended Conference at 14th D.A. H.Q.	
"	30.4.17.		In view of our taking over another part of the front- though not moving positions- and coming under orders of 14th D.A. in near future, Batteries were warned to increase dump at guns to 5,000 rounds per Battery. The Brigade temporarily came under the orders of 18th D.A. at an uncertain hour during the last 24 hours.	

L. A. C. [illegible]
Lt Col Comd 280th Bde RFA

2353 Wt. W2544/1454 700,000 5/15 D. D. & L. A.D.S.S./Forms/C. 2118.

Original

Vol 18

56th

War Diary

280th Bde R.F.A.

May 1917

Army Form C. 2118.

Instructions regarding War Diaries and Intelligence Summaries are contained in F. S. Regs., Part II. and the Staff Manual respectively. Title pages will be prepared in manuscript.

WAR DIARY
or
INTELLIGENCE SUMMARY.
(Erase heading not required.)

28th (City of London) BRIGADE, R.F.A.

Place	Date	Hour	Summary of Events and Information MAY, 1917.	Remarks and references to Appendices
MENINEL	1.5.17.		At 4.0 a.m. 18-pdrs. joined in a feint attack- a creeping barrage from front line of enemy and then return. Bombardment lasted 8 minutes. D/280 fired also for same period on targets in rear. 11.0 a.m. Bde. H.Q. moved up near MENINEL. Noon: Brigade came under Orders of 14th Div. Arty. At 12.50 p.m. D/280 joined in a Corps concentrated Howitzer bombardment of Village of VIS en ARTOIS for 10 minutes.	
"	2.5.17.		All Batteries fired in succession all day and night on our apportioned front.	
"	3.5.17.		Another grand attack opened at 3.45 a.m. Enemy put up a most vigorous barrage forthwith and in addition liberally sprinkled the countryside with gas and tear shell near H.Q. and Batteries. Our attack was in vain. Enemy counter-attacked at about 11.0 a.m. and threw back our Infantry to trench from which they started. Alarms all day. Twice ~~XXXXXX~~ again during the day Batteries were firing 2 rounds per gun per minute on counter attacks. In the evening another attack was resisted vigorously for about 30 minutes and all night Batteries maintained a slow rate of fire. A day of great effort which appeared to be fruitless in results obtained. The 18-pdr. Batteries were under heavy shell fire all day but were able to replenish ammunition supply to 800 rounds per gun without horse casualties. Personnel casualties 14 only.	
"	4.5.17.		Enemy very active. Our Batteries remained quiescent until the evening when bombardment of roads and crossings was opened and kept up all night.	
"	5.5.17.		A similar programme of fire as previous day was carried out. At 10.15 p.m. a S.O.S. alarm. Every Battery for miles on either flank opened out rapid rate of fire. Apparent from the start that the alarm was false. Batteries of the Brigade quickly cut down rate of fire and finally ceased at 11.15 p.m.	
"	6.5.17.		Remarkable change in temperature- a drop of 25 degrees- though with a rise in barometer. Batteries carried out usual harassing fire.	
"	7.5.17.		18-pdr. Batteries carried out small programme of fire and a little sniping during the day. D/280 alone dealt with night fire as the flashes from the 18-pdrs. are plainly visible by the enemy. Enemy splashed the whole countryside with 8" Instantaneous-fused shells pretty nearly all the day and added a few gas shells in the evening.	
"	8.5.17.		A day very similar to the 7th. Enemy not quite so offensive.	

2353 Wt. W2544/1454 700,000 5/15 D. D. & L. A.D.S.S./Forms/C. 2118.

Instructions regarding War Diaries and Intelligence Summaries are contained in F. S. Regs., Part II. and the Staff Manual respectively. Title pages will be prepared in manuscript.

~~WAR DIARY or~~ INTELLIGENCE SUMMARY. 28th (City of London) BRIGADE, R.F.A.

(Erase heading not required.)

Army Form C. 2118.

Place	Date	Hour	Summary of Events and Information — MAY, 1917.	Remarks and references to Appendices
HENINEL	9.5.17.		Enemy comparatively quiet. All Batteries of the Brigade carried out harrassing fire. Visibility exceptionally favounable for seeing tracks used by enemy.	
"	10.5.17.		Harrassing fire on both sides. 93rd. Battery withdrawn to Wagon Line ~~XXXXXXX~~ for one weeks' rest.	
"	11.5.17.		Comparatively quiet day. A, C, & D/280 carried out small programmes and did some little sniping. Three of the Brigade Wagon lines shelled by enemy and were evacuated. A few casualties to O.R. and horses sustained. Enemy in the night paid vigorous attention to all roads and tracks and approaches from Gun line to Wagon lines. Bde. H.Q. vicinity ~~was well~~ is now usually heavily shelled ~~XXX~~ all night.	
"	12.5.17.		Enemy less active. Batteries directed fire during night and early morning on enemy routes and tracks.	
"	13.5.17.		The same inactivity - and yet activity in the form of harassing fire on rearward tracks of the enemy. All batteries at various parts of the day took turns in annoying enemy.	
"	14.5.17		A similar day to above. Enemy more active and yet one sees indications possibly of a withdrawal of some of his guns to another sphere - his fire seeming to be directed with a view to showing how many guns he still has on this front.	
"	15.5.17.		Enemy much less active. We maintained our usual proportion of fire during the day, and at night increased fire at long range on his approaches as it was believed that he was withdrawing to another line of defence.	
"	16.5.17.		Hostile fire practically ceased all day. We increased our fire in rear of enemy's line and maintained slow and irregular fire all night.	
"	17.5.17		Slight evidence that enemy had got his guns again into position - though little of his fire was directed against our front. Gas shells were fired into a wood occupied by enemy during this night.	

2353 Wt. W2544/1454 700,000 5/15 D. D. & L. A.D.S.S./Forms/C. 2118.

Instructions regarding War Diaries and Intelligence Summaries are contained in F. S. Regs., Part II. and the Staff Manual respectively. Title Pages will be prepared in manuscript.

Army Form C. 2118.

WAR DIARY
or
INTELLIGENCE SUMMARY. 280th (City of London) BRIGADE R.F.A.

(Erase heading not required.)

Place	Date	Hour	Summary of Events and Information MAY, 1917.	Remarks and references to Appendices
MENINEL.	18.5.17.		93rd Battery after 8 days rest returned to position vacated on 10th and took over a portion of the Brigade front. Desultory fire on enemy front system was maintained all day and night.	
"	19.5.17.		A day very similar to every other day during the past 10 days. Enemy doing systematic counter battery work on positions within 100 yards of our battery positions and H.Q. Apparently our positions camouflaged so successfully that his aeroplanes had not found them.	
"	20.5.17.		5.15 a.m. Feint attack- creeping barrage and then a jump back on to enemy front line. During the day, harrassing of enemy. Bde. H.Q. heavily shelled twice.	
"	21.5.17.		Brigade Commander visited G.O.C.R.A., 18th Division. In afternoon severe shelling in neighbourhood of H.Q. 8.0 p.m. - Brigade transferred to 18th Div. Arty. Barrage lines and Brigade Zone moved slightly further south- no movement of Batteries however. Batteries maintained usual fire continuously in turn, all day on enemy front and rear system and approaches.	
"	22.5.17.		Very quiet day. We carried out usual harrassing fire, spending about 700 18-pdr., and 250. 4.5" How. rounds.	
"	23.5.17.		Steps taken by all Batteries to dig themselves in deeply, and also to construct permanent O.P's. Fire carried on as usual. Enemy comparatively quiet.	
"	24.5.17.		Activity of enemy very slight. We maintained usual fire every hour of the 24, but increased by 50% our fire from 10.0 p.m. to 3.0 a.m. as a relief of the enemy was suspected.	
"	25.5.17.		Enemy exceptionally vigorous with his 8" barrage across the valley in which are situated the Batteries of the Brigade. For some 6 hours Bde. H.Q. which is in the barrage line were somewhat in some suspense.	
"	26.5.17.		Orders received for A/280, C/280 and D/280 to withdraw for a rest to Wagon line, also Bde. H.Q. Never was a rest more needed or appreciated. Bde. H.Q. took up quarters in a field in MERCATEL and all guns and detachments were pulled out and in respective wagon lines by 11.0 p.m. 93rd. Battery came under orders of O.C., 281st Bde.	
"	27.5.17.		An easy training and Sports programme carried out by all units during the day.	

2449 Wt. W14957/M90 750,000 1/16 J.B.C. & A. Forms/C.2118/12.

Army Form C. 2118.

WAR DIARY

~~or~~ ~~INTELLIGENCE SUMMARY~~ 28th (City of London) BRIGADE, R.F.A.

(Erase heading not required.)

Instructions regarding War Diaries and Intelligence Summaries are contained in F. S. Regs., Part II. and the Staff Manual respectively. Title pages will be prepared in manuscript.

Place	Date	Hour	Summary of Events and Information — M A Y, 1917.	Remarks and references to Appendices
MERCATEL DISTRICT	28.5.17.		A period devoted to rest, recreation, and short phases of training in H.Q., A, C, and D/280 Batteries.	
"	29.5.17.		Enemy put over with long range guns, a few small calibre shells in vicinity of wagon lines, no casualties.	
"	30.5.17.			
"	31.5.17.			

[signature]

Lieut. & Adjutant,
for Lieut. Colonel,
Commanding, 280th Brigade, R. F. A.

2353 Wt. W2544/1454 700,000 5/15 D. D. & L. A.D.S.S./Forms/C. 2118.

Original

Vol 19

War Diary

June 1917

280th Bde R.F.A.

Army Form C. 2118.

Instructions regarding War Diaries and Intelligence Summaries are contained in F. S. Regs., Part II. and the Staff Manual respectively. Title Pages will be prepared in manuscript.

WAR DIARY

or

~~INTELLIGENCE SUMMARY~~ 280th (City of London) BRIGADE, R.F.A.

(Erase heading not required.)

Place	Date	Hour	Summary of Events and Information JUNE, 1 9 1 7.	Remarks and references to Appendices
MERCATEL & HENINEL.	1.6.17. to 5.6.17.		Brigade H.Q., A/280 ~~and~~ C/280 Batteries still at rest and otherwise fully occupied at SPORTS	
HENINEL.	6.6.17.		Brigade H.Q. and Batteries at rest returned to the line, H.Q. to a position near ST. MARTIN, and C/280 to a position slightly South of HENINEL. Batteries carried out necessary registration.	
"	7.6.17.		At Noon, Group consisting of 109th, 93rd., A., C., and D/280 Batteries, formally took over task of covering left Brigade of the 18th Division.	
"	8.6.17.		Usual daily harrassing fire with special "spurts" of fire at 10 p.m. and 2 a.m. Apparently no special object in these bursts of fire other than to mislead the enemy. O.C. Brigade visited C.R.A., 21st Div. Arty. with a view to the Brigade coming under the 21st Division shortly.	
"	9.6.17.		Usual harrassing fire. Enemy very quiet on a whole.	
"	10.6.17.		6. a.m. Brigade came under orders of 21st Division for special enfilade tasks on that portion of the HINDENBURG Line still held by enemy. Group consisting of 93rd, A., and D/280, all of which Batteries retained old positions. C/280 and 109th Batteries remained at old positions, but subject to orders of 18th C.R.A., through O.C. 280th Brigade. Group H.Q. remained in same position. The Battery B/123 of 37th Division was more or less in the Group.	
"	11.6.17.		Registration on new Zones proceeded. 93rd. Battery position heavily shelled by 5.9"'s. No casualties, but one gun knocked out.	
"	12.6.17.		Nothing of interest to place on record.	
"	13.6.17.		6 p.m. Group consisting of 93rd., A., and D/280 and B/123 Batteries definitely constituted. C/280 joined Group, Commanded by O.C., 124th Brigade of same 37th Divisional Arty, attached 21st Div	

2449 Wt. W14957/M90 750,000 1/16 J.B.C. & A. Forms/C.2118/12.

Army Form C. 2118.

Instructions regarding War Diaries and Intelligence Summaries are contained in F. S. Regs., Part II. and the Staff Manual respectively. Title Pages will be prepared in manuscript.

WAR DIARY or INTELLIGENCE SUMMARY

(Erase heading not required.)

280th (City of London) Brigade, R. F. A.

Place	Date	Hour	Summary of Events and Information — JUNE, 1917.	Remarks and references to Appendices
ST.MARTIN & HENINEL	14.	6.17.	~~XXXXX~~ Registration only	
"	15.	6.17.	At 2.50 a.m. Group joined in with all other Batteries of 21st Div. Arty. in feint attack in support of an attack on our immediate right by 58th Division (our own 2nd. Line) (Territorials)	
"	16.	6.17.	At 3.10 a.m. an attack on our front to finally clean up the HINDENBURG LINE S.W. of FONTAINE -les-CROISILLES still held by enemy. 18-pdr. Batteries fired almost true enfilade for about 10 minutes only, but D/280 was kept on a slow rate of fire for upwards of 14 hours. This attack was a failure- enemy having had previous warning of our attack apparently- and put down his protective barrage at least 3 hours before Zero.	
"	17.	6.17.	A quiet day. D/280 alone fired a few rounds on FONTAINE. B/123 was taken out of the Group. C/280 returned to the Group and occupied their position. Transfer of personnel and guns was effected by Midnight.	
"	18.	6.17.	For many hours it was a moot point whether the Brigade was under the orders of the 21st., 18th., or 50th Div. Arty. The matter was settled finally after about 8 hours, when, after having already received orders from both 18th. and 50th D.A., the Brigade found itself still part of the 21st D.A.	
"	19.	6.17.	No change. Little activity on either side.	
"	20.	6.17.	At 10. a.m. Brigade passed under control of 33rd Div. Arty. From 11 a.m. to Noon and from 7 to 8 p.m., bursts of fire by all Batteries on TUNNEL TRENCH. Just short of 2000 rounds "A", "AX", and "BX" being used up.	
"	21.	6.17	Similar programme as previous day.	

2449 Wt. W14957/M90 750,000 1/16 J.B.C. & A. Forms/C.2118/12.

Army Form C. 2118.

WAR DIARY
or
INTELLIGENCE SUMMARY

(Erase heading not required.)

Instructions regarding War Diaries and Intelligence Summaries are contained in F. S. Regs., Part II. and the Staff Manual respectively. Title Pages will be prepared in manuscript.

280th (City of London) BRIGADE, R.F.A.

JUNE, 1917.

Place	Date	Hour	Summary of Events and Information	Remarks and references to Appendices
ST. MARTIN & HENINEL	22.	6.17.	Same programme shoot as on 21.6.17.	
"	23.	6.17.	do	
"	24.	6.17.	At Midnight an attack on TUNNEL TRENCH. Fire maintained for nearly 2 hours. Attack failed. Usual programme of fire at 11.50 a.m. and 7.35 p.m. in preparation for another attempt to gain this objective.	
"	25.	6.17	At 11.50 a.m an attack was ordered once again on TUNNEL TRENCH, but at the last moment was cancelled. All Batteries marched out to Wagon Lines during the night, and the Brigade passed under control of the 56th D.A. Same programme of fire carried out during the day as for last 4 days	
MERCATEL	26.	6.17.	Bde. H.Q. removed to Wagon Lines at MERCATEL.	
"	27	6.17	Refitting and resting.	
HENDECOURT	28.	6.17.	Brigade marched to VIIth Corps Rest Camp for refitting and rest.	
"	29.	6.17.	Refitting and resting.	
"	30.	6.17.		

L. A. C. [illegible]

Lt Col Comd
280th Bde RFA

Instructions regarding War Diaries and Intelligence Summaries are contained in F. S. Regs., Part II. and the Staff Manual respectively. Title pages will be prepared in manuscript.

WAR DIARY
or
INTELLIGENCE SUMMARY. 280th (City of London) Brigade, R.F.A

(Erase heading not required.)

Army Form C. 2118.

Vol 23

Place	Date	Hour	Summary of Events and Information	Remarks and references to Appendices
BEAUMETZ	1.10.17.		500. BX. fired into enemy wire during the day. Usual fire directed XXXXXXX during night on tracks in rear of enemy, and on keeping open wire cut. C/280 moved two of its guns to a new position near Village of DOIGNIES.	
"	2.10.17.		Remaining guns of C/280 removed and old position handed over to a Battery of 36th Division.	
"	3.10.17.) 4.10.17.)		Concentrated fire by all Batteries on certain targets, and usual night fire.	
"	5.10.17.		Guns and detachments of A/280 (who were under orders of 281st Brigade, R.F.A.) moved from their positions and went under direct orders of A/281; A/280 Battery being practically split up as a Battery and its guns used to reinforce Battery.of A/281. This condition brought about owing to the many guns in the Divisional Artillery being at the Repair Workshops or at Wagon lines too worn out to be safe for fire.	
"	6.10.17.) 7.10.17.)		Very quiet period.	
"	8.10.17.		Enemy 5.9's directed (300. rds.) at A/280 position vacated but 3. days ago. Left section of C/280 partly in line of fire. Casualty to one gun only.	
" "	9.10.17) 21.10.17)		Nightly bombardments, A. AX, BX., and gas shell interspersed at irregular intervals and uncertain times, and in various quantities.	
"	22.10.17.		After preliminary wire cutting in divers places, to deceive the enemy, an attempt to raid enemy trenches in front of DEMICOURT by means of BANGALORE TORPEDO was made XXXXXXXXX in the small hours of the morning, but was frustrated by hostile machine gun.	
" "	23.10.17 26.10.17		Usual nightly programmes continued; occasional day shoots by 4.5" How. with aeroplane co-operation.	

2353 Wt. W2544/1454 700,000 5/15 D. D. & L. A.D.S.S./Forms/C. 2118.

Army Form C. 2118.

WAR DIARY

or

~~INTELLIGENCE~~ SUMMARY.

(Erase heading not required.)

280th (City of London) Brigade, R. F. A.

Instructions regarding War Diaries and Intelligence Summaries are contained in F. S. Regs., Part II. and the Staff Manual respectively. Title pages will be prepared in manuscript.

Place	Date	Hour	Summary of Events and Information	Remarks and references to Appendices
BEAUMETZ.	27.10.17.		Enemy ~~hostile~~ Batteries exceptionally active against DOIGNIES; one 18-pdr. put out of action slight damage to a few dug-outs. Lt-Col. E.A.C. Southam, D.S.O. having proceeded to Div. Arty to the place of the G.O.C.R.A. while on leave. Lt-Col. W.E. Batt assumed command.	
"	28.10.17.		Quiet day. Orders received to find further gun positions in order to accommodate two more 18-pdr. and one more 4.5" How. Batteries.	
"	29.10.17.		Hostile Batteries again active; no damage done.	
"	30.10.17.		Sites for new pits selected and work started.	
"	31.10.17.		Enemy artillery again active, otherwise a quiet day.	

W.E. Batt

Lieut.Colonel,
Commanding, 280th Brigade, R. F. A.

2353 Wt. W2544/1454 700,000 5/15 D. D. & L. A.D.S.S./Forms/C. 2118.

56 D T

Nov. 1917

War Diary.

Original.

280th Brigade R.F.A.

Vol 24

Secret.

To 56th Divnl. Arty.

Herewith War Dairy for month of November 1917.

280TH
(CITY OF LONDON),
BRIGADE,
R.F.A.
No. C/667.
Date 30.11.17.

H Leslie Dobb
Lieut.
for Lieut. Colonel,
Commanding 280th Brigade, R.F.A.

Instructions regarding War Diaries and Intelligence Summaries are contained in F. S. Regs., Part II. and the Staff Manual respectively. Title pages will be prepared in manuscript.

WAR DIARY
or
INTELLIGENCE SUMMARY.
(Erase heading not required.)

280th (City of London) Brigade, R.F.A.

Army Form C. 2118.

Place	Date	Hour	Summary of Events and Information — N O V E M B E R 1917.	Remarks and references to Appendices
DEMICOURT	1.11.17. to 8.11.17.		Usual night firing programmes and harrassing fire by day. Work begun on new Battery positions in DEMICOURT and HERMIES.	
	9.11.17.		Ammunition for new positions to the extent of 600. rounds per gun coming by rail to HERMIES and thence by pack to new positions.	
	10.11.17.) 12.11.17.)		Working day and night on new positions. Ammunition carrying continued.	
	13.11.17.		Brigade wagon lines moved from HAPLINCOURT; A/280 and 93rd Batteries to BANCOURT, C/280 to D.A.C. H.Q., between BANCOURT and BAPAUME; D/280 to FREMICOURT (168th Inf. Bde. Lines); H.Q. to Div. H.Q. lines FREMICOURT. Orders received during the day to turn out every wagon to take up ammunition to METZ. This brought about the curious situation of a Brigade having to move in one direction and carry ammunition in another at the same time. The difficulty was only overcome by moving kits, etc., by motor lorry.	
	14.11.17. to 18.11.17.		Work on DEMICOURT and HERMIES positions continued. On 15th, 281st Brigade started work on positions just to E. of BOURSIES to which this Brigade, subject to the success of operations could move. On night of 18th, one section of each Battery moved into their respective positions; C/280 and D/280 to DEMICOURT, 93rd and A/280 to HERMIES.	
	19.11.17.		Lt-Col. W.E. BATT proceeded to HERMIES to command a Group consisting of 173rd Brigade, RFA together with 93rd and A/280 Batteries. Major E.R.C. WARRENS to DEMICOURT in command of a SUB-GROUP consisting of C/280 and D/280 Batteries for counter-Battery work.	
	20.11.17.		Batteries barraged from ZERO (6.20 a.m.) as per programme, up HINDENBURG LINE from HAVRINCOURT to CAMBRAI Road. Operations proceeded up to time and the barrage in spite of no registration whatever, was pronounced excellent. On the night 20/21st, the 3. 18-pdr. Batteries pulled out and occupied further positions in BOURSIES, the 4.5" How. Battery remaining in DEMICOURT, the whole of the four Batteries coming again under single command of Lt-Col. W.E. BATT.	
	21.11.17.		At 11.0 a.m. Batteries were called on to support an attack on BOURLON WOOD at extreme range. In the afternoon, Wagon lines moved up; 93rd, A and C/280 to LEBUCQUIERE, D/280 and H.Q. to BEAUMETZ.	

2353 Wt. W2544/1454 700,000 5/15 D. D. & L. A.D.S.S./Forms/C. 2118.

Instructions regarding War Diaries and Intelligence Summaries are contained in F. S. Regs., Part II. and the Staff Manual respectively. Title pages will be prepared in manuscript.

WAR DIARY
or
INTELLIGENCE SUMMARY.

(*Erase heading not required.*)

Army Form C. 2118.

280th (City of London) Brigade, R.F.A

Place	Date	Hour	Summary of Events and Information — N O V E M BE R, 1917.	Remarks and references to Appendices
DEMICOURT etc.	22.11.17.		At 7 a.m. Batteries opened on S.O.S. lines in response to call of LIASON OFFICER with 109th Inf. Bde. Operations commenced at 10.30 a.m. with bombardment of enemy trenches between MOEUVRES-DEMICOURT and INCHY-LOUVERVAL road, followed by creeping BARRAGE at 11.30 a.m. Operations were unsuccessful, due to enemy counter-attack in the evening.	
	23.11.17.		Durther unsuccessful attempts to gain above mentioned line.	
	24.11.17.		A day of attack and counter attack, our positions held with the exception of a short piece of trench in the neigbbourhood of INCHY.	
	25.11.17.		Further attack at Mid-day to retake those elements of trenches lost in German counter- attack of 24th. This attack was successful and the enemy immediately countered; Batteries were called to fire on their S.O.S lines until late in the evening by which time the attack was beaten off.	
	26.11.17.		Temporary return of H.Q. to BEAUMETZ because it became necessary to demolish the DEMICOURT H.Q. in order to widen the road for double traffic.	
	27.11.17.		Feint attack on trenches in HINDENBURG FRONT LINE west of INCHY at 6-20 a.m, batteries barraged for 15 minutes only. 3-20 p.m. - Enemy attack on TADPOLE COPSE area in front of INCHY beaten off.	
	28.11.17		Harassing fire during the night.	
	29.11.17		Nothing of importance to report, harassing fire throughout the night. Lt. Col. L.A.C. SOUTHAM, D.S.O. resumed command of the Brigade, having returned from leave.	
	30.11.17.		Enemy counter-attack on large scale against ground won by us. Our barrage was maintained from 9.30 a.m. to dark. A large number of fleeting opportunity targets were engaged, by us, including Batteries on the move.	

L. A. C. Southam Lt Col.
Comm'g 280th Bde RFA

2353 Wt. W2544/1454 700,000 5/15 D. D. & L. A.D.S.S./Forms/C. 2118.

Original

180th Bde RFA

War Diary

December 1917

280 Bde RFA
Vol 25

Instructions regarding War Diaries and Intelligence Summaries are contained in F. S. Regs., Part II. and the Staff Manual respectively. Title pages will be prepared in manuscript.

Army Form C. 2118.

WAR DIARY
or
INTELLIGENCE SUMMARY. 280th (CITY OF LONDON) BRIGADE, R.F.A.

(Erase heading not required.)

Place	Date	Hour	Summary of Events and Information DECEMBER 1917.	Remarks and references to Appendices
BOURSIES.	1st.		Massed enemy attack on our new line, batteries fired all day and the enemy was successfully checked on Divisional Front.	
	2nd.		Quiet morning, batteries fired on S.O.S. Lines in response to Infantry call. 51st. Divisional Artillery takes over from 56th.	
	3rd.		295th. Brigade, R.F.A. comes under the command of Lieut. Colonel. L.A.C. SOUTHAM, D.S.O commanding Right Group with two 18pdrs. in rear of and to South of DOIGNIES and the 4.5" How. battery in D/280's DEMICOURT POSITION.	
	4th.		Orders received to move batteries to rear positions, A/280 in old position to WEST of DOIGNIES, C/280 in old position to EAST of DOIGNIES, 93rd. Battery to position near DOIGNIES - DEMICOURT ROAD to EAST again of C/280. The howitzer battery D/295 also moved from DEMICOURT to DOIGNIES. This was done in conjunction with the withdrawal from the CAMBRAI battle front. 173rd. Brigade also came under Right Group as a further sub-group with positions in HERMIES.	
	5th.		Enemy made determined attacks on our abandoned lines, keeping up a heavy bombardment on the trenches from 10-0 a.m. to 12 Noon when white lights were seen in his trenches; shortly after this his troops were seen in his old front line and his barrage lifted forward. While his barrage was down the GROUP kept up fire on the old S.O.S. lines to delude the enemy. On his being seen in the abandoned trench the GROUP fire was diverted to harrassing and super fire. An intense bombardment of this trench was carried out by 4.5" Hows. and HEAVY ARTILLERY GROUPS from 3-30 to 3-45 p.m.	
	5th		Quiet day sniping at movement. Harrassing fire by night, 3 Officers, 45 Trench Mortar men, 1 Officer 20 O.R's R.E. attached to the Group for assistance. These units were offered voluntary, a fact at once new and exceptionally welcome in the experience of the Brigade.	
	7th.		Usual sniping by day and harrassing fire throughout the night. 173rd. Brigade, R.F.A. left to strengthen the MORCHIES GROUP.. two single guns put into forward positions to engage TANKS as it was rumoured that the enemy intended to attempt an attack with tanks.	
	8th 9th. 10th		Sniping by day, harrassing fire by night.	

2353 Wt. W2544/1454 700,000 5/15 D. D. & L. A.D.S.S./Forms/C. 2118.

Instructions regarding War Diaries and Intelligence Summaries are contained in F. S. Regs., Part II. and the Staff Manual respectively. Title pages will be prepared in manuscript.

Army Form C. 2118.

WAR DIARY
or
INTELLIGENCE SUMMARY. 280th (CITY OF LONDON) BRIGADE, R.F.A.

(Erase heading not required.)

Place	Date	Hour	Summary of Events and Information DECEMBER 1917.	Remarks and references to Appendices
	11th.		D/280 Battery in process of relief by D/310. This was carried out by D/280 taking over the Guns of D/173 who in its turn toof over the Guns of D/310.. The Command of the Group passed at 4-0 p.m. to O.C. 255th Brigade who completed his relief of 295th Brigade during the morning.	
	13th.		At 6-0 a.m. an intense bombardment of the enemy system between MOEUVRES and TADPOLE COPSE (INCHY EN ARTOIS) was carried out as a counter irritant for a suspected attack on BULLECOURT.	
	12th & 13th.		Group and 18pdr. Batteries relieved by 5th A.F.A. the relief being of personnel only, this Brigade taking over the Guns of 5th Brigade stripped. Small stores were in part made up by taking over those indented for by 5th Brigade who had taken over Guns from YPRES much the worse for wear and sadly deficient in small stores and spare parts. On completion of relief Brigade withdrew to its Wagon Lines in the BAPAUME - BANCOURT areas, Brigade Headquarters remaining at OFFICERS REST HOUSE, BAPAUME for night 13th/14th.	
	14th.		Brigade moved to COURCELLES LE COMTE assisted by 5 lorries lent by the courtesy of O.C. 5th. Brigade, A.F.A.	
	15th.		March continued to HABARCQ; here on night 15th/16th orders were received to change guns and procure small stores etc. from 281st Brigade R.F.A. at MONTENES COURT as this Brigade was not for the moment going into the line. This procedure was carried out and aptly described as "refitting at the trot."	
	16th.		Brigade marched to its wagon lines 1 Kilo N.E. of ST. NICOLAS on the ARRAS - BAILLEUL road.	
	17th.		3 Guns, A/280, 3 Hows D/280 and 1 section each of 93rd & C (personnel only) move into new positions on GAVRELLE FRONT, 93rd Battery & C/280 taking over positions of B/170 and C/170 who were moving to cover CENTRE Brigade.	
	18th.		Remainder of Brigade move into new positions also 1 more gun A/280,	
	19th.	9-0 a.m.	2 Sectors of the Divisional Front taken over, thus reinforcing the Divisional Artillery by one Brigade. Night firing on enemy communications, one more How. in position for D/280.	
	20th.		Nothing to report.	
	21st/24th.		" " "	
	25th.		All quiet on front.	
	26th/30th.		Normal.	

2353 Wt. W2544/1454 700,000 5/15 D. D. & L. A.D.S.S./Forms/C. 2118.

Army Form C. 2118.

Instructions regarding War Diaries and Intelligence Summaries are contained in F. S. Regs., Part II. and the Staff Manual respectively. Title pages will be prepared in manuscript.

WAR DIARY
or
INTELLIGENCE SUMMARY.

280th (CITY OF LONDON) BRIGADE, R.F.A.

(Erase heading not required.)

Place	Date	Hour	Summary of Events and Information DECEMBER 1917.	Remarks and references to Appendices
	31st.		11-0 p.m. Enemy ~~symbolized~~ signalized the approach of New Year by harassing fire on Front System. Midnight. Batteries reciprocated.	

Major.
for Lieut. Colonel,
Commanding 280th Brigade, R.F.A.

2353 Wt. W2544/1454 700,000 5/15 D. D. & L. A.D.S.S./Forms/C. 2118.

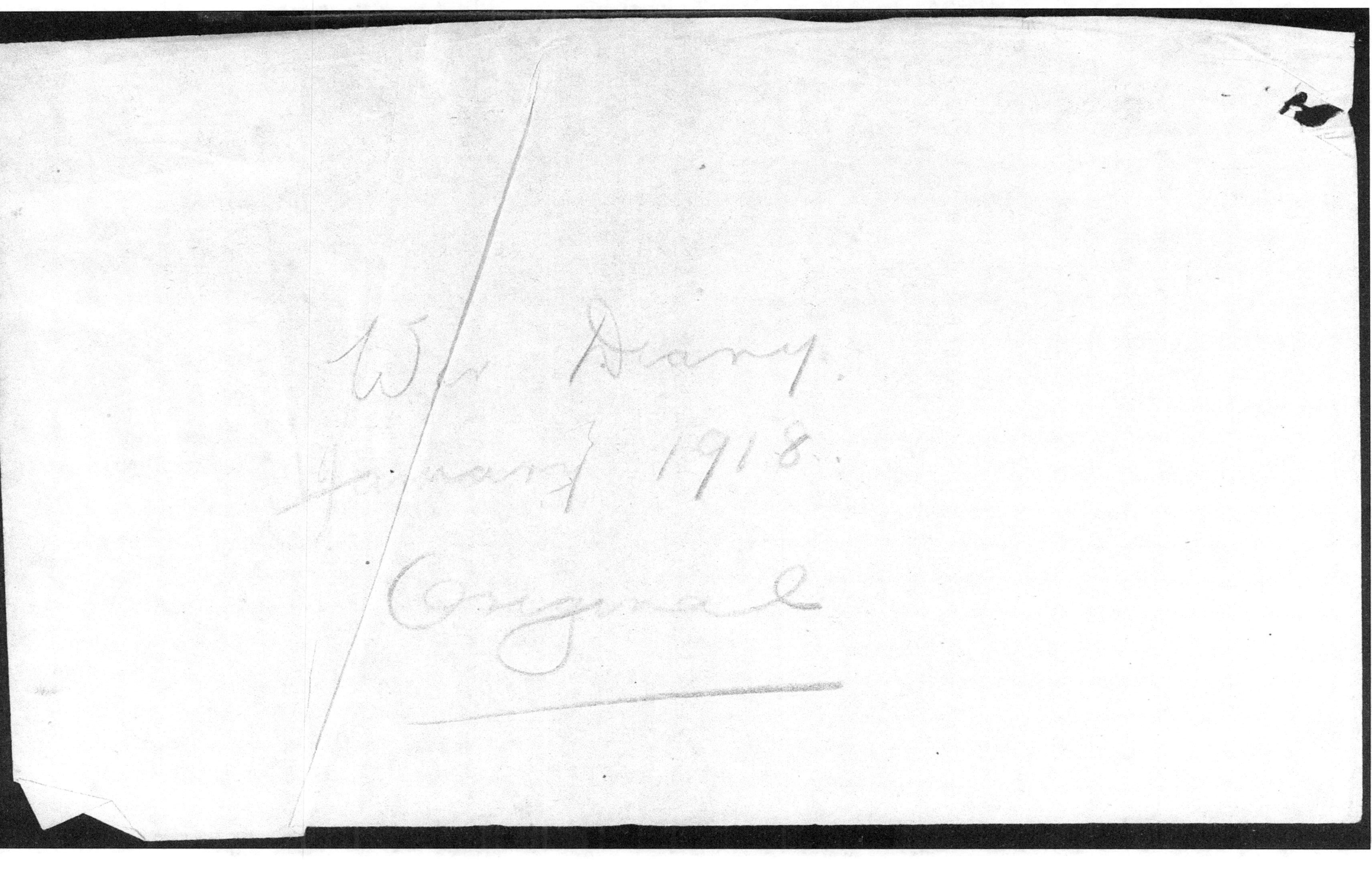
War Diary.
January 1918.
Original

Army Form C. 2118.

Instructions regarding War Diaries and Intelligence Summaries are contained in F. S. Regs., Part II. and the Staff Manual respectively. Title pages will be prepared in manuscript.

WAR DIARY
or
INTELLIGENCE SUMMARY. 280th (CITY OF LONDON) BRIGADE, R.F.A.

(*Erase heading not required.*)

Place	Date	Hour	Summary of Events and Information JANUARY 1918.	Remarks and references to Appendices
	1st. & 2nd.		Normal days.	
	3rd.		Demonstration barrage for the benefit of U.S. General Officer visiting the division.	
	4th - 8th.		Quiet days. Occasional retaliatory shoots on offensive Trench Mortars, bad weather preventing any active operations on either side.	
	9th.		62nd. Div. Arty. took over command from 56th Div. Arty.	
	10th 11 th & 12th.		Reconnaissance of rear defence positions & O.P's in view of forthcoming relief by personnel of 62nd Div. Arty. and the possible subsequent necessity to reinforce the line.	
	13th.		Officers of 310th Brigade at Headquarters preparatory to taking over the Group on 15th.	
	14th.		Relief of 1 section per Battery by Batteries of 310th Brigade.	
	15th.		Remaining 2 sections relieved on night 15th/16th. Brigade Headquarters at noon 15th. re-established for 24 hours at Officers Club, ARRAS.	
	16th.		Brigade, ~~less Headquarters~~, march into rest area, 93rd Battery to BERLES (MONCHEL), A/280 to FREVIN-CAPELLE, C/280 to CAPELLE FERMONT, D/280 to VANDELICOURT, marching empty ammunition being exchanged with the relieving Brigade. Brigade H.Q. established at BERTHENCOURT.	
	17th - 20th.		Cleaning up, Billetting and General refitting.	
	21st.		Inspection by G.O.C. Division & C.R.A. Great satisfaction expressed at the excellent results in spite of extremely adverse weather conditions.	
	22nd - 31st.		Intensive Training.	

[signature]
Lieut.Colonel,
Commanding 280th Brigade, R.F.A.

2353 Wt. W2544/1454 700,000 5/15 D. D. & L. A.D.S.S./Forms/C. 2118.

Original

Vol 27

250 Bde.

War Diary

February 1918

Instructions regarding War Diaries and Intelligence Summaries are contained in F. S. Regs., Part II. and the Staff Manual respectively. Title pages will be prepared in manuscript.

WAR DIARY
or
INTELLIGENCE SUMMARY.
(Erase heading not required.)

Army Form C. 2118.

28th (City of London) Brigade, RFA

Place	Date	Hour	Summary of Events and Information — FEBRUARY, 1918	Remarks and references to Appendices
BETHENCOURT etc.	1.2.18 -14.2.18		Brigade continued its rest and training.	
	15.2.18.		Personnel of one section per Battery relieved corresponding units of 310th Brigade, RFA in the GAVRELLE-OPPY sector.	
	16.2.18		Remaining sections and Bde. HQrs completed the relief, forming the Right Group, consisting of Batteries of 28th Brigade, RFA, 109th Bty. and 1. section of D/281 of 281st Bde. RFA.	
	17.2.18. 18.2.18. 19.2.18.		Much work put in in reserve positions, selecting and digging Anti-tank gun sites.	
	19.2.18.		Enemy raid in front of ARLEUX. Slow protective barrage by Northern Batteries of Group.	
	20.2.18. - 28.2.18.		Usual day sniping; night firing carried out by advanced sections and by Roving 18-pdr. gun.	
	38.2.18.		Smoke and T.S. barrage on trenches south of GAVRELLE, supporting raid by 2nd Guards Brigade.	

W. [signature]
Lieut. Colonel,
Commanding, 28th Brigade, R. F. A.

2353 Wt. W2544/1454 700,000 5/15 D. D. & L. A.D.S.S./Forms/C. 2118.

56th Div.

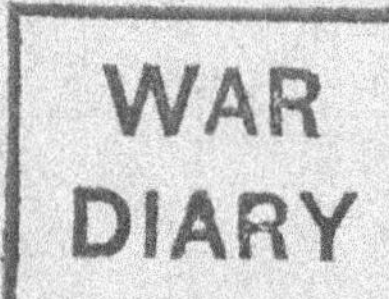

Headquarters,

280th BRIGADE, R.F.A.

M A R C H

1 9 1 8

Attached:-

Report on Operations
28th March, 1918.

280 Bde R.F.A.
(56 D)

Vol 28

Original

War Diary
for
March 1918

Army Form C. 2118.

Instructions regarding War Diaries and Intelligence Summaries are contained in F. S. Regs., Part II. and the Staff Manual respectively. Title pages will be prepared in manuscript.

WAR DIARY or INTELLIGENCE SUMMARY. 280th (CITY OF LONDON) BRIGADE, R.F.A.

(Erase heading not required.)

Place	Date	Hour	Summary of Events and Information MARCH 1918.	Remarks and references to Appendices
GAVRELLE.	1st - 5th.		Harassing fire by day and night. Aeroplane registration etc. Building Reserve positions, improving existing ones, and the usual avalanche of courses and fatigues all combined to make work in plenty for all ranks.	
	6th.		An early morning raid by GUARDS DIVISION South of GAVRELLE in which batteries of this Group assisted, proved successful.	
	7th.		Quiet day, it appears worthy of comment that each battery now manns 2 Lewis Guns (taken on the establishment) and that three batteries of the brigade have 7 guns, each one having an Anti-Tank gun in position. Needless to say the extra materiél does not carry with it extra personnel.	
	8th.		Nothing unusual.	
	9th.	6-45am.	A Dummy Bombardment by batteries of the Group South of OPPY with smoke to support a raid North of OPPY which proved successful. 4 prisoners.	
	10th.	5-0am.	Supported raid by 3rd GUARDS BRIGADE well South of GAVRELLE by means of dummy barrage.	
	11th.		Harassing fire by day and night on tracks and roads to interfere with suspected enemy relief.	
	12th.		Standing to at dawn in anticipation of enemy attack on the ARRAS Sector. Forward sections of 109th Battery, D/280 & D/281 brought back to main positions.	
	13th - 15th.		Increased harassing fire at nights wire cutting by day with 4.5" Hows. 2 Hows. put forward into position behind GAVRELLE to cut wire.	
	16th.	10pm.	Raid by 169th Infantry Brigade on enemy trenches in front of GAVRELLE. Supported by the Divisional Artillery and the Guards Divisional Artillery. The enemy trenches were very heavily manned ~~but~~ the Raiding Party succeeded in killing a few enemy but returned without any prisoners.	
	17th - 19th.		Normal days. Harassing fire at night. Good visibility made Sniping very possible.	
	20th.		Night of 20th/21st. D/280 send forward 2 more Hows. to their position forward of the Ridge and behind GAVRELLE. Extensive Hostile Artillery activity along the front in conjunction with the beginning of his offensive operations on the Western Front. Much Retaliation given, Batteries were continually in action from 5-0 a.m. to 9-0 a.m.	
	21st.		Quiet day, harassing fire by 18 pdrs. Gas shoot by 4.5" Hows.	

Instructions regarding War Diaries and Intelligence Summaries are contained in F. S. Regs., Part II. and the Staff Manual respectively. Title Pages will be prepared in manuscript.

or

INTELLIGENCE SUMMARY 280th (CITY OF LONDON) BRIGADE, R.F.A.

(Erase heading not required.)

Place	Date	Hour	Summary of Events and Information MARCH 1918.	Remarks and references to Appendices
	22nd.		Night of 22nd/23rd. 2 Hows. again moved from the forward position to the main position behind the Ridge as the Tactical Situation and the action of the enemy South of the Divisional front led to the supposition that an attack was imminent on the front.	
	23rd.		No enemy action developed but considerable hostile shelling of our front system and the consistent enemy advance in the MONCHEY sector together with the Tactical withdrawal of the XVII Corps on our Right still made it a very probable factor. In addition to this, afternoon reports showed his front system and his FRESNES ROUVROY Line packed with troops. This movement was engaged throughout the afternoon by batteries of this Brigade.. The detached Xn of A/286 was withdrawn to its main position as it was in view of MONCHEY LE PREUX, and, to meet any eventuality that might arise, 93rd Bettery reconnioitred a position S.W. of BAILLEUL.	
	24th.		Many Camouflaged emplacements presumed to be gun positions seen on the front, this gave further colour to the idea of an enemy attack. Furthermore connected shell holes behind the enemy front system at OPPY and GAVRELLE suggested the possibility of the enemy's intention to attack with Gas Projectors. These holes were registered by 18 pdr. batteries and a barrage arranged to deal with this situation should it arise.	
	25th.		Considerable sniping opportunities taken, usual night firingon tracks etc.	
	26th.		Early morning barrage on enemy front line as hostile attack was expected to develop. Much sniping during the day, harassing fire at night. Wagon Lines moved from their forward position East of ROCLINCOURT to new positions on ARRAS - SOUCHEZ Road N.E. of ECURIE.	
	27th.		Very quiet day. Special harassing fire at night. 169th Infantry Brigade extended their line further North, Group S.O.S. Lines amended accordingly.	
	28th.	3-0am	Enemy opened intense barrage on the Front at the same time putting a terrific barrage on the Battery Positions. No attack developed until 7-20 a.m. Fighting ensued without cessation until 2-0 p.m. when the Germans had forced their way through our 1st. defensive system. A local attack on the BAILLEUL - WILLERVAL LINE failed during the afternoon. 109th Battery rejoined the Group at Noon as the 281st Brigade had been reinforced by A/52. During the night all batteries but D/280 were withdrawn to positions selected to cover the BAILLEUL - WILLERVAL line. 109th Battery left the Group and B/281 took their place. Ammunition supply was arranged by Wagon & Pack from the old or forward Wagon Line in front of ROCLINCOURT. The widening of the front made the line extremely thinly held but the Moral was excellent and the enemy, it is certain, came far short of his intentions in spite of immensely favourable numbers in men and guns.	

2449 Wt. W14957/M90 750,000 1/16 J.B.C. & A. Forms/C.2118/12.

Instructions regarding War Diaries and Intelligence Summaries are contained in F. S. Regs., Part II. and the Staff Manual respectively. Title pages will be prepared in manuscript.

Army Form C. 2118.

WAR DIARY or INTELLIGENCE SUMMARY. 280th (CITY OF LONDON) BRIGADE, R.F.A.

(Erase heading not required.)

Place	Date	Hour	Summary of Events and Information MARCH 1918.	Remarks and references to Appendices
	29th		No further developments, many sniping targets, hostile batteries in the open etc. presented themselves and were made use of by batteries. 4th Canadian D.A. arrived to take over the Divisional Artillery who were to move out of action on the morning of the 30th with the G.O.C. Division. The Brigade Commander of the 3rd Canadian Field Artillery Brigade arrived at Group H.Q.	
	30th.	1 pm	Command of the Group passed to Lieut.Colonel MACDONALD, D.S.O. the 28th Group Commanded by Lieut.Colonel W.E. BATT, C.M.G. becoming a Sub-Group. Harassing fire carried out all night.	
	31st.		Quiet day, enemy artillery activity considerable. During the day the Brigade again became a separate GROUP. LT COL WE BATT CMG proceeded on leave to ENGLAND. MAJOR D D THOMSON MC took over command of the BDE	

[signature]
for Lieut.Colonel,
Commanding 280th Brigade, R.F.A.

2353 Wt. W2544/1454 700,000 5/15 D. D. & L. A.D.S.S./Forms/C. 2118.

56th Div. Arty.

RIGHT GROUP REPORT
OF THE OPERATIONS OF THE 28th MARCH 1918

The report of Liaison Officer with Right Battalion, sent herewith, gives the series of dispositions of that Battalion. This Officer, Lieut. G.S. JONES was in telephonic communication the whole of the day and sent back intelligence of the greatest importance. Unfortunately the communications to three O.P's, TANK, HOCKEY and TENNIS were cut at an early hour. Lieut. C.J. EDWARDS, A/280 at TANK endeavoured to repair the wire and get in touch but was finally compelled to withdraw after losing one of his Signallers. Similarly, attempts to repair the wires to HOCKEY and TENNIS were unavailing. Finally, about 10 am observation was established at two places on the ridge by runners and wire. By these means, many targets were dealt with, particularly the following:-

At Noon the 4.5" Hows. did great execution against masses of the enemy at the junction of the BAILLEUL-GAVRELLE Road with MARINE Trench.

At about 2.0 pm., the 4.5" Hows. silenced a enemy 7.7cm. Battery in C.19.a.central.

The 18-pdrs. dealt with masses of the enemy in the wire in GAVRELLE and later in the sunken BAILLEUL-GAVRELLE Road. The Batteries were heavily shelled all day but fortunately the casualties to personnel were light, while 3 guns of A/280 were destroyed by shell fire and two at ARLEUX, abandoned to the enemy. Lieut. G.J. HALFREY fought this section until ordered to withdraw when he blew up the guns by putting a round both in muzzle and breech. He burnt his dug-outs and only withdrew with dial sights and breech blocks as the 18-pdr. barrage of the Division on our left came down on top of them.

After the Infantry withdrew to the RED LINE a heavy attack developed on BAILLEUL EAST post, about 3.30 pm. which was repulsed.

The situation then became quiet except for shelling of the RED LINE and communications. This Artillery retaliated when asked and harassed the enemy all night.

The day's expenditure of the three 18-pdr. Batteries of 280th Brigade, R.F.A. was, approximately, 11,000 and of the 4.5" How. Battery 3,000 rounds.

Lieut.Colonel,

29.3.18. Commanding, 280th Brigade, R.F.A.

INTELLIGENCE REPORT
OF LIAISON OFFICER
RIGHT BATTALION.

3-18.

5 a.m. Situation report from all Coys. "All quiet".

0 " Hostile barrage came down upon RED LINE and NAVAL Trench, consisting chiefly of gas shell of all calibres intermixed with a few heavy shell. Situation in front line at TOWEY and WATER POSTS remained quite quiet.

) " Hostile barrage increased greatly in intensity and included the front line posts and the whole length of TOWEY ALLEY. Heavy T.M.s supplied the chief weight of the bombardment on the posts in the front line, i.e. TOWEY and WATER.

" Hostile barrage lifted off to TOWEY C.T. between NAVAL Trench and RED LINE, including KEILLER POST in which RT. BATTN.H.Q. were established, and concentrated upon TOWEY POST, WATER POST, NAVAL and MARINE Trenches and RED LINE. From this line until 7.0 a.m. these barrage lines remained intense.

" Barrage lifted from front line posts to NAVAL and MARINE Trenches and the S.O.S. Signals went up all along Divisional front. Enemy Infantry attacked in great strength.

" Information was received that TOWEY POST was still holding out.

" Garrison of GAVRELLE POST reported back in NAVAL Trench; that TOWEY POST had fallen. This report was quickly followed by another, brought in by Runner, that WATER POST had also been captured and our S.O.S. barrage was brought down to a line running North and South through WATER POST and the enemy appeared to be forming in front of NAVAL Trench.

"
ox) Observers reported that the enemy had broken through to the North through GAVRELLE VILLAGE and to the South through the Brigade on our right and appeared to be outflanking us. At this time, Capt. ~~XXXXXX~~ LOUNDES, who had been in command of TOWEY POST, reached the NAVAL LINE with 40 of his garrison, having bombed his way down TOWEY ALLEY after he had been surrounded.

" Intelligence Officer at Battn. on our left came into Battn. H.Q. and reported that the remainder of his own Battn. had been driven out of MARINE Trench but had established a block at the junction of MARINE Trench and THAMES ALLEY where they were holding on. The situation on the right appeared to be becoming serious also, and the enemy was seen bringing up his Field guns over the open. NAVAL LINE meanwhile was easily holding its own.

" An enemy 77m.m. Battery opened fire on TOWEY ALLEY seemingly at point blank range. It was impossible to locate its position accurately but it appeared to be situated in the old No-man's-land at about C.25.a.8.5.

0 a.m. A report came in that the blocks at both ends of the NAVAL LINE and that the enemy had commenced to bomb up the trench from each end and also down TOWEY ALLEY towards the junction of that C.T. with the NAVAL Trench. It was then decided to withdraw Battn. H.Q. to the RED LINE. Before any move could be made it was reported that the NAVAL LINE had been forced to give way and by the time the garrison of KEILLER POST and the Battn. H.Q. Staff had been got out into TOWEY C.T., the remainder of XXXX the NAVAL LINE garrison XXXXXXXX arrived with the information that the enemy were only 50 yards up the trench bombing his way down. The enemy could now be seen in open order rapidly advancing down each side of the C.T. over the open. Both parapets of the C.T. were immediately manned and the Battn. withdrew slowly down TOWEY ALLEY towards the RED LINE, holding the enemy well in hand the whole time. The RED LINE was reached about 11.0 a.m. with the loss of very few men. Unfortunately during this withdrawal, communication with the rear was impossible.

A bombing block was established 300 yards East of the RED LINE up TOWEY ALLEY and the enemy was entirely checked. Information was soon brought in that blocks had been made in the other main C.Ts along the front and the enemy was completely held in check all along the RED LINE.

0 a.m. Communication was again established through DITCH POST.

From this time onwards throughout the remainder of visibility, much movement of parties of from 20 to 50 men could be seen, chiefly along the main BAILLEUL-GAVRELLE Road, the main ARRAS-GAVRELLE Road and along the NAVAL-MARINE LINE, chiefly at the junctions with TYNE ALLEY, THAMES ALLEY and TOWER ALLEY. These parties were engaged by our guns with great success.

An attempt to force an entry of the RED LINE by way of NORTH TYNE ALLEY was smashed by Artillery fire.

56th Divisional Artillery.

280th (City of London) BRIGADE R.F.A.

APRIL 1918.

Instructions regarding War Diaries and Intelligence Summaries are contained in F. S. Regs., Part II. and the Staff Manual respectively. Title pages will be prepared in manuscript.

WAR DIARY
or
INTELLIGENCE SUMMARY.
(Erase heading not required.)

Army Form C. 2118.

280th (City of London) Brigade R.F.A.

Place	Date	Hour	Summary of Events and Information April, 1918	Remarks and references to Appendices
GAVRELLE.	1st.		One Section of C/280 moved during the night to a position just S.E. of ROCLINCOURT, and E of ROCLINCOURT - ST. LAURENT BLANGY Road. Many sniping targets engaged. Enemy artillery active all day.	
	2nd.		Remainder of C/280 moved to New Position. 93rd Battery moved a few hundred yards to a flank as the position was under direct observation from MONCHY-LE-PREUX. H.Qrs moved to rear position H.5.b.30.05. S.E. of ROCLINCOURT.	
	3rd.		Quiet day. Light harassing fire carried out. No night firing, the Brigade being in the line mainly for S.O.S. purposes, and to rest prior to joining the Division which was out to refit.	
	4th		Nothing to report.	
	5th		Quiet day.	
	6th		Quiet day.	
	7th.		Warning orders received in the morning of a relief by the 12th AUSTRALIAN F.A. Brigade, which was duly carried out by the evening, three batteries of 281st Brigade being relieved, and H.Qrs., and 93rd Battery of this (280th) Bde., thus reducing the super-imposed Brigades on the Divisional Front by 50%. The Brigade withdrew to the Wagon Lines at MADAGASCAR CORNER, (A.26.d), for the night.	
AGNY.	8th.		The Brigade marched under orders from 56th Division to Southern Positions near AGNY. Guns were left at old Wagon Line to hand over to Units of 4th Divisional Artillery, the Brigade relieved being the 1st Canadian Brigade F.A. Thus, on the Anniversary of April 9th, 1917, when the Brigade was in action at BEAURAINS for the Spring Offensive, it found itself within a few yards of its old positions ready to oppose the further advance of the enemy's Great 1918 Offensive.	

D. D. & L., London, E.C. (A8094) Wt W2771/M2031 750,000 5/17 Sch. 52 Forms/C2118/14

Army Form C. 2118.

WAR DIARY
or
INTELLIGENCE SUMMARY.
(Erase heading not required.)

280th (City of London) Brigade R.F.A.

Instructions regarding War Diaries and Intelligence Summaries are contained in F. S. Regs., Part II. and the Staff Manual respectively. Title pages will be prepared in manuscript.

Place	Date	Hour	Summary of Events and Information April 1918.	Remarks and references to Appendices
AGNY.	9th		Quiet day.	
	10th		Quiet day. 29th Brigade R.F.A. 4th Division came into Action to thicken the Line, and divisional front.	
	11th		Considerable Enemy activity in the early morning. No action developed. C/280 moved to a position slightly further EAST.	
	12th to 18th		Normal days. A great amount of work done during this period in salving and putting into use R.E. material from a very large dump at RONVILLE abandoned by reason of the Enemy advance from MONCHY.	
	19th		A minor and temporarily successful infantry operation gave much Gun Fodder in the way of sniping targets, in that the Enemy, who had an inter-battalion Relief in progress, was thrown into considerable confusion. He, however, attacked our outposts at 6.p.m. with success and the result that dawn on the 20th found us in our old line once again.	
	20th		Normal day.	
	21st		Normal day.	
	22nd		Normal day.	
	23rd		Divisional front enlarged by extension North to the SCARPE 15th Divisional Area.	
	24th		Barrage in support of a raid which obtained prisoners but gave no identifications.	
	25th		Normal day.	
	26th		Orders received to cut down all fire to a minimum, it being recognised that Artillery Personnel, due to its lack of rest out of the line, and the amount of harassing fire, and other work while in the line, can become worn out just as their material.	
	27th		Normal day. Lt Col W.E. Batt C.M.G. confirmed in command of Bde vice Lt Col Southam D.S.O. evacuated	
	28th		Normal day.	
	29th		Feint raid to cover raids by the 2nd Canadian Division on the Right which proved highly successful. Section of 93rd Battery moved to forward position East of ARRAS - BUCQUOY Road	
	30th		Normal day	

W. E. ? Batt
Lieut. Colonel, Commanding 280th Brigade R.F.A.

D. D. & L., London, E.C. (A8094) Wt W1771/M2031 750,000 5/17 Sch. 52 Forms/C2118/14

WR 30

280th (City of London) Brigade R.F.A.

War Diary May 1918.

Original.

Instructions regarding War Diaries and Intelligence Summaries are contained in F. S. Regs., Part II. and the Staff Manual respectively. Title pages will be prepared in manuscript.

WAR DIARY
or
INTELLIGENCE SUMMARY.
(Erase heading not required.)

280th Brigade (City of London) R.F.A.

Army Form C. 2118.

Place	Date MAY.	Hour	Summary of Events and Information	Remarks and references to Appendices
AGNY.	1st - 3rd.		Quiet, nothing to report.	
	4th - 8th.		Harrassing fire largely increased since a hostile attack was expected in conjunction with impending operations threatened by the 2nd German Army against AMIENS.	
	7th.		The Brigade supported a successful raid by the CANADIANS against NEUVILLE VITASSE.	
	8th - 11th.		Quiet days. The amount of harrassing fire gradually decreasing though so arranged as to bring down a great volume of fire about dawn. This policy, combined with nightly Gas shoots, produced an irritant effect on the Enemy with the result that on the morning of the	
	12th.		12th inst he adopted the same policy about our Front System.	
	13th - 16th.		Nothing of import. Harrassing fire still carried out, though expenditure remained lower. Gas bombardments every night when conditions were suitable eventually caused a long suffering enemy to retaliate though to no great extent. His harrassing fire remained active and was principally directed to Roads and Tracks used by transport and was applied by means of sudden and irregular hurricane Bombardments.	
	17th.		Hostile artillery ative. Destructive shoot on D/280. One Gun Destroyed. No casualities to personnel.	
DAINVILLE.	18th.		Brigade H.Q. moved to Railway Cutting just E. of DAINVILLE, the cellars in AGNY proving too damp for health.	
	19th.		Normal day.	
	20th.		Normal day.	
	21st.		2nd Canadian Raid supported by 56th Division. Successful, 4 prisoners being captured. No casualities.	
	22nd.		Another Raid by CANADIANS on NEUVILLE VITASSE. Successful, dummy barrage by Batteries of this Brigade.	
	23rd.		Wagon Lines at BERNEVILLE bombed and casualities caused to C/280.	
	24th		Normal day.	
	25th.		Enemy artillery increased about 7.p.m.	
	26th.		Enemy artillery continued very ative. Registration for forthcoming Raid by 18-pdrs.	
	27th.		Intense bombardment from 2.am. to 4.am. on Corps on the Right. Much Gas on Division on the Right of this Brigade.	
	28th.		Quiet day. Raid by 167th Infantry Brigade at 11.pm. Many enemy killed, 2 prisoners, and 4 Machine Guns. Special letter from Brigadier-General commanding Inf. Bde., congratulating Artillery on the excellence of the barrage.	
	29th.		Inspection of Battery positions by G.O.C. Division.	
	30th - 31st.		Normal days.	

Lieut. Colonel,
Commanding 280th Brigade, R.FA.

D. D. & L., London, E.C. (A8204) Wt. W1771/M2031 750,000 5/17 Sch. 52 Forms/C2118/14

Vol 31

Secret

Original
War Diary
June 1918.

Instructions regarding War Diaries and Intelligence Summaries are contained in F. S. Regs., Part II. and the Staff Manual respectively. Title pages will be prepared in manuscript.

WAR DIARY
or
INTELLIGENCE SUMMARY. 280th (City of London) Brigade, R.F.A.

(Erase heading not required.)

Army Form C. 2118.

Place	Date	Hour	Summary of Events and Information June 1918.	Remarks and references to Appendices
DAINVILLE.	1st.		Raid by 168th Infantry Brigade North of CAMBRAI ROAD, very successful, 27 prisoners.	
	2nd.		Supporting Raid by 2nd CANADIAN DIVISION (19 prisoners, 3 Machine Guns & 2 Trench Mortars captured) At 11-0 p.m. a heavy enemy barrage was put down on our trenches in responce to which batteries opened for 15 minutes on their S.O.S. Lines.	
	3rd.		NORMAL DAY, nothing to report. The many complaints received from the Infantry and from Batteries that enemy Aircraft were too frequently not engaged by Anti-Aircraft Guns, a form of working LIAISON between Field Brigades and Anti-Aircraft Sections was instituted with a view to inducing them to obtain additional range by taking up more advanced positions and of making clear to those complaining some of the difficulties that Anti-Aircraft Sections have to meet.	
	4 - 7th.		Normal days. Several Instructional Shoots carried out by batteries.	
	8th.		Enemy Raid on the CANADIAN DIVISION on the Right. Protective Barrage put down for short interval by batteries.	
	9th - 11th.		Normal days.	
	12th.		Successful Raid by 169th Infantry Brigade opposite TILLOY-LES-MIFFLAINES. Supported by batteries of the Group.	
	13th.		Quiet day.	
	14th.	1-0am.	Dummy Barrage to assist Raid by CANADIAN DIVISION South of NEUVILLE VITASSE which proved a success. Enemy Artillery extremely inactive.	
	15th.		Quiet day.	
	16th	9-0am.	Enemy Aeroplane brought down near NEUVILLE VITASSE, was destroyed by D/280.	
	17th.		Hostile Artillery activity increasing.	
	18th.		Nothing to report.	
	19th - 23rd.		Quiet days. Several Instructional shoots carried out.	
	24th.		Demonstration to assist successful Raid by 15th Division just North of RIVER SCARPE.	

D. D. & L. London, E.C. (A8:04) Wt W1771/M2031 750,000 5/17 Sch. 52 Forms/C2118/14

Instructions regarding War Diaries and Intelligence Summaries are contained in F. S. Regs., Part II. and the Staff Manual respectively. Title pages will be prepared in manuscript.

WAR DIARY
or
INTELLIGENCE SUMMARY.
(Erase heading not required.)

Army Form C. 2118.

Place	Date	Hour	Summary of Events and Information	Remarks and references to Appendices
	25th.		The Brigade assisted in Barrage for Raid by 6th. C.I.B. on NEUVILLE VITASSE. 1 Officer and 21 O.Rs. were taken prisoners.	
	26th - 30th.		Normal days. Hostile Artillery very inactive. until 30th when an increase was noticed	
			30.6.18.	
			[signature] Lieut.Colonel, Commanding 280th Brigade, R.F.A.	

D. D. & L., London, E.C. (A8004) Wt W1771/M2031 750,000 5/17 Sch. 52 Forms/C2118/14

Original

WO 95/3?

WAR DIARY.

280th (City of London) Brigade R.F.A.

July 1918.

SECRET

To: 56th Div. Arty.

C/3667

Herewith Original of War Diary for month of JULY, 1918.

Lieut-Colonel,
Commanding, 28^{0}th Brigade, R.F.A.

1-8-18.

Army Form C. 2118.

WAR DIARY
or
INTELLIGENCE SUMMARY.
(Erase heading not required.)

Instructions regarding War Diaries and Intelligence Summaries are contained in F. S. Regs., Part II. and the Staff Manual respectively. Title pages will be prepared in manuscript.

280th (City of London) Brigade, RFA.

J U L Y, 1918

Place	Date	Hour	Summary of Events and Information	Remarks and references to Appendices
DAINVILLE	1.7.18.		Hostile Artillery very active during the day.	
	2.7.18.		Enemy's Batteries still rather more active than usual.	
	3.7.18.		Normal day.	
	4.7.18.		An unusually large amount of movement observed and fired on with success. A direct hit was obtained on an occupied gun pit and about 20. Casualties were caused.	
	5.7.18. to 8.7.18. inc.		Quiet days. Hostile Artillery very inactive.	
	9.7.18.		Destructive shoot on 6" Battery position on road just in rear of detached Section, 93rd. Bty.	
	10.7.18. 11.7.18.		Normal days.	
	12.7.18.		Destructive shoot on hostile T.M. successfully carried out by D/280.	
	13.7.18.		C/280 registered on junction of Tracks with K.B. observation.	
	14.7.18.		10 c.m. Gun rather active during the day on Level crossing G.31.d.	
	15.7.18. to 18.7.18.		Quiet days. D/280 carried out one destructive shoot each day on hostile T.M.'s	
	19.7.18.		The 1st Canadian Division Infantry relieved that of 3rd C.D. on night of 18th/19th. The Brigade fired a large number of times in retaliation during the day at request of Infantry.	
	20.7.18.		Several retaliation shoots again carried out. 1. Section of each Battery relieved during the evening by 311th Brigade, R.F.A.	
BERNEVILLE	21.7.18.		Quiet day. Remainder of Batteries & Brigade H.Q. relieved by 311th Brigade, R.F.A. and proceeded to Wagon Lines at BERNEVILLE.	
FREVIN-CAPELLE	22.7.18.		The Brigade marched from BERNEVILLE to following areas; H.Q.-A/280 and C/280 to FREVIN-CAPELLE; 93rd & D/280 to ACQ.	
	23.7.18. to 30.7.18.		Brigade carried out training in neighbourhood of MONT ST. ELOI.	
	31.7.18.		1. Section of each Battery relieved 1. Section of Batteries 1st Canadian D.A. in their old positions between BEAURAINS and ACHICOURT.	

[signature]
Lieut-Colonel,
Commanding 280th (City of London) Brigade, RFA.

D. D. & L., London, E.C. (A8094) Wt W1771/M2031 750,000 5/17 Sch. 58 Forms/C2118/14

Instructions regarding War Diaries and Intelligence Summaries are contained in F. S. Regs., Part II. and the Staff Manual respectively. Title pages will be prepared in manuscript.

Army Form C. 2118.

WAR DIARY
or
INTELLIGENCE SUMMARY. 280th (City of London) Brigade, R.F.A.
(Erase heading not required.)

Place	Date	Hour	Summary of Events and Information AUGUST 1918.	Remarks and references to Appendices
	1st.		Remaining sections of Batteries relieved 1st C.D.A. during the evening and Brigade H.Q. was relieved during the afternoon.	
	2nd-4th.		Quiet days. Batteries carried out registration and usual night firing.	
	5th.		Hostile Artillery considerably more active than usual chiefly registration.	
	6th.		Hostile Artillery carried out a number of area shoots in battery area.	
	7th.		Enemy's batteries again active. The enemy has apparently had his "circus" in the area during the past few days.	
	8th.		Brigade carried out bombardment of approaches to NEUVILLE VITASSE in connection with projection of gas.	
	9th.		Quiet day.	
	10th.		Hostile artillery rather more active than usual on Front line and Battery areas.	
	11th.		Quiet day.	
	12th.		Considerable increase in hostile shelling. 93rd Bty and A/280 main positions received about 20 Rounds 21cm. How. There was also several enemy "Joyride "shoots on battery areas.	
	13th.		Quiet day.	
	14th.		Batteries assisted Brigade on Left to repulse hostile raid.	
	15th.		Quiet day. One section of each battery relieved by 15th Division.	
	16th.		Remainder of batteries relieved.	
	17th.		Brigade Concentrated at BERNEVILLE.	
	18th -21st.		Brigade still at BERNEVILLE awaiting orders.	
	22nd.		Brigade Commander and Battery Commanders proceeded up the line early in the morning near BOISLEUX-AU-MONT to reconnoitre position. At night Batteries took up positions Sheet 51.B. S.15.b. N.E. of BOIRY ST.MARTIN with a view to supporting an attack on the enemy's lines in front of BOIRY BECQUERELLE and BOYELLES, and Brigade H.Q. was established E. of BLAIRVILLE. Batteries were heavily gassed during the night.	
	23rd		Infantry attacked at 5.00 a.m. under Barrage of this and other Brigades assisted ~~with~~ by Tanks and met with instant success. The villages of BOYELLES and BOIRY BECQUERELLE were captured and important strong point known as BOIRY WORK and trenches N. and S. thereof were finally reached. Many prisoners were returned. In the evening Batteries moved forward to position S.W. of BOISLEUX ST. MARC and Brigade H.Q. was established near the station at BOISLEUX AU MONT. Battery Wagon Lines moved to WAILLY.	
	24th		A quiet day, but much ammunition humping.	
	25th		At 7.00 a.m. this Brigade supported an attack on SUMMIT Trench which the Infantry carried together with a considerable number of prisoners. At 5.40 p.m. orders were received to advance	

Instructions regarding War Diaries and Intelligence Summaries are contained in F. S. Regs., Part II. and the Staff Manual respectively. Title pages will be prepared in manuscript.

WAR DIARY
or
INTELLIGENCE SUMMARY.
(Erase heading not required.)

Army Form C. 2118.

Place	Date	Hour	Summary of Events and Information	Remarks and references to Appendices
Continued	25th		and B.Cs. went forward followed by their Batteries, and came into action just in time to support a further attack at 7.30 p.m. Our Infantry met with great resistance, and only smallx progress was made. Brigade H.Q. were moved to near Crucifix near BOISLEUX ST. MARC.	
	26th		This Brigade put down a Barrage at 3.00 a.m. and again at 7.30 a.m. to support our Infantry Operations with a view to improving our positions on the Hill between BOIRY BECQUERELLE and CROISELLES. Very stubborn fighting ensued but our Infantry wereable to make some smallx gains. Wagon Lines moved to near BOISLEUX AU MONT. S.5.c. and S.11.d. (Sheet 51.B.)	
	27th		168th Infantry Brigade attacked at 9.30 a.m. with the object of capturing CROISELLES. This Brigade supported the attack. Heavy opposition was encountered from M.Gs. advantageously sited in Sunken Roads and old trenches around the village, and although elements of our troops entered the village it could not be held. At 8.00 p.m. the Brigade advanced to positions of the Left Front in order to bring enfilade fire to bear on the HINDENBURG LINE E. of CROISELLES. Brigade H.Q. moved to a vacated Battery position E. of BOIRY BECQUERELLE.	
	28th		At 12.30 p.m. 56th Division continued the attack in order to deal with the M.Gs. which had held up the advance the day before. One Brigade made a flanking attack down the HINDENBURG LINE from the N.W. whilst the other made a holding frontal attack. All objectives were reached but numerous M.G. Nests, completely surrounded, held on till nightfall when they were finally cleared out.	
	29th		In the early morning Batteries moved up into positions N.E. of CROISELLES and Brigade H.Q. was established N.W. of this village. At 1 p.m., 167th Infantry Brigade continued the attack, this Brigade putting down a barrage for 4 hours. As before, Machine guns gave considerable trouble before BULLECOURT was captured.	
	30th		Division was heavily counter attacked at 7 a.m. and slightly pressed back. Brigade put down a protective barrage for several hours during the morning and much sniping was done at parties moving over the open- 600. rds. alone being spent by one Battery on this work.	
	31st		Enemy again counter attacked at about 1.30 p.m. Batteries engaged firing for many hours. All units of the Brigade suffered a few casualties from H.E. and gas shell.	

Lieut-Colonel,
Commanding, 280th Brigade, R.F.A.

D. D. & L., London, E.C. (A8104) Wt W1771/M2031 750,000 5/17 Sch. 52 Forms/C2118/14

Original

War Diary

Sept 1918

Army Form C. 2118.

Instructions regarding War Diaries and Intelligence Summaries are contained in F. S. Regs., Part II. and the Staff Manual respectively. Title pages will be prepared in manuscript.

WAR DIARY
or
INTELLIGENCE SUMMARY. 280th (City of London) Brigade, R.F.A.

(Erase heading not required.)

Place	Date	Hour	Summary of Events and Information SEPTEMBER 1918.	Remarks and references to Appendices
	1st.			
	2nd.		Brigade Headquarters removed to U.19.b.6.4. N.W. of BULLECOURT. Brigade Headquarters Wagon Lines to T.17.a.9.1. Guns to positions between BULLECOURT and LONGATTE.	
	3rd.		Brigade Headquarters removed to QUEANT, Batteries to East of PRONVILLE.	
	4th.		Wagon Lines moved to EAST of QUEANT, 93rd Battery EAST of PRONVILLE.	
	5th.		In the morning orders were received to move Batteries EAST of PRONVILLE and Brigade Headquarters to PRONVILLE.This move was actually in progress when orders were received for the Brigade to withdraw and concentrate for the night at CROISILLES. Batteries pulled up in T.18 and Headquarters in T.17.c. before midnight, The Brigade for the day being under the orders of the 63rd Division. During the day D/280 fired a 10.5cm enemy battery on to the City of CAMBRAI.	
	6th.		Brigade again under the orders of the 56th Division and transferred from 17th Corps to 22nd. Corps and marched to Wagon Lines in the HENINEL Valley.	
	7th.		Brigade Headquarters and Battery Positions near DURY and RECOURT reconnoitred in the morning and occupied in the evening. Wagon Lines moved to CHERISY. Gun Position area bombed by enemy during the night.	
	8th.		All Batteries working on new Battery and Section gun positions in P.12., 18 and 29. (Sheet 51B).	
	9th - 11th.		All batteries very busy improving conditions, making new gun-pits and getting up ammunition. Heavy enemy shelling of battery areas all day and night.	
	12th.		Enemy much less active. Heavy rains which made tracks and roads most difficult for for transport.	
	13th - 15th.		Considerable Hostile Fire all day and most of the night on Battery Areas. Bombing at night.	
	16th.		Much less hostile fire. D/280 carried on Wire Cutting and 93rd Battery considerable sniping on roads in enemy territory.	

D. D. & L., London, E.C.
(A8:04) Wt W1771/M2031 750,000 5/17 Sch. 52 Forms/C2118/14

Army Form C. 2118.

Instructions regarding War Diaries and Intelligence Summaries are contained in F. S. Regs., Part II. and the Staff Manual respectively. Title pages will be prepared in manuscript.

WAR DIARY
or
INTELLIGENCE SUMMARY. 280th (City of London) Brigade, R.F.A.

(Erase heading not required.)

Place	Date	Hour	Summary of Events and Information SEPTEMBER 1918.	Remarks and references to Appendices
	17/18th.		Persistent shelling of areas in occupation of Brigade Headquarters and Batteries. Considerable bombing too at nights.	
	19th.		Hostile shelling much reduced, rumours to the effect that enemy was in process of withdrawing from North of SENSEE River.	
	20/21st.		Preparations for getting up a large supply of ~~xxxx~~ Gas, Smoke and other shell to forward positions for a battle.	
	22/23rd.		Considerable shelling by enemy of main routes to Battery positions.	
	24th.		A Section of enemy 7.7cm guns put into action near SAUDEMONT for the purpose of firing 2,000 rounds enemy Yellow Cross Gas Shell into BOIS DE QUESNOY..	
	25th/26th.		Little hostile H.E. fire but some gas shelling of Battery area.	
	27th.		Zero hour 5-20 a.m. This Brigade participating in a big Canadian Corps attack on BOURLON WOOD area in which 56th and 11th Divisions took part. For 13 hours and 20 minutes the Brigade's task was to maintain a smoke screen on the left flank of the attack and also bombard areas (later to be occupied by our Infantry) with 4.5" How. Gas Shell and some 1600 rounds of enemy 7.7cm Yellow Cross Shell. (Gun detachments for the two enemy guns were supplied by all Batteries of the Brigade). The prolonged battle proved exhausting for detachments, Enemy did not, most unexpectedly, much worry the Batteries during the battle except with a small amount of gas shell towards the end and at night. Operations appear to have been a great success. Our Barrage and that spent on innumerable fleeting targets given us by the R.A.F. consumed over 17,500 rounds of BNO, A, AX, AS and Yellow Cross Shells.	
	28th		At 7.30 p.m. this Brigade put down a creeping barrage in arrangement with B.G.C., 167th Infantry Brigade with a view of capturing ARLEUX, North of PALLUEL which had been occupied as a result of the operations of the previous day. Our Infantry were successful in entering the Village but later in the night the enemy strongly counter attacked under heavy barrage which extended to PALLUEL and our Infantry were driven back. Our Battery areas suffered from enemy gas bombardment.	
	29th		Owing to a re-adjustment of the Front, 4th Division extended its Zone to the Right and took over most of the Zone covered by the 167th Infantry Brigade. As a consequence, the 189th Army Bde. R.F.A. relieved this Brigade in the night of the 29th and H.Qrs and Batteries with-	

Instructions regarding War Diaries and Intelligence Summaries are contained in F. S. Regs., Part II. and the Staff Manual respectively. Title pages will be prepared in manuscript.

WAR DIARY
or
INTELLIGENCE SUMMARY.

280th (City of London) Brigade, RFA

(Erase heading not required.)

Army Form C. 2118.

Place	Date	Hour	Summary of Events and Information	Remarks and references to Appendices
			(Continued)	
	29th		drew into Mobile Reserve at Wagon Lines which were established near VILLERS-lez-CAGNICOURT.	
	30th		H.Qrs and Batteries remained in Mobile Reserve at Wagon Lines. Some casualties were caused to personnel of D/280 by a casual enemy shell.	

[signature]
Lieut-Colonel,
Commanding, 280th Brigade, R. F. A.

D. D. & L. London, E.C. (A8091) Wt W11/1M431 750,000 5/16 Sch. 52 Forms/C2118/14

280. Bde. R.F.A.

Original
War Diary

October 1918

Instructions regarding War Diaries and Intelligence Summaries are contained in F. S. Regs., Part II. and the Staff Manual respectively. Title pages will be prepared in manuscript.

Army Form C. [illegible]8.

WAR DIARY
or
INTELLIGENCE SUMMARY. 280th (City of London) Brigade, R.F.A.

(Erase heading not required.)

Place	Date	Hour	Summary of Events and Information OCTOBER 1918.	Remarks and references to Appendices
	1st.		Brigade relieved 250th Brigade, R.F.A. in neighbourhood of OISY-LE-VERGER and as before formed part of a protective flank.	
	2nd.		Considerable hostile shelling of battery areas.	
	3/4th.		Quiet days.	
	5/6th.		Brigade Wire cutting R.21.b.	
	7th.		168th Infantry Brigade established posts in AUBENCHEUL but were compelled later to withdraw.	
	8th.		Took part in barrage to assist operations on our N.W. Our Infantry again occupied AUBENCHEUL.	
	9/16th.		A quiet period, the enemy retiring rapidly on the North.	
	17th.		Came under orders of 4th Canadian D.A.	
	18th.		Brigade moved to R.4.c. North of AUBIGNY-AU-BAC and remained for the night in state of readiness.	
	19th.		Batteries advanced to S.E. of FRESSAIN with wagons alongside Guns. Brigade H.Q. at R.4.b.3.8. early in morning. In the afternoon batteries again advanced to MARCQ bringing Wagon Lines alongside.	
	20th.		Brigade moved South across SENSEE CANAL at WASNES-AU-BAC to RAMILLIES (93rd Battery to ESWARS) coming there under the direct orders of XXII Corps.	
	21st.		Brigade in Army Reserve when every opportunity was taken to effect a very necessary re-organization and the bringing together stores and essentials that had had to be left in the rear owing to rapid and frequent marches.	
	22/29th.		Refitting and training. Considerable work put in in re-roofing barns and houses which enabled all men and horses to exist under conditions approximating comfort. The cleaning up of our locality, burying of dead and also many horses kept all units very fully occupied. At 20.15 hours orders received to be ready to march and at 22.30 hours the Brigade marched off for THIANT.	
	30th.		Brigade arrived at THIANT between 04.00 and 05.00 hours and bivouacked, At about 09.00 hours it was learned definitely that we were to go into action East of MAING and that we were under the orders of the 49th Division. Positions were reconnoitred during the morning and ammunition taken up to positions that night.	
	31st.		Guns put into action and further supplies of ammunition taken up in preparation for a big battle at 05.15 hours November 1st. Battery positions all in the open fields about 2,000 yards from our front line.	

[signature]
Lieut.Colonel,
Commanding 280th Brigade, R.F.A.

D. D & L., London, E.C.
(A8204) Wt W1771/M2031 750,000 5/17 Sch. 52 Forms/C2118/14

To: 56th Div. Arty.

280th (CITY OF LONDON) BRIGADE. R.F.A.

No. D/923

Date.

Herewith Original of War Diary

for month ending November 30. 1918

[signature]

Lieut-Colonel
Commanding 280th Brigade
R.F.A.

30. 11. 18.

Army Form C. 2118.

280 Bde R.F.A.

Instructions regarding War Diaries and Intelligence Summaries are contained in F. S. Regs., Part II. and the Staff Manual respectively. Title pages will be prepared in manuscript.

WAR DIARY
or
INTELLIGENCE SUMMARY.
(Erase heading not required.)

NOVEMBER 1918

98 36

Place	Date	Hour	Summary of Events and Information	Remarks and references to Appendices
THIENT (Sheet 51 A. N.E)	1.11.18		0515. Attack by 49th Division in conjunction with Canadians on the left and 4th Division on the right. All objectives taken early but forward posts driven in during the day. Positions reconnoitred S.E. of FAMARS but not occupied.	
	2.11.18		Attack by 4th Division to adjust ~~reverses during~~ yesterday's ~~fighting~~ line at 0530. Brigade did not fire. C/280 detailed as special Battery to work with Infantry Battalion Commander.	
	3.11.18		Enemy retiring; Batteries moved to positions East of SAULTAIN. Bde.H.Qrs at BETTERAVE Fme. S. of FAMARS. Group consisted of 280th, 246th and 77th F.A. Brigades. ~~XXXXXXXXXXXXXXXXXXXXXXXXXX~~	
	4.11.18		Brigade H.Qrs at SAULTAIN; Batteries in position 2000 yards W. of SEBOURG. Harrassing fire during afternoon and evening. 246th Brigade in Corps Reserve. 77th Brigade under orders from 56th Div. Arty.	
	5.11.18		Barrage to assist Infantry in an advance from SEBOURG to ANGREAU at 0530. Brigade H.Qrs in SEBOURG. Batteries just E. of the Village. Attack successful; some elements penetrated East of the GRAND RHONELLE river but eventually withdrew, under pressure, until the morning.	
	6.11.18		Spent at SEBOURG. Infantry straightening their line. Heavy Artillery moving up.	
	7.11.18		Barrage put down at 0900. 49th and 51st D.A. in the line to reinforce, but enemy again retired so the day was spent in bringing up Batteries. Reconnaissance of route SEBOURG-ONNEZIES made with view to early move to that district. A/280 Wagon Line moved to ROISIN.	
	8.11.18		Batteries advanced to positions East of ONNEZIES with their Wagon lines. Brigade H.Qrs at ONNEZIES.	
	9.11.18		Batteries moved West of FAYT-LE-FRANC for barrage at 0800 hrs., limbered up and advanced but were not required again owing to enemy's too rapid retreat. H.Qrs moved to LA FOLIE. A/280 and 93rd. Wagon Lines at ERQUENNES; C/280 at LA FOLIE; D/280 Sheet 51- D.7.a.4.0.	
	10.11.18		Brigade moved to BLAREGNIES, ~~XXXXXXXXXXXXXXXXXXXXXXX~~ where it rested all day.	
	11.11.18		ARMISTICE at 1100 hours. Brigade remaining at BLAREGNIES and engaged in cleaning up, etc.	
	12.11.18		Collecting Ammunition and forming it into dumps.	
	13.11.18 to 24.11.18		At BLAREGNIES.	
	25.11.18		Preliminary Reconnaissance of area of GOEGNIES-CHAUSSEE.	
	27.11.18		Brigade moved to GOEGNIES-CHAUSSEE.. Brigade H.Q., A/280, C/280 and D/280 Batteries being in the Village; 93rd. Battery at BETTIGNIES.	
	28.11.18 to 30.11.18		Settling in at GOEGNIES-CHAUSSEE. Considerable difficulty experienced in finding billets suitable for winter quarters owing to congestion in the area. Considerable time was given during last fortnight of the month to the promotion of the Army Education Scheme, Captain	

D. D. & L., London, E.C. (A8764) Wt W1771/M2031 750,000 5/17 Sch. 52 Forms/C2118/14

Instructions regarding War Diaries and Intelligence Summaries are contained in F. S. Regs., Part II. and the Staff Manual respectively. Title pages will be prepared in manuscript.

WAR DIARY
or
INTELLIGENCE SUMMARY.
(Erase heading not required.)

NOVEMBER 1918

Army Form C. 2118.

Place	Date	Hour	Summary of Events and Information	Remarks and references to Appendices
	30.11.18		(Continued) H.V. HUMMEL, M.C. being appointed 280th Brigade Education Officer. Inter-Unit Sports were arranged and Committees formed to give additional impetus to Football, Boxing, Cross-Country Running, etc.	

[signature]

Lieut-Colonel,
Commanding, 280th Brigade, R. F. A.

D. D. & L., London, E.C.
(A8004) Wt W1771/M2031 750,000 5/17 Sch. 52 Forms/C2118/14

To: 56th Div. Arty.

Herewith Original of War Diary for month ending December 31st 1918.

31.12.18.

Lieut-Colonel,
Commanding, 280th Brigade, RFA.

Army Form C. 2118.

Instructions regarding War Diaries and Intelligence Summaries are contained in F. S. Regs., Part II. and the Staff Manual respectively. Title pages will be prepared in manuscript.

WAR DIARY
or
INTELLIGENCE SUMMARY.
(Erase heading not required.)

DECEMBER 1918.

37

Place	Date	Hour	Summary of Events and Information	Remarks and references to Appendices
GOEGNIES CHAUSSEE	5.12.18		H.M. the KING passed through the Village of GOEGNIES-CHAUSSEE and was given an enthusiastic welcome by the Brigade and Infantry Battalion quartered in the Village.	
			There was nothing further of note to record during the whole month, but, nevertheless, time was more than occupied by Recreation, Education, and Demobilization which was commenced by sending away 30 Miners and Pivotal Men. The Wagons of the Brigade were in continuous use removing Refugees and doing cartage work for the local inhabitants.	
			Christmas passed with the usual festivities.	

[signature]

Lieut-Colonel,
Commanding, 280th Brigade, R.F.A.

D. D. & L., London, E.C.
(A8-04) Wt W1771/M2031 750,000 5/17 Sch. 58 Forms/C2118/14

VR 38

56 DW

Original
War Diary
January 1919

280th
(CITY OF LONDON)
BRIGADE,
R.F.A.

No. D/1474.

Date.

To:- 56th Div. Arty.

Herewith Original of War Diary for month ending January 31st 1919.

[signature]

Lieut. Colonel,
Commanding 280th Brigade, R.F.A.

31-1-19.

Army Form C. 2118.

WAR DIARY
or
INTELLIGENCE SUMMARY. 280th (City of London) Brigade, R.F.A.

(Erase heading not required.)

Instructions regarding War Diaries and Intelligence Summaries are contained in F. S. Regs., Part II. and the Staff Manual respectively. Title pages will be prepared in manuscript.

Place	Date	Hour	Summary of Events and Information JANUARY 1919.	Remarks and references to Appendices
GOEGNIES - CHAUSSEE.			The Brigade remained at GOEGNIES-CHAUSSEE. Demobilization proceeded and parties of men were from time to time dispatched to the Dispersal Stations. Horses were inspected and classified and some of these sent away. At the end of the month the personnel had been reduced to 14 Officers and 649 O.Rs (100 of whom were on leave and possibly demobilized in England) and 513 horses.	
	7th.		The Brigade marched past the G.O.C., R.A., 56th Division (the Corps Commander who had arranged to inspect the Brigade being prevented by illness). The G.O.C., R.A. expressed himself very pleased with the turn out.	
			A Section Football ~~XXXXXXXXXXX~~ League was organised within the Brigade and other matches played with other Units in the Division.	
			31-1-19. [signature] Lieut.Colonel, Commanding 280th Brigade, R.F.A.	

D. D. & L., London, E.C. (A8204) Wt W1771/M2031 750,000 5/17 Sch. 52 Forms/C2118/14

VARIOUS RE-ORGANIZATIONS OF THE 280th BRIGADE, R.F.A.

1. The Brigade came to France composed of three 4-gun 18-pdr. Batteries; A, B and C/280.

2. On the 11th May 1916 the Brigade was re-organized into one of four 4-gun 18-pdr. Batteries. The fourth Battery which was called D/280 was the 93rd. Battery, under the command of Major COOPER, transferred from some other Division.

3. On the 28th May 1916, the 93rd. Battery ceased to be D/280 and was transferred to the 283rd Brigade, R.F.A. and the original 1/11th London Howitzer Battery became D/280.

4. On or about the 5th November 1916, the Brigade was re-constituted into four Batteries of 6. guns made up as follows:-

A/280: 4. guns A/280 and 1. Section of B/280

93rd: (transferred from 283rd Brigade, R.F.A)
4. guns 93rd. Bty. and 1. Section transferred from C/283.

C/280: 4. guns C/280 and the remaining Section transferred from B/280.

D/280: Did not get its additional Section until some time in January 1917, when it was made up by the addition of a section from the 500th Battery.

5. There is no ~~XXXXX~~ further information in this Office with regard to either the 500th Battery or ~~XXX~~ D/126.

280th
(CITY OF LONDON)
BRIGADE,
R.F.A.

No. D/1717
Date.

56th Div. Arty.

Herewith Statement regarding the various re-organizations of the Brigade required by you.

for Lieut-Colonel,
Commanding, 280th Brigade, R. F. A.

21.2.19.

HISTORY OF THE 280th (City of London) Brigade, R.F.A.

The 280th (City of London) Brigade, R.F.A. as now constituted comprises, in addition to Headquarters :-

A/280 Battery, R.F.A.(T.F.)
93rd Battery, R.F.A.(Regulars)
C/280 Battery, R.F.A.(T.F.)
D/280 Battery, R.F.A.(T.F.)

Rather more than half the Brigade, viz., Headquarters, A and C Batteries were formed from the 1/1 London Brigade, R.F.A., and D/280 is the original 1/11th London Battery of the 1/4th London Howitzer Brigade, R.F.A. with a section of the 500th Battery R.F.A. (New Army).

The 1/1 London Brigade, R.F.A. being the parent of the 280th Brigade R.F.A. its early history is now traced, but that of the 93rd Battery R.F.A., and of the 1/11th London (Howitzer) Battery will be inserted in the narrative at the point therein at which these Batteries were incorporated in the Brigade.

The 1/1 London Brigade, R.F.A. was originally the 1st London (City of London) R.G.A.(Volunteers) and was an amalgamation of two or more units including the old 1st Surrey Artillery. It became a very strong unit consisting of 16 companies divided into 2 Wings each commanded by a Lieut. Colonel, the whole being under Lieut. Colonel W. Hope V.C. as Lieut. Colonel Commandant.

At the time of the South African War its strength rose to 1500, and when the City Imperials were formed a strong contingent formed part of the Artillery of that Force.

At the transfer, in 1908, of the Volunteers to the Territorial Army there was a shortage of Field Artillery, and at the request of the War Office the Brigade changed over, en masse, to Field and from it were formed 3 Field Artillery Brigades which were located in different parts of London.

The principal one became the 1st City of London Brigade R.F.A.; its first Commanding Officer being Colonel J. Stollery, V.D., and, as in the case of all Units bearing the City's name, it was under the City of London Territorial Association for administrative purposes.

For 4 years the Brigade struggled on under very adverse circumstances as it had no proper quarters and was obliged to carry out drills and store its guns and wagons in hired buildings such as wharves, etc., but eventually the Association built for it what are, perhaps, the finest Headquarters in London. These were situated in Handel St., Bloomsbury, and included a Riding School and stabling for 13 horses.

During the 7 years preceding the War the Brigade attended Camp either with the Division or at an Artillery Centre where Gun Practice was obtained.

On the outbreak of War the whole of the mobilization arrangements were carried out at Handel Street, and at the end of August 1914, the Brigade, complete with horses, guns, wagons, and stores, marched out of London and trekked with the Division through Surrey and Sussex to Maresfield Park, Uckfield, where until the middle of November, 1914, strenuous training was carried out in preparation for its eventual transfer overseas. Training was continued under canvas until early in November 1914, when on a saturday morning orders were received by wire to be prepared to move at two hours notice to a destination unknown. On the following Monday the Brigade entrained at HAYWARDS HEATH, and after a long journey detrained at WEST CRAMLINGTON, near NEWCASTLE.

From here the Batteries were hurried to the Coast at BLYTH, and the guns were moved into action in positions on the Sand Dunes with the 1st Battery North of the town at CAMBOIS, and the other two South, the Brigade Ammunition Column being billeted in SHANKHOUSE. From this time until early in April 1915 the Brigade formed part of the 1st Line troops to meet an enemy invasion. The guns were manned every morning for an hour before dawn, and 'Stand To' continued till it was possible to see 3,000 yards out to sea. The cold bleak northern climate was very trying to the London troops who were billeted under conditions not dissimilar to what they afterwards found in France. For a long time such close villigance was maintained that the guns were not allowed to be removed from their positions, but early in 1915 the regulations were relaxed to allow the Brigade to train with the 1st Northumberland T.F. Infantry Brigade and many interesting and instructive xxxx field days took place under Brigadier General Riddell. Early in April the Northumberland Infantry Brigade marched away from BLYTH, and within a few days were engaged in the 2nd Battle of YPRES where many, including General Riddell, were killed.

A few days after their departure the 1st London Brigade, R.F.A. also left BLYTH, not as it hoped to proceed overseas, but to go South. It entrained for Sussex, and was billeted for a few weeks around UCKFIELD in SUSSEX. From here it entrained for SALISBURY PLAIN, and did practice preliminary to going overseas. From the Plain it went to IPSWICH and rejoined the 1st London Division which was now composed entirely of 2nd and 3rd line troops under Command of General Cooper. Once more intensive training began, but the men were all the time straining to get overseas to take part in real fighting.

From here the 2nd City of London Battery was sent to KETTERING, to become Instructional Battery to the No.3.T.F.Artillery Training School. Officers and NCO.Os. were called upon to act as Instructors, and the Battery horses and equipment were placed at the disposal of the School for five weekdays out of six.

During this period the Brigade was inspected by the Inspector-General of R.H.& R.F.A., and reported upon favourably, and finally, to the great joy of everyone, orders were received toward the end of September.1915 for the Brigade to proceed to BORDON to refit and re-equip for service overseas. The old 15-pdr guns were handed over to the 2nd line Brigade as well as harness and equipment, and the personnel together with about 50% of the horses which had been passed for overseas service entrained to BORDON. Arriving there the Brigade found that it was to form part of the 36th Divisional Artillery. It took over guns and equipment of the New Army Units of that Division, and on the 3rd Oct. 1915, sailed from SOUTHAMPTON.

The Brigade was under Command of Lieut. Colonel L.A.C.Southam, with Majors R.P.Jones, W.E.Batt, and H.N.Clark as the three Battery Commanders, and Capt. G.G.J.Brady as Commander of the B.A.C.

Arriving in HAVRE on the morning of the 4th., the Brigade entrained and detrained at LONGEAU, and was billeted in the AMIENS Area. Intensive training soon began under the C.R.A., Brigadier-General R.J.G. Elkington, C.M.G., who arrived to take over his new Command a few days after the Brigade had arrived.

On the 9th October the Brigade moved up into the line and went into action near COLINCAMPS. It was attached to the 29th Brigade, R.F.A. of the 4th Division, and the object was to test its efficiency for the line. It remained in action for 10 days during which time each Battery fired about 50 rounds and were passed fit. The sector was very quiet, and no casualties were suffered. The Brigade then marched back into its original area.

On the 25th October 1915 the Brigade was inspected by H.M. King George V on the AMIENS-DOULLENS Road.

In December the original New Army Artillery of the 36th (Ulster) Divisio arrived from England, and the 1/1 London Brigade, R.F.A. with the rest of the London Divisional Artillery became the Divisional Artillery of the 38th (Welsh) Division, entraining from PONT REMY on the 11th Dec. 1915 to AIRE, in which area it was billeted until 1st Jan. 1916 when it was transferred to the 16th (Irish) Division. On the 6th Jan. 1916 the Brigade moved up into action at LOOS, taking over from French Batteries. The relief was complete and the whole Brigade in action on the night of the 7th. This sector had not completely quieted down after the active operations of the Autumn, and as the British position was a sharp salient the enemy were able to shoot at our Batteries from both flanks. All ranks gained valuable experience, and some effective shoots took place, especially on the trenches around the famous DOUBLE CRASSIER. On the evenings on the 26th and 27th the Brigade was relieved by the 3rd London Brigade R.F.A. and marched back into billets at LIERES. At the time of coming out of the line the enemy were very active, probably in celebration of the Kaiser's birthday. During the three weeks in action the Brigade suffered its first casualties, having a few men killed and wounded.

On the 24th Feb. 1916 the Brigade left the 16th Division to join the 56th, which was then being formed. Prior to xxxx leaving the Brigade was inspected by Major-General Hickie, Commanding the 16th Division, and complimented both on its smart appearance and the good work it had done.

It detrained at PONT REMY on 24th Feb. 1916, and went into billets at FONTAINE-SUR-SOMME. From there it marched by easy stages to HERNEUVE and HERNEUVIETTE, arriving on 14th March. Here the Brigade recommenced training with the 167th Infantry Brigade, and interesting and instructive field days took place.

From here also Major H.N.Clark Commanding 1/3rd London Battery was despatched to England to command a 2nd line Brigade, and Capt. G.J.C. Brady was transferred from the Bde. Amm. Col. to command this Battery.

Between the 2nd and 5th April 1916 the 1st and 2nd Batteries moved up into the line at ARRAS to reinforce the 14th Divisional Artillery. Three sections were placed in silent forward positions, and the remaining section of the 2nd Battery was placed into position near ARRAS Station to enfilade the trenches around the BEAURAINS Salient. All ranks worked hard on making good positions, and comfortable accommodation for the personnel.

On the 15th April 1916, the 93rd Battery, under Command of Major G.S. Cooper, joined the 56th Div. Arty., and was attached to the 1st London Brigade.

On the 8th May 1916, the Brigade, less the details in action at ARRAS, moved from their billets at REBREUVE and REBREUVIETTE to PAS.

On the 11th May 1916 the nomenclature of the Brigade was changed from 1/1 London Brigade, R.F.A. to 280th Brigade, R.F.A., and the Units were named as under :-

1/1st City of London Battery became	A/280.
1/2nd " " " "	B/280.
1/3rd " " " "	C/280.
93rd Battery "	D/280.

The 93rd Regular Battery was formed in 1898, but did not take part in the South African War. At the Outbreak of War it was serving in INDIA, where it had sent a contingent to the DURBAR of H.M. King George V at DELHI. It formed part of the Divisional Artillery of the LAHORE Division, and came to FRANCE with that Division, landing at MARSEILLES on the 28th Sept. 1914. It was then commanded by Major de Bruy. It proceeded via ORLEANS to BAILLEUL, and went into action on 24th Oct. 1914 at LAVENTIE, relieving a French Cavalry Division. The next day it fired its first rounds in a German attack which was driven back. On 11th Nov. 1914 it took part in the repulse of the Germans of that date. On 1st Dec. 1914 it moved back to rest at ROBECQ, and moved into the line again on the 6th at FESTUBERT, near where it remained for a time with a short period of rest, taking part in the capture and loss of the RICHEBOURG Ridge. The months of January and part of Februmgy were spent at rest at OCHILLES, and then the Battery moved back into the line near NEUVE CHAPELLE. It fired heavily for about a week, and suffered its first casualties. On April 23rd the Battery moved North to YPRES and took part in the 2nd Battle of YPRES, where gas was used for the first time. Some casualties were sufferred. On 7th May the Battery moved South again to the LAVENTIE Area, and took part in the bombardment for the FESTUBERT Battle of 17th May, 1915. The Battery remained in this area until November, having a quiet time except for the unsuccessful attack by the LAHORE Division on 25th Sept. 1915. During this time Captain (afterwards Major) G.S.Cooper took command. On 2nd Dec. 1915, it moved North to DICKEBUSCH, to assist the 2nd Canadian Division. It remained here until 19th Dec. 1915 suffering casualties from gas, and then moved out to WULVERDINGHE, where it left the LAHORE Division and was broken up to form two 4-gun Batteries. Capt. G.S.Cooper remained with the main part of the Battery which on 28th Feb. 1916 moved down to the coast at Cape GRIS NEZ for a month's rest and training. On 15th April 1916 the 93rd Battery under Command of Major G.S.Cooper joined the 56th Division.

On the 17th May 1916 the Brigade Ammunition Column left the Brigade and came under orders of the O.C., 56th D.A.C. It was subsequently disbanded when B.A.Cs. were abolished. Many of its personnel returned to the Brigade as reinforcements, others were absorbed by the D.A.C., and a few were sent to the Base.

On 28th May 1916 the 93rd Battery ceased to be D/280 and was transferred to the 283rd Brigade, R.F.A., while the original 1/11th London Howitzer Battery, under Command of Capt. E.R.C.Warrens, became D Battery of the 280th Brigade, R.F.A. This Battery was formerly a Unit of the 4th London (Howitzer) Brigade,R.F.A. This Brigade was formed on 1st April 1908 from the 2nd West Kent Volunteer Garrison Artillery, an old established Regiment which had sent a contingent to the South African War. Prior to its transfer to the Territorial Force it had been armed with old pattern Howitzers, but was not horsed. It was therefore well versed in high angle fire. The 4th London Brigade mobilized at its headquarters at HITHER GREEN, and marched out of London at the end of August 1914 with the other Units of the 1st London Divisional Artillery.. When the 1st London Brigade R.F.A? went to BLYTH, the 4th went to EDINBURGH where it remained all the winter acting as part of a mobile force in readiness to meet invasion. Its stay in

[ED]INBURGH was notable for the extreme discomfort of the barracks which had never been completed. The Brigade moved South in the spring and was afterwards billeted alongside the 1st London Brigade at WARREN, IPSWICH, the Officers combining with those of the 1st London Brigade in forming a Mess. The subsequent history of the Brigade is similar to that of the 1st London Brigade except that it went for a time into action in front of MERVILLE in December 1915. The 1/11th Battery was commanded on mobilization and until August 1916 by Major F.H.Bowater, and on that Officer proceeding to England to command a Brigade the command of the Battery devolved upon Captain (afterwards Major) E.R.C.Warrens. When made up to a 6-gun Battery in December 1916, it obtained its 3rd section from a New Army Unit, the 500th Battery, R.F.A.

BATTLE OF GOMMECOURT.

Work was now commenced and was soon in full blast on gun positions in front of HEBUTERNE for the great attack which was shortly to take place. On the night of the 1st/2nd June the guns and details of A and B Batteries were withdrawn from ARRAS and joined the Brigade. Working parties had already preceeded them. The time spent in ARRAS was, so far as war conditions allowed, a very happy one. Only two or three light casualties were sufferred, and with sufficient hard work and recreation the health and good spirits of the men were well maintained. The respective Brigade Commanders of the 14th Divisional Artillery to which the Batteries had been attached expressed themselves delighted with the good behaviour and the good work of the Batteries. The active section of B/280 had taken part in some effective bombardments of BEAURAINS and had cut wire as part of the general preparation for the big attack.

All Batteries now worked hard on preparation of positions for the attack on the GOMMECOURT Salient. At this time the trend of thought among Artillery Commanders, influenced doubtless by many months of trench warfare, favoured the erection of large and strong gun-pits. Consequently huge dumps of material were collected and a standard gun-pit was designed, and the plans issued to Batteries to guide them in the preparation and erection of these pits. Unfortunately the exegensies of the preliminary preparations were such that most Batteries had to move positions after doing much work on originally selected sites.

By the 17th June the guns of all Batteries of the Brigade including the 93rd Battery which was attached for tactical purposes were in position and registration took place. On the 19th June A/280 was detached from the 280th Brigade Group to be one of the wire cutting Batteries of the 282nd Brigade Group.

On the 24th June the Preliminary Bombardment commenced. Zero Day was to be notified later, and after some postponemnts was finally fixed for 1st July 1916. Between the 24th June and this date a very elaborate Artillery programme was carried out. A/280 cut wire, B/ and C/280 enfiladed the enemy trenches from the North, and D/280 and the 93rd bombarded frontally. For this operation D/280 was not in the 280th Brigade Group. A prodigious amount of ammunition was fired, and in light of later experience it must be admitted that much of it was wasted. On the 1st July the attack was launched by the 56th Division on the Southern Side GOMMECOURT Salient. The 280th Brigade Group commenced with a preliminary bombardment and at 7.30 a.m. began the creeping and other barrages for the actual assault. The guns remained in action during the whole of the day their barrage conforming to the fluctuating fortunes of the Infantry, and by nightfall when our Infantry were back in their own trenches the gunners, thoroughly exhausted by a week's preliminary firing and by a long and heavy day literally flung themselves down besides the guns and slept like logs. The expenditure of ammunition for the four 18-pdr Batteries of 4 guns each averaged 2600 rounds, and that of the Howitzer Battery 1600 during the attack and subsequent retirement. Lieut. G.E.Fisher performed courageous and useful work on Zero Day as Brigade F.O.O., and Captain H.V.Hummel assisted the Brigade Commander to work out the very complicated system of barrage for the attack.

During this battle and the long preliminary bombardment the Brigade's casualties were comparatively light. The enemy had not in those days perfected his policy of area strafing on Battery positions, and such counter-battery shoots as he did were of the ponderous type which gave the Battery personnel time to get clear before much damage was done. However some Batteries found that the enormous Third Army gun-pits were very large targets unless well camouflaged and after the battle when Battery positions were re-arranged it was found advisable to leave some of these large erections empty. They continued, however, to attract a good deal of fire from the enemy which might have done more harm in other directions

From now until the end of August after the front had quieted down, the Brigade spent a fairly peaceful time. Batteries of the Brigade, in different Groups, were spread over an area from BIENVILLERS to HEBUTERNE. Only in the distance did the gunners hear the incessant rolling of the guns in the big fight down South. However all considered that their turn would come, and finally on the night of 31st August the Brigade was withdrawn and bivouaced at the Wagon Lines.

The BATTLE of the SOMME.

On 1st Sept. 1916 the Brigade marched to the SOMME, and arrived at Wagon Lines near BRAY on the afternoon of the 5th. One section of A/280 moved into position near HARDECOURT that afternoon, and the next day the other Battery Commanders went forward to reconnoitre. It was a memorable day for those taking part in the reconnaissance. The shell-ravaged ground, the leafless tree-trunks, the unburied dead, and the litter of twisted wire and broken trenches brought home to them the hard nature of the operations in which they were going to take part.

By the 8th all Batteries of the Brigade were in action except that one section of C/280 was left out as a Divisional Pool and was made up with one section of the 109th Battery R.F.A. while the 93rd Battery similarly left a section out and reinforced B/281 with its other section.

The Brigade remained in acti[illegible] until the 31st Oct. approximately 8 weeks. During this time it advanced three times and took part in the major operations of the 9th September for the attack on GINCHY and GUILLEMONT; on the 15th September for the attack on LEUZE and BOULEAUX WOODS; on the 25th September for the attack on MORVAL. In addition during October, from its positions near MORVAL, it supported a number of minor attacks on the system of trenches known as HAZY, RAINY, FOGGY, etc., in front of Le TRANSLOY. In addition to the actual operations the Brigade did a large amount of shooting on S.O.S. calls, on wire cutting, and on harassing fire. For the whole period of 8 weeks the 4-gun Batteries averaged rather more than 500 rounds per day, and this expenditure put a very heavy burden on the horses. During the whole of the month of October after heavy and incessant rain the terrain became so bad that it was almost impossible to get vehicles up to the positions. All semblance of a road stopped short at GUILLEMONT, and from there onwards for more than a mile the going was atrocious. Improvised ammunition carriers were made out of the baskets from the ammunition wagons, and for the last part of the operations all ammunition, rations, and water went up by pack animals. It was most difficult to get material up to the guns and in consequence Officers and men suffered a good deal of discomfort.

Enemy shelling was by this time being directed very methodically on Battery areas and all Batteries suffered casualties. Majors H.P.Jones of A/280 and E.A.C.Warrens of D/280 were severely wounded early in the operations, the former being permanently disabled from further active service.

Casualties to the horses were caused more by the hard work than by enemy shells, and about 10% either died or were evacuated for debility. This figure however compares very favourably with many other Units engaged in the same operations.

Finally on the 31st October, some three weeks after the Infantry had been withdrawn, the Batteries of the Brigade were relieved by Batteries of the 8th Divisional Artillery. The withdrawal of the guns proved a very difficult task, and one section of A/280 which was not relieved until darkness had set in, got stuck in the mud and took three days to be got out. The remainder of the Brigade marched away from the SOMME on the 1st November and kept going till the afternoon of the 6th, when it arrived at Wagon Lines near MAROEUIL, and went into action on the following day on the NEUVILLE ST VAAST front in support of the 3rd Canadian Division.

At this time the Brigade was made up to 6-gun Batteries and was finally constituted as it now is by breaking up B/280 and transferring one section therefrom to each of A/280 and C/280 and by adding to the 93rd Battery one section of C/283, a New Army Battery. At the same time the 93rd Battery was transferred from the broken-up 283rd Brigade to the 280th Brigade, R.F.A. D/280 did not get its additional section until a later date. The Batteries were then commanded :-

A/280 Battery by Captain [illegible]. Bird.

93rd Battery by Major D. Thomson,
C/280 " Major G.C.J. Brady,
and D/280 " Major W.E. Batt.

This sector proved to be a very quiet one, there was scarcely any hostile artillery fire and the only source of trouble were the Minnenwerfer and the constant fear of Mines for which the sector was noted. The Batteries were able to take advantage of the comparative rest to get refitted and reclothed after the trying time on the SOMME, and with good stabling and little work the horses soon picked up. On the 1st December, after a very peaceful period of trench warfare, the Brigade was relieved by the 10th Canadian Brigade, R.F.A., and marched to the NEUVE CHAPELLE Area to cover its own Infantry.

WINTER IN FLANDERS.

All ranks were delighted to return to their own Infantry, and it was also a joy to be among the hospitable inhabitants of FLANDERS. After over six months spent in dug-outs it was a great luxury for Gunners to be billeted in houses where they were often sharing accommodation with the inhabitants. The sector proved to be very quiet. The enemy was almost entirely restricted to shooting the front trenches, with occasional straafs of gun positions. A lot of work was done on alternate positions, but although many of the positions occupied by the Batteries had been in existence over two years only on one occasion was a Battery shelled out. LAVENTIE, a town some 3,000 to 4,000 yards from the line, was never shelled and was almost fully occupied by inhabitants, many good houses remaining. The end of the month of January 1917 was notable firstly for the very hard weather which was experienced, and secondly for the series of operations which took place with regard to the establishment [illegible] maintainance of Raids in the enemy lines. These operations kept the gunners busy nearly every night for several days. A policy of annoying the enemy and wearing down his moral was maintained, and harassing fire was kept up both by day and night. Many combined Artillery and Trench Mortar shoots took place under the orders of the Infantry Brigade Commanders.

During this period [illegible]/280 was made up to a 6-gun Battery by the addition of a section from the 560th Battery. Major E.R.C. Warrens having returned from England, where he had gone wounded, took over his old Battery and Major W.E. Batt took over A/280.

On the 5th March the Brigade was relieved by the 246th Brigade of the 49th Division, and billeted for that night and the next at CALONNE-SUR-LYS.

THE BATTLE OF ARRAS.

On the morning of the 7th March the Brigade marched to the ARRAS Front. It was a most trying journey as the weather was bitterly cold and the roads frozen hard. On the 10th the Brigade arrived and billeted in LUCHEUX being very crowded. After four days spent in minor field operations it marched on the 14th to SIMENCOURT, and on the 17th preliminary reconnaissance was made by the O.C. Brigade and Battery Commanders of gun positions at ACHICOURT for the coming battle. On the 18th the Brigade moved into positions at ACHICOURT, but immediately received news that the enemy had retired from BEAURAINS. Further positions were then selected in the old No Man's Land, just South of BEAURAINS and work was immediately commenced therein and large quantities of ammunition taken up. On the 20th the guns were placed into these positions. Work was continued and the enormous dump of 1[illegible],000 rounds per Battery was hurried up. On the 25th orders were received to find advanced positions for two 18-pdr Batteries and these were selected in MERCATEL. Work was commenced on these and the guns moved in on the 30th. Very fine work was done by the drivers in taking up ammunition to forward positions, the approaches to which were constantly shelled.

Wire cutting was now commenced and proceeded with vigour until the 4th April the first day of the bombardment. From now until Zero Day a heavy bombardment and wire cutting programme was carried out.

On the 9th April at 7.45 a.m. the attack was launched. A long and complicated barrage programme was carried out by the Brigade, and the Batteries did some effective observed shooting to assist the Infantry in clearing up minor situations. The experience of the Infantry and a subsequent inspection proved that all wire allotted to the Brigade had been well and truly cut. On the two following days the Batteries fired at long range in support of mopping-up and minor operations. On the 12th April 1917

[In] the worst possible weather the Brigade advanced to positions in front [of] NEUVILLE VITASSE. Snow was thick on the ground and it was bitterly cold, so that the gunners were only too glad to work hard to keep xhxmx xsixsx warm - digging themselves and their guns well into the mud. Early next morning a programme shoot was fired to assist the further advance of our Infantry. For the next few days the Batteries did a little shooting at long range and remained in readiness to advance, this, however did not take place till the 17th April. On the 23rd a programme shoot was carried out to assist the further attack, and on the 25th the Batteries moved to their final positions in front of HENINEL. On the 28th the Brigade assisted in an attack by the Corps on the Left, and again on the 1st May it supported an attack by the 18th Division. On the 3rd May the Brigade fired a long and complicated programme to support an attack of that date. By this time the enemy resistance had been organised and many enemy batteries concentrate[d] on the front. Also for the first time a policy of organised harassing fire on Battery areas seemed to be instituted. Consequently when our guns opened up on the 3rd May the enemy retaliated with vigour. Fortunately the Batteries had dug themselves in well, and the resultant casualties were few. Nevertheless the 3rd May will long be remembered by gunners who took part in the operations by reason of the many hours of heavy firing and the disappointing results of the operations, which combined produced great mental and physical depression.

Thereafter this sector began to quieten down, though for a long time the enemy frequently and heavily bombarded the gun positions. By the x 10th May it was possible for the Batteries to be given a rest. The 93rd Battery was withdrawn to its Wagon Line until the 18th, and on the 26th A/280, C/280, and D/280 were similarly allowed to withdraw to their Wagon Lines in the neighbourhood of MERCATEL.

SUMMER 1917.

This period of rest was much appreciated by all ranks who had been strenuously engaged since the end of March in very bad weather. Battery and Brigade Sports were organised, and as much recreation enjoyed as possible.

The Batteries returned to the line on xxx 6th June, and engaged in an attack on TUNNEL TRENCH of the HINDENBURG LINE on the 16th, which was repeated on the 24th.

On the 26th the whole Brigade was withdrawn, and on the 28th proceeded to the VII Corps Rest Station at HENDECOURT, where it remained until 5th Ju[ly] when it marched to the YPRES Area, xxx arriving at OUDEZEELE on the 13th Ju[ly] 1917. This proved to be a very clean and comfortable village where all ranks were well billeted. Favoured with fine weather cricket and other sports became the order of the day, and the Brigade set itself out to enjoy what was in fact the only real rest it had had since the GOMMECOURT Offensive. The Brigade, however, was not permitted to fully enjoy this rest, and on the 17th July a party of 4 Officers and 182 Other Ranks proceeded up the line to the neighbourhood of the BLUFF for ammunition duties with the VI Corps Heavy Artillery. In fact many of the gunners actually manned the heavy guns. They returned on the 25th having suffered considerable casualties from gas.

THE THIRD BATTLE OF YPRES.

On the 29th the Brigade marched to Wagon Lines East of DICKEBUSCH, and were held in readiness to reinforce the front near ZONNEBEKE. On the 2nd and 3rd August the Brigade relieved the 45th Brigade of the 8th Division, taking over their guns in positions near HOOGE. From thence onwards began the most terrible time the Brigade has ever experienced in this War. The enemy shelled the Battery positions night and day. This shelling was generally more in the nature of harassing fire with occasional more serious counter-battery shoots. The ground being so wet digging was impossible and the personnel lived in holes in the ground a few inches deep covered with corrugated iron. By seeing that no more than one or two lived in each bivouac casualties were minimised, while a careful arrangement of the supply of ammunition at early dawn when apparently the enemy guns were taken off their tasks ready for S.O.S. purposes, kept the casualties to horses and drivers within bounds. Nevertheless casualties were heavy and most batteries lost about 100% of their gun-line strength in killed and wounded.

The Brigade supported major operations on the 10th, the 12th, the 16th and the 22nd August. It also fired on S.O.S. Calls on an average every other evening besides having a very heavy day on the 24th August when the enemy counterattacked in strength. On the 31st the Brigade pulled out to its Wagon Lines at VIJVERHOEK which had incidentally been shelled almost continuously by long range guns during the whole month. Fortunately the only damage caused by this long range gunnery was to a few horses and material. At the Gun-line, however, the shelling was the heaviest in the experience of the Brigade. On the 16th and 17th the whole of the guns of D/280 were put out of action. Enemy shell fire and exploding ammunition practically blew them to pieces, and except for the actual tubes of three Howitzers nothing was found worth salving. On this occasion Cpl. S. Ford received a D.C.M., Sgt. H.W. Linney a Bar to his M.M. and Sgt. R. Inskipp a M.M. for rescuing wounded men from the gun position under a continuous rain of enemy shells and bursting ammunition. In addition to the continuous shelling the weather was generally wet and both at gun and wagon lines much discomfort and misery was inflicted on all ranks.

On the 1st September the Brigade marched to ESQUELBEC for entrainment to the South, and it was the fervent hope of all ranks that never again would they see the YPRES Salient.

THE CAMBRAI FRONT.

On the 3rd September the Brigade arrived at BAPAUME, and occupied temporary lines under canvas on the outskirts of the destroyed town. On the nights of the 6th and 7th the Brigade relieved the 40th Brigade R.F.A. of the 3rd Division in the line at DOIGNIES. Brigade Wagon Lines were established on the outskirts of the broken village of HAPLINCOURT. This sector proved to be a very quiet one and with fine weather all ranks and the horses settled down to recover from the 5 weeks grueling in the YPRES Battle. Grazing was unlimited and the large uncultivated tracks of grass afforded excellent training ground for driving and riding drill. A lot of hard work was put into improving gun positions and building alternate positions and work was commenced on winter standings for the horses. About two months' hard work provided very excellent stabling for every horse in the Brigade. In addition Nisson Huts were erected for the men as well as cook-houses, forges and recreation rooms.

The Lord Mayor of London, who is Honorary Colonel of the Brigade, visited it during October and was highly delighted with the appearance of both men and horses.

During this period Captain J.V.Gray was appointed to Command A/280 in the place of Major W.E. Batt promoted to Lieut. Colonel.

At the end of October it became apparent that something was going to happen on this peaceful front, and under direction of the G.O.C.,R.A., 36th Division the Brigade began to build new gun positions in front of HERMIES and to fill them with ammunition to the extent of 600 rounds per gun. This work was attended with the utmost secrecy. Nothing was done when visibility was good, and every sod that was cut was carefully camouflaged. On the night of the 18th November one section from each Battery occupied the new positions, and on the following night the remainder of the Battery with the personnel moved in. About this time the Wagon Lines were vacated and the Batteries were squeezed up with the transport Units of the Division in order to allow reinforcing Artillery to come into the Brigade Wagon Lines. On the night of the 19th Lieut. Colonel W.E. Batt, Commanding the Brigade in the absence of Lieut. Colonel L.A.C. Southam on leave, moved up to Advanced Headquarters in front of HERMIES, and took over the Command of a Group consisting of the 173rd Brigade R.F.A. of the 36th Division with A/280 and the 93rd Battery. C/280 and D/280 became a sub-group at DEMICOURT for counter-battery work under Major E.R.C. Warrens D.S.O.

The night was very quiet until the early morning when the enemy apparently became aware that something was going to happen. The Battery positions were then harassed by enemy shell fire, and some casualties caused. At 6.20 a.m. on the 20th November the Artillery programme was commenced and consisted of a series of barrages moving from Right to Left as the Infantry worked Northwards up the HINDENBURG LINE. These barrages had to be fired without any previous registrations and on Lines which had been laid out magnetically by night. In spite of this they were fired within 150 yards of the advancing Infantry, and pronounced after the attack as excellent. An Officers' Patrol, consisting of Lieut. E.A. Shipton, M.C., [illegible]280 and Lieut. F.P. Hodge A/280 with the necessary signallers, advanced with the Infantry, and succeeded in maintaining telephonic communication during the whole day. This party came under machine gun fire at short range and one signaller was instantly killed. By strenuous endeavour it kept the line, and sent back information of the highest importance.. Lieut. F.P. Hodge was awarded the Military Cross.

That night the 18-pdr Batteries made a flank movement to BOURSIES, and returned to the 56th Division.

The 36th Division was very appreciative of the hard preliminary work and the excellent shooting on the day of the attack, and subsequently recommended the acting Brigade Commander for the C.M.G. which was awarded him in the New Years' (1918) Homours List.

At 11 a.m. on the morning of the 21st the Brigade supported at long range an attack on BOURLON WOOD, and on subsequent days until the 27th engaged in supporting the operations. During these operations Lieut. T.A.C. Davies when acting as F.O.O., accompanied by one signaller with a rifle captured 16 of the enemy. For this Lieut. Davies received a Bar to to his M.C., and the signaller received the M.M.

On the 30th November one of the heaviest days in the Brigades' history was experienced. Early in the morning the enemy heavily attacked TADPOLE COPSE and the trenches held by the 56th Division. From 9 a.m. until dark the guns rained shells on the advancing Infantry and enemy guns. Lieut. E.A. Shipton M.C. who was Brigade F.O.O. on this day had the unique experience of directing the fire of his, and other, Batteries into masses of Infantry and knocking out an enemy Field Battery endeavouring to come into action East of the CANAL DU NORD. The enemy again attacked next day, and the Brigade fired all day.

On the 4th December the Batteries were withdrawn to their original positions in BOURSIES in conjunction with the withdrawal of the Infantry from TADPOLE COPSE. The disappointment of the men was very keen. After the success of the initial operations and the stout resistance of our Infantry on the 30th November it was a severe blow to have to retire.

On the 5th the enemy heavily bombarded the evacuated trenches and advanced to their old lines offering very good targets to the guns. The succeeding days were quiet, and on the 12th and 13th the Brigade was relieved by Batteries of the 5th A.F.A. Brigade and marched to ARRAS.

THE DEFENCE OF VIMY.

On the 16th December the Brigade occupied Wagon Lines between SAINT CATHERINES and BAILLEUL, and on the nights of the 17th and 18th the Brigade moved into positions just South of BAILLEUL, relieving the 170th Brigade of the 31st Division. This front was a very quiet one but much harassing fire was done and a certain amount of enemy counter-battery work was directed on the Battery positions. Work was begun on rear positions in preparation for the expected enemy offensive. On the 14th and 15th January 1918 the Brigade was relieved in accordance with the Corps plan of keeping one Division of three in rest, and on the 16th proceeded to the AUBIGNY Area where the Brigade and Batteries were billeted in the villages of BETHANCOURT, BERLES, FREVIN-CAPELLE, and CAPELLE FERMONT.

This period was used in cleaning up and refitting. The G.O.C., Division, General Sir C.A. Hull K.C.B., and the G.O.C.,R.A., Brigadier-General R.J.G. Elkington C.M.G., D.S.O., inspected the Brigade and expressed themselves very satisfied with its appearance. Intensive training also took place.

On the 15th and 16th the Brigade went back to the line into its old positions. The period which ensued was notable for numerous raids by our troops; by hard work on rear positions; and harassing fire by roving guns and sections. Anti-tank guns were also placed in position.

On the 27th February Lieut. Colonel L.A.C. Southam D.S.O. unfortunately broke his ankle while acting as C.R.A., and Lieut. Colonel [illegible] Watt C.M.G. was appointed to command.

K As March wore on the rumours of the impending enemy attack became more persistent and all possible precautions were taken, including the reconnaissance and selection of positions to a considerable depth in rear.

harassing fire on the enemy lines was increased, and all ranks were warned to be in readiness for an attack.

Finally, after several false alarms, the enemy attacked on the morning of the 28th March. On the evening before D/280, which had occupied a forward position, was withdrawn to a rear position but the projected move of a forward section of the 93rd near ARLEUX was cancelled. At 3 a.m. the Brigade opened fire, and continued all day. Unfortunately at an early hour all telephone lines to Observation Posts were cut, but Lieut. G.S. Jones, C/280, who was Liason Officer with the Infantry Battalion managed to keep in communication practically all day and by about 10 a.m. an O.P. was established on the RIDGE by using a combination of Runners and telephone line. These runners did excellent work under heavy fire all day, one of them Gunner J.S. Mayhew received the M.M.

Heavy fire was poured into the advancing enemy and into the hostile guns endeavouring to advance into action. About 10 a.m. our Infantry were compelled to retire to the second line of resistance. This operation envolved the abandonment of the forward section of the 93rd Battery. Accordingly orders were sent to the Officer in Charge. He fired all his ammunition, and when our own barrage descended on his guns he blew them up as well as his dug-outs, and retired with his detachments, bringing away his wounded. For his courageous behaviour he was awarded the M.C. All this time the Batteries were being heavily shelled by the enemy. Three guns of A/280 were knocked out at an early hour, and many casualties suffered, including Major G.J.C. Brady C/280 who was severely wounded.

Ammunition was rushed up, and the guns remaining in action continued firing at a rapid rate until dark. Some 17,000 rounds were fired and there can be no doubt that heavy and important casualties were inflicted on the enemy.

That night the three 18pdr Batteries were withdrawn to rear positions across the BAILLEUL-ARRAS Road and the Brigade continued in action under the Canadians until the 8th when it was relieved by the 12th Australian F.A. Brigade, and proceeded at once to AGNY where it went into positions almost identical in situation to those occupied for the ARRAS Offensive of the year before. Capt. A.V. Reid took over command of C/280 rendered vacant by the casualty to Major G.J.C. Brady.

On arrival at these new positions the sector was still lively and the enemy did a good deal of harassing fire. A captured German Map showed that some of the gun positions were known to the enemy and these were moved. On our part we carried out sniping by day, and harassing fire by night. The front gradually assumed quiesence , and the enemy's fire took on more the nature of occasional organised counter-battery work. Also the Brigade supported several very successful raids by our own Infantry and the Canadians on our Right. On the 17th April D/280 position was heavily shelled and one gun was utterly destroyed, but casualties to personnel were slight. Work was put in hand in three series of rear positions . As the weather improved the enemy was very active at night bombing and casualties were suffered in the Brigade Wagon Lines at BARNAVILLE.

As the summer advanced the enemy became very tame on this front and practically all activity was on our side. During June sections were almost daily pulled out for training in the Back Areas, and the men devoted the long summer evenings to cricket and other recreations. The Brigade organised a Polo Club which played two afternoons a week at an old Aerodrome near WAGNONLIEU. This proved very attractive to Officers of the Division and neighbouring Units, the G.O.C. Division being a regular patron. Unfortunately, after several weeks, the enemy began to shell the ground which was in view from MONCHY, and the G.O.C. Division was reluctantly compelled to veto the amusement.

On the 21st July the Brigade was relieved by the 311th Brigade, A.F.A., and marched the next day to billets in the ACQ Area where intensive training was at once commenced. This, however, was not fated to last, and on the nights of the 30th and 31st July the Brigade marched back and occupied its old positions near BEAURAINS.

After a quiet period of a fortnight the Brigade moved out to Wagon Lines on the 15th and 16th August, being relieved by the 15th Division.

BULLECOURT - AND AFTER.

On the morning of the 22nd the Brigade and Battery Commanders reconnoitred forward positions near BOISLEUX-AU-MONT, and that evening the Batteries occupied them taking up 400 rounds of ammunition per gun. On the following morning the Brigade supported the Infantry attack, and fired a long programme. The attack waxx highly successful and the Brigade moved forward that night. Ontx the 26th the Brigade again supported a morning attack, and at 5 p.m. received orders to advance to support an attack at 7.30 p.m. The notice was so short that Batteries literally galloped into action, all ranks being keenly excited to arrive in time which was successfully accomplished. The Brigade did heavy firing in support of the attacks on CROISILLES and BULLECOURT, and inflicted heavy casualties on the enemy.

During the reconnaissance of positions near CROISILLES Lieut C.J. Edwards A/280 performed a very courageous act. A Battery Officer, having advancedxintaxthexopenxxx 2/Lieut T.O.O'Dell, having advanced into the open was shot down at short range by enemy machine gun fire. Lieut. C.J. Edwards and Sgn. C.F. Kew crawled forward over about 200 yards of exposed ground, and dragged 2/Lieut O'Dell into safety. They undoubtedly saved his life as his leg was shattered and he was bleeding to death. Lieut C.J. Edwards was awarded the M.C., and Sgnr. C.F.Kew the M.M.

The Brigade continued to advance almost daily, and occupied 8 different positions in quick succession. After our own Divisional Infantry had been withdrawn from the line it continued to fight under orders of the 40th Division, and then of the 63rd Division.

Very heavy work was thrown upon the drivers in carrying up ammunition and being ready at all times to advance. The enemy shelling consisted mainly of gas bombardments and the Battery Areas became so saturated with poison that it was impossible to prevent the effects being felt. Practically every Officer, including the Brigade Staff, had lost their voices, and many had their eyes affected more or less. Fortunately most of the casualties returned to duty after short rests at the Wagon Lines or in Hospital.

On the morning of the 3rd September the enemy retreated so fast that it was difficult to keep touch with him. On this morning the Intelligence Officer, Lieut. R.F.Hodge M.C., made a daring reconnaissance on horseback riding almost to the CANAL DU NORD to the advanced outpost line of the Infantry. He came under rifle and shell fire and his horseholder Dvr. D. Walford had his horse shot under him. The latter was awarded the M.M. On the morning of the 5th, just as Batteries were moving into positions East of PRONVILLE orders were received to withdraw to CROISILLES. All ranks and the horses were terribly fatigued, but it was with a feeling of regret that the Brigade turned back after the exciting and successful advance of of the preceeding few days. As the Batteries moved back through QUEANT the roads were heavily shelled, but with extraordinary good luck they came through with very slight casualties.

A feature of the operations was the excellence of the communications due to the splendid organisation of the Brigade Signal Section under Lieut. R.A.Inglis, who received a M.C.

On the 7th September the Brigade moved into fresh positions near DURY relieving an Artillery Brigade of the 1st Division. These positions were of a very elementary nature and work was commenced forthwith, and forward positions constructed and occupied at RECOURT WOOD and SAUDEMONT. The role of the Division at this time was forming a protective flank with the enemy on two sides of a square.xxx A good deal of shelling was experienced by the Batteries, mainly gas. Towards the end of the month the Brigade was engaged almost daily in putting down heavy flank barrages to assist operations on our Right, and to cover reconnaissances in force on our Front. On the 27th September the Brigade fired a very heavy programme, expending some 16,000 rounds to support the attack of our Infantry across the CANAL DU NORD and the capture of SAUCHY CAUCHY and SAUCHY LESTREE.

On the 29th the Brigade withdrew to its Wagon Lines to VILLERS-lez-CAGNICOURT into Corps Mobile Reserve.

On the 1st October the Brigade relieved the 285th Brigade R.F.A. near OISY-LE-VERGER, and once more formed part of a protective flank. Wire-cutting was engaged in on the 5th and 6th in front of AUBENCHEUL, which was occupied by our Infantry on the 8th, and later, under the Canadians the Brigade was engaged in following the retreating enemy.

On the 20th October the Brigade withdrew to [illegible] in Army Reserve, and immediately commenced to refit and clean up. The G.O.C. Division arranged to inspect the Brigade but on the eve of the day arranged, viz 29th October, orders were received xxxx late in the evening to march to THIANT. After an all-night march the Brigade arrived early on the morning of the 30th, and at once selected positions and commenced work thereon and laying up ammunition.

TOWARDS MONS - THE LAST PHASE.

On the night of the 31st October the guns were placed in position, and on the following morning a heavy programme was fired to support the advance of the 49th Division. This barrage was one of the heaviest of the war, and subsequent inspection of the ground showed that most terrible execution had been wrought on the German Infantry. From that time onward operations became a pursuit of the enemy.

Our own Divisional infantry came into the line on the 4th November, and the Brigade supported them in attacks on SEBOURG, ANGREAU, and the country beyond. To increase mobility xxx a policy of leapfrogging Artillery Brigades was instituted and in addition C/280 XXXXXX was detailed as a special Battery to advance in close support with the Infantry. This battery did some good work, and its commander, Act/Major A.V. Reid was awarded the M.C. The Brigade continued to press forward, and on the 11th November found itself in temporary Reserve at BLAREGNIES. It was about to move forward into action when orders were received to cease fire for the Armistice at 11 a.m. The hour came and passed without any incident, and the Brigade settled down to clean up and refit.

A detachment of the Brigade was sent to MONS to march past General Sir H.S. Horne K.C.B., K.C.M.G., Commanding the First Army, on that Officer's Official Entry into the Belgian City.

Thereafter Education, Recreation, and Demobilization kept the Brigade busy.

x x x x x

On the 8th December the Brigade, with the 1st London Regiment, gave H.M. the KING a rousing reception on his passing through the village of GOEGNIES-CHAUSSEE where it was billeted.

The Brigade was commanded onx the cessation of hostilities by Lieut. Colonel W.M. Batt, C.M.G., and Batteries as follows :-

A/280 by Major J.V. Gray, M.C.
93rd by Major A. Thomson, M.C.
C/280 by Major A.V. Reid, M.C.
D/280 by Major E.H.G. Warrens, D.S.O.

x x x x x

STATISTICS.

An analysis of the Brigade casualties shows that in this respect it has been exceedingly fortunate. No doubt, however, this good fortune can be ascribed in no small measure to the way in which experienced Officers and men returned to the Brigade after being sick or wounded. By strenuous efforts of the Brigade Office and of the Officers and men concerned many were able to avoid the apparent policy of sending them to other Units, and happily rejoined their old Brigade. Many experienced Officers also preferred to remain with their own Unit in subordinate positions rather than go in promotion to other Units.

The total casualties due to enemy shell fire and rifle fire were :-

	Officers.	Other Ranks.
Killed...	1.	57.
Wounded...	26.	354.
Missing...		1.

Total 439.

The one missing man was a signaller on the [illegible] who apparently wandered into the enemy lines in the dark and was either killed or captured.

Guns utterly destroyed 2. Guns damaged but repaired 60 and 2 Guns abandoned to the enemy after being blown up.

A rough estimate of the rounds fired by the Brigade during the time it formed part of the 56th Division is upwards of half a million.

x x x x x

The following Decoration have been awarded to Officers and Men of the Brigade :-

C.M.G. Lieut. Colonel W.E. Batt.

D.S.O. Lieut. Colonel L.A.C. Southam. Majors H.R.P. Jones, E.R.C.Warrens, G.C.J.Brady.

M.C. and Bar. Lieut. T.H.C.Davies.

M.C. A/Majors D.Thomson, J.V.Gray, A.V.Reid; Captains H.V. Hummel, G.Mallett, H.J.P.Oakley, W.G.Grant.
Acting Captains F.K.Headington, F.M.Cade, F.E.Redfern.
Lieutenants W.D.Loudon, E.A.Shipton, R.C.Oliver, F.P. Hodge, G.J.Palfrey, C.J.Edwards, H.L.Wood, R.S.Inglis, C.E.Gould.
2/Lieut J.C.Reed.(since deceased).

D.C.M., M.M. and Bar. Cpl. S.Ford.

M.M. and Bar. B.S.M.Linney H.W., Cpl. Phillips J.R., Bdr. Presbury W.W. Bdr. Moss R.A., Cpl.Sgnr. Snodgrass C.

M.M. and M.S.M. Sgt. Flannagan J.L., BSM McCARTNEY

M.M. B.S.M.Bellamy W.H., Sgt.Norris H.C., Cpl.Braithwaite, Cpl.Cook, Sgt.Graham J., Bdr.Donovan H., Bdr.Taylor B., Bdr.Browne N., Sgt.Inskipp W., Sgt.Minns D., Pioneer W.Doyle, Cpl.Williams E., Bdr.Blann, Bdr.Sporton H.C., Bdr.Lockwood G., French Interpreter Chiron, Gnr.Harding F.C., Sgt.Maunder F.J., Gnr J.S.Mayhew, Gnr Williamson A, BQMS Lovell H.R., Gnr.Tunney J., Cpl.Belger A., Bdr. Wilson, Cpl.Matthews F., Gnr.Topley G., Cpl.Winning P., Cpl.Fletcher W.T., Gnr.Kew C.F., Sgt.Napper E., B.Q.M.S. Gore A.F., Sgt.Wallen A., Cpl.Ansell W., Dvr.Walford D., Dvr.Reed J.G., Dvr.Halligan C., Sgt.Francis F.W., Dvr.Gavin T., Sgnr.Clabbon F.W., Bdr.McGrath J., R.S.M. McCartney J.F., Signr.Whitelegg J.R.
Sgt Spencer, Sgt Townsend Bdr Burch

M.S.M. R.S.M. W.J. Lancaster.
B.Q.M.S. Moore. A. B.S.M. Turner W.S.
Sgt. H. Rumney. BQMS Rowland T
BQMS C. Webster
Cpl Fitter Gunthorpe AE.

In addition many other original members of the Brigade have won Decorations in other Units to which they had been transferred, notably :-

D.S.O. Major H.N. Clark.

M.C. Major W.B. Telling.

D.C.M. R.S.M. Bedloe F.C. Farr. Sgt. Apps W.

The following Foreign Decorations have been awarded to Officers and Other Ranks :-

French CROIX DE GUERRE. A/Major A.V. Reid M.C.

Belgian CROIX DE GUERRE. Lieut. Colonel L.A.C. Southam D.S.O.
B.S.M. Leslie W. Cpl. Wilson C.J.

ADDENDUM.

After line 50, page 1, - 'Transfer overseas', insert :-

During this period Colonel [illegible] Stollery, who had commanded the Brigade for so long, was informed that he was over the age for Foreign Service, and the Command of the Brigade passed to Lieut. Colonel [illegible] Southam, Colonel Stollery proceeding to London to take over Command of the newly formed Second Line Brigade much to the regret of all ranks of his old Unit.

Reorganisation of Bde from 3 Batteries to 4 Batteries – being 4 gun Batteries only

R of B from 4 18 Pr Batt to 3 15 Pdr

5 1 How Batt still 4 g

R of Batt into 6 guns or 6 hows

Any inf as regards D/126 & 500 How Batt

Army Form C. 2118.

WAR DIARY
or
INTELLIGENCE SUMMARY. 280th (City of London) Brigade, R.F.A.

(*Erase heading not required.*)

Instructions regarding War Diaries and Intelligence Summaries are contained in F. S. Regs., Part II. and the Staff Manual respectively. Title pages will be prepared in manuscript.

Place	Date	Hour	Summary of Events and Information February 1919.	Remarks and references to Appendices
GOEGNIES-CHAUSSEE.			Severe weather was experienced during the early part of the month. Nothing worthy of note occurred during the month. Demobilization proceeded very slowly. About 50% of the Brigade horses were disposed of either by sale or despatch to Base Remount Depots. No Stores were handed in during the month. Much time was devoted to Sport particularly football. The civilian population engaged itself to a very considerable extent in compiling claims for damages against the Brigade. On investigation most of these claims were found to be either imaginary or for damage done by the Enemy when in this area - or in two cases for damage alleged against the British troops when they retreated through the area in 1914. The avariciousness displayed on the part of the civilians did not tend to improve the relationship between them and those who had reclaimed their Country. Apparently in case of Strikes or possibly in fear of "Bolshevism" orders were again received to support the Belgian Military Authorities in case of disturbances in the area. The epidemic of "Influenza" whilst affecting the civilians and causing many deaths did not, happily, affect the troops of the Brigade.	
	27-2-19.		Lieut.Colonel, Commanding 280th Brigade, R.F.A.	

D. D. & L., London E.C. (19344) Wt W5300/P713 750,000 3/18 E 688 Forms/C2118/16.

To:- 58th Div. Arty. D/1894

Reference S.G.451/27.

Herewith 4 small incidents in triplicate which it is thought may be the sort of thing required.

Lieut.Colonel,
20-[illegible]-18. Commanding 290th Brigade, R.F.A.

RECORD OF INSTANCES OF GALLANT CONDUCT ON THE PART OF THE ARTILLERY DURING THE RECENT WAR.

1. It has been suggested by various Artillery Officers at different times during the last two years that some steps should be taken to recall many of the incidents which have taken pl place during the last four years shewing the skilful and courageous handling of guns under various tactical circumstances.

2. Such a record, if carefully edited, should beof inestimable value for carrying on the best traditions of the Regiment and teaching all ranks what can be done, and should be done, under varying circumstances.

The past year has given many openings for initiative and tactical skill in handling guns both in offence and defence. Accurate and concise accounts of such opportunities successfully grasped, will be no less value for the instruction of future generations than records of gallant conduct for their emulation.

3. With this object in view it is proposedto collect from R.A. Units the details of such incidents while the stories are still vividly impressed in the memories of various spectators. The main difficulty rests in giving the battle picture sufficiently clearly, and yet in sufficiently compressed form, to enable the reader to understand the opperations as a whole, so that he may appreciate the skillful handling of the guns as a portion of that whole.

4. Narrative should be, if anything, on the side of lengthiness and detail, and good plans and maps should be attached so as to assist the future editor in compressing the stories without missing the salient points for the instruction of future gunners.

5. Care should be taken in all naratives to include the following details:-

(a) Name, number or designation of the unit.
(b) Name of the Officer, N.C.O or man in command.
(c) Exact date and time of the occurence.
(d) Formation to which unit belonged at the time of the occurence.
(e) Clear description of the locality, mentioning well known places in the vicinity and avoiding local, and possibly, obscure names.

6. Narratives when completed should be forwarded to R.A. Headquarters, First Army, through the normal R.A. Channels. On receipt these narratives will be examined, tabulated, where necessary retyped and maps or diagrams copied if required.

The complete collection of narratives will in due course be forwarded to R.A., G.H.Q., for dispatch to the editor selected.

Reference SC 451/27

Narratives of Incidents in 280 Bde RFA

1). On the morning 28th March 1918 the 56th Division was holding the Southern Spur of the VIMY RIDGE and the 280 Bde RFA was covering the 169 Infantry Brigade holding GAVRELLE. A Section of the 93rd Battery RFA of the 280 Bde RFA occupied a forward ~~outpost~~ position near ARLEUX a few hundred yards behind our front line trenches and from which position it was able to enfilade an intricate system of trenches in front of a post known as MILL POST near GAVRELLE. An enemy attack was hourly expected and the enemy's preliminary bombardment commenced at 3 am on the 28th March. The evening before the withdrawal of this forward section had been discussed but the position was so valuable that it was decided to risk its loss. At 7.20 am the Germans attacked in great strength overwhelming the Infantry forward posts. The remaining ~~British~~ Infantry ~~fought most~~ defended ~~determinedly~~ the main line of resistance most ~~stub~~ stubbornly but by 10 am [illegible] evident that there was danger of the enemy getting behind our troops and a withdrawal to the next defensive line was ordered. This line was behind the 93rd forward section and consequently the OC 280 Bde telephoned to the Section Commander Lieut. G J Palfrey MC and ordered him to fire away all his ammunition and as the infantry retired to destroy his guns and retire with them. This order was duly carried out. Lieut Palfrey fought his section under shell and rifle fire until our barrage had crept back to his section. He then placed a round in muzzle and bore thus shattering the muzzle of each gun, set fire to his dug outs and papers and retired carrying his dial sights and breech blocks. The detachments bearing their wounded were able by making a circuitous route to reach the main Battery Position in safety. The coolness and determination of Lieut Palfrey and his detachments were worthy of greatest praise.

2/ On the 22 August 1917 the
280 Bde R.F.A. occupied positions
near HOOGE ~~[illegible]~~ immediately NORTH
of ZOUAVE WOOD. ~~A Battery~~
~~[illegible]~~ Owing to the impossibility of
digging and bringing up material
the guns had little cover. At
7 a.m. the Brigade was called upon
to fire a barrage programme in
connection with an infantry attack.
Soon after the start of the programme
an enemy shell burst behind
No 6 gun of A Battery 280 Bde
(commanded by Major W. E. Batt). Of
the detachment of four one was
killed and two severely wounded.
The fourth Gunner P. Harding M.M.
assisted the Battery Medical Orderly
to carry away the two wounded
men and then literally removed
the remains of the dead man
from the mechanism of the gun.
~~[illegible]~~ ~~[illegible]~~ Owing to the casualties
it was impossible for the moment
to ~~[illegible]~~ detach men from other
~~[illegible]~~ sub-sections, ~~[illegible]~~ and
Gunner Harding though suffering
from shock and concussion

finished the programme firing his gun unaided for 40 minutes. In the circumstances it was a wonderful feat of endurance

---

3/ On the 19 August 1917 D Battery 280 Bde RFA (Commanded by Major E.R.C. Warrens DSO) was in action North of ZONNEBEKE near ~~the~~ ~~the~~ HALFWAY HOUSE. During the morning the enemy put down a terrific bombardment upon this and neighbouring batteries. Very soon ammunition was set on fire and the Battery Commander ordered the detachments to clear the Battery Position. On a muster being made it was found that two men were absent. By this time the Battery position was an inferno. Enemy shells and dumps of our own ammunition were bursting continually.

~~At~~ Sergts Lummey H.W., Inskipp W and Cpl Ford S. at once volunteered to return and search the position. This they did at imminent risk of their lives and found one wounded man in a [illegible] whom they brought away. They were hardly clear when a terrific explosion occurred. ~~On~~ a subsequent inspection showed that of the six guns nothing was left but scrap metal and more than one had utterly disappeared.

4/ On the 25th August 1918 the 280 Bde occupied positions S.W. of BOISLEUX St MARC. At 5 pm orders were received to advance the Bde to support an attack on the trenches between BOIRY BECQUERELLE and CROISELLES at 7.30 that evening. The wagon lines were some distance from the guns and utmost despatch was necessary. All Battery Commanders immediately went forward selected their positions worked out their barrages and put their guns in shell holes into action in time. In particular C/280 commanded by Major A.V. REID M.C. had an exciting time. The ground sloped gently up to SUMMIT trench which was our Infantry front line. Behind a small intervening rise most of the Divisional Artillery had found positions, which determined Major Reid to advance further under the enemy crest to a position some 600 yards behind our Infantry. As the Battery moved up the intervening crest was heavily bombarded with enemy gas shell. The Battery leader Lieut E. L. Wood MC was in a dilemma. To stop, ~~to~~ adjust gas masks and make a detour would mean being late for the barrage programme. He decided to make a dash for it. Giving the signal to gallop, he ~~pushed~~ dashed his Battery through the gas barrage and got into action just in time to commence the programme. His casualties were small. The incident shows that after nearly three years of trench warfare a ~~Batt~~ well ~~[illegible]~~ trained Battery is able to rise to the occasion.

Army Form C. 2118.

Instructions regarding War Diaries and Intelligence Summaries are contained in F. S. Regs., Part II. and the Staff Manual respectively. Title pages will be prepared in manuscript.

WAR DIARY
or
INTELLIGENCE SUMMARY. 280th (City of London) Brigade, R.F.A.

(Erase heading not required.)

Place	Date	Hour	Summary of Events and Information MARCH 1919.	Remarks and references to Appendices
GOEGNIES-CHAUSSEE,	1st - 9th.		The slow disintegrating process of demobilization proceeded.	
	10th.		The 93rd Battery, R.F.A. left the Brigade to join the 18th Army Brigade, R.F.A. marching out with 3 Officers, 115 O.Rs. and 71 Horses.	
	16th & 17th.		The Brigade's Guns and Ammunition Wagons were transported to JEMAPPES by Motor Lorry haulage.	
	19th.		The Balance of the Brigade - Brigade Headquarters, A, C & D/280 was moved by Motor Lorry to FLENU about 3 miles West by South of MONS. Here excellent ~~XXXXXXX~~ Billet accomodation was found and most men had beds in view of the fact that the billet strength of the Brigade was but 160 approx.	
FLENU.	25th.		The Brigade was ordered to find a Guard of 2 Officers and 160 O.Rs. to preserve order and stop pilfering at MONS Station.	
	26th.		The town of JEMAPPES where the Brigade had all its Guns and Wagons parked was placed in Quarantine on account of Small-Pox. This caused some slight inconvenience and necessitated a further call on the Brigade's depleted personnel for the purpose of picqueting this Town.	
	27th.		Embargo on JEMAPPES lifted. The last few men eligible and available for the normal machinery of demobilization were dispatched. The residue now consisted of 59 O.Rs per Battery (10 O.Rs H.Q) and a few O.Rs. awaiting posting to the Army of the Rhine.	
	28th.		The total animal strength of the Brigade to-day being reduced to 4 Mules - Rations, Stores etc. are being delivered by Motor Transport. Guard at MONS Station relieved.	
	29th.		A Guard of 1 Officer & 15 O.Rs. again ordered to be posted at MONS Station. This detachment forming part of a main Guard found by the 56th Divisional Artillery.	

[signature]
Lieut.Colonel,
Commanding 280th Brigade, R.F.A.

D. D. & L., London E.C.
(10344) Wt W5300/P713 750,000 3/18 E 888 Forms/C2118/16.

Army Form C. 2118.

Instructions regarding War Diaries and Intelligence Summaries are contained in F. S. Regs., Part II. and the Staff Manual respectively. Title pages will be prepared in manuscript.

WAR DIARY
or
INTELLIGENCE SUMMARY. 280th(City of London) Brigade, R.F.A.

(Erase heading not required.)

Place	Date	Hour	Summary of Events and Information APRIL 1919.	Remarks and references to Appendices
FLENU.			The Brigade remained at FLENU. Balance of the conscripts and the few O.Rs. and Officers who volunteered were dispatched to the Army of the Rhine, reducing the Ration Strength to approximately 130 men.- Rations and Ordnance were delivered by M.T. The four mules of the Brigade being used for Post, Coal-fetching and the rolling of a Cricket Pitch. Stores were sent to a large Warehouse at JEMAPPES which necessitated the maintenance of another Guard in addition to those already maintained at MONS Station and at the JEMAPPES Gun Park. Owing to the fact that there was so little to occupy the minds of all those remaining in the Brigade considerable ennui developed. In an attempt to stay the further rapid development of mental and physical atrophy efforts were made to play Football, Cricket, Racquets, Golf etc. xxxxxx Whist Drives and Dances were organised and Lectures given. Dances were difficult as the local men were hard to placate if our men danced with their women folk. A considerable amount of leave was granted to all ranks so that they might visit places of interest in Belgium and France, whilst leave to England continued good. Men who had only been able previously to go home once in 20 - 24 months now going home again after 5 months absence from home. At this period of the year Spring was felt to have arrived and there were a few indications of this visible at FLENU. But the verdure was overshadowed by the blackness of the atmosphere and the hugh slag or spoil heaps which abound in this area, locally known as the "Borinage".	

Major,
Commanding 280th Brigade, R.F.A.

D. D. & L., London E.C.
(10349) W1 W5300/P713 750,000 3/18 E 688 Forms/C2118/16

DIARY OF EVENTS of 56th. DIVISION
for the period 5/2/1916 to 11/11/1918.

1916.

Febry. 5th.-26th.	Division formed - HALLENCOURT Area.
Febry. 27th.	Division moved to DOMART Area.
Febry. 28th.- March 10th.	Division remained DOMART Area.
March 11th.	Division moved DOULLENS Area.
March 12th-13th.	Division remained DOULLENS Area.
March 14th.	Division moved to LE CAURCY Area.
March 15th. - May. 5th.	Division remained LE CAUROY Area.
May. 6th.	Division moved to DOULLENS Area.
May. 7th.	Division moved to HENU Area.
May. 8th.	Division took over Line GOMMECOURT Sector.
May. 9th.-14th.	Division in line GOMMECOURT Sector.
May. 15th. - June 30th.	Division remained in Line GOMMECOURT Sector and preparation made for Battle of GOMMECOURT which included a new system of Trenches along the whole Divisional Front.
July. 1st.	BATTLE OF GOMMECOURT.
July 2nd.-3rd.	Division in Line GOMMECOURT Sector.
July 4th.	Division took over FONQUEVILLIERS-HANNESCAMPS Sector.
July 5th. - Aug. 20th.	Division remained FONQUEVILLIERS-HANNESCAMPS Sector.
Aug. 21st. - Septr. 2nd.	Division marched South to ST.RIQUIER Area.
Septr. 3rd.	Division moved forward to HAPPY VALLEY.
Septr. 4th. - Octr.10th.	Division engaged on SOMME Front. Division took over Line near FALFEMONT FARM 4/9/1916 and was withdrawn to MEALTE for one day (28/9/1916) during this period.

Principal Actions.

LEUZE WOOD	...	...	7th.-9th/9/1916.
LOOP TRENCH.	...	...	15/9/1916.
COMBLES	...	...	26/9/1916.
LE TRANSLOY (Brown Line)	...	...	1/10/1916 and 7/10/1916.

Octr. 11th.	Division withdrawn to CITADEL (Somme Area)
Octr. 12th.	Division moved to PICQUINY Area.
Octr. 13th-22nd.	Division remained PICQUINY Area.
Octr. 23rd-26th.	Division entrained north to LA GORGUE Area.
Octr. 27th.	Division took over line VIEILLE CHAPELLE Sector.
Octbr. 28th.- Mch.3rd.1917	Division remained in VIEILLE CHAPELLE Sector, gradually moving North to just East of LAVENTIE. During this period Division held posts in German Front Line (Bertha, Flame etc.)

1917.	
Mch. 4th.-13th.	Division left LAVENTIE Area 4/3/1917, and marched to WILLEMAN Area, but was immediately recalled and Division proceeded to ARRAS Front.
Mch. 14th.	Division took over Line ACHICOURT Sector.
Mch 15th.-17th.	Division remained ACHICOURT Sector.
Mch. 18th.	Enemy withdrew, and BEAURAINS captured, our line halting just west of NEUVILLE VITASSE.
Mch. 19th -) Apl. 8th.)	Division in NEUVILLE VITASSE Sector preparing for Attack.
Apl. 9th -) Apl. 19th.)	ARRAS BATTLE.
	NEUVILLE VITASSE 9/4/1917.
	HEININEL (Rum Jar) 12/4/1917.
	WANCOURT TOWER 14/4/1917.
Apl. 20th.	Division moved to WANQUETIN Area.
Apl. 21st-27th.	Division remained WANQUETIN Area.
Apl. 28th.	Division returned to Battle WANCOURT Sector
Apl. 29th. -) May. 2nd.)	Division remained WANCOURT Sector.
May. 3rd.	CAVALRY FARM.
May. 4th-20th.	Division engaged in minor operations around CAVALRY FARM, TOOL TRENCH etc.
May. 21st.	Division moved to WARLUS Area.
May. 22nd-23rd.	Division remained WARLUS Area.
May. 24th.	Division moved to HABARCQ Area.
May. 25th -) June 9th.)	Division remained HABARCQ Area.
June 10th.	Division took over Line WANCOURT Sector.
June 11th -) July 3rd.)	Division remained WANCOURT Sector.
July 4th.	Division moved to LE CAUROY Area.
July 5th-22nd.	Division remained LE CAUROY Area.
July 23rd.	Division moved North to EPERLECQUES Area.
July 24th -) Aug. 5th.)	Division remained EPERLECQUES Area.
Aug. 6th.	Division removed to RENINGHELST-ABEELE Area.
Aug. 7th-11th.	Division remained RENINGHELST-ABEELE Area.
Aug. 12th.	Division took over line GLENCORSE WOOD Sector.
Aug. 13th-15th.	Division remained GLENCORSE WOOD Sector.
Aug. 16th.	Battle for GLENCORSE WOOD & INVERNESS COPSE.
Aug. 17th.	Division remained in line.
Aug. 18th.	Division moved to RENINGHELST-STEENVOORDE Area.
Aug. 19th-23rd.	Division remained RENINGHELST-STEENVOORDE Area.
Aug. 24th.	Division moved to EPERLECQUES Area.
Aug. 25th-29th.	Division remained EPERLECQUES Area.
Aug. 30th.	Division moved South to BAPAUME Area.
Aug. 31st.) Septr. 3rd.)	Division remained BAPAUME Area.
Septr. 4th.	Division took over Line LAGNICOURT-MORCHIES-LOUVERVAL Sector.
Septr. 5th.) Novr. 19th.)	Division remained in Line.
Novr. 20th.	First Battle for CAMBRAI (TADPOLE COPSE)

1917.	
Novr. 21st-29th.	Division continued to be engaged in Battle for CAMBRAI.
Novr. 30th.	Enemy Counter Attack (MOEUVRES-TADPOLE COPSE)
Decr. 1st.	Division remained in Line.
Decr. 2nd.	Division withdrawn to BAPAUME Area.
Decr. 3rd.	Division moved to FOSSEUX Area.
Decr. 4th.	Division remained FOSSEUX Area.
Decr. 5th.	Division moved to ROCLINCOURT Area.
Decr. 6th.	Division remained ROCLINCOURT Area.
Decr. 7th.	Division took over VIMY RIDGE Sector (GAVRELLE-OPPY)
Decr. 8th. - Jan. 3rd. 1918.	Division remained in Line.
Jan. 4th.	Division moved to VILLERS CHATEL Area.
Jan. 5th - Feb. 6th.	Division remained in VILLERS CHATEL Area.
Feb. 7th.	Division took over Line VIMY RIDGE Sector.
Feb. 8th - Mch. 27th.	Division remained in Line.
Mch. 28th.	Enemy attacked <u>SCARPE VALLEY (GAVRELLE)</u>
Mch. 29th.	Division remained in Line.
Mch. 30th.	Division moved to ECOIVRES Area.
Mch. 31st - Apl. 6th.	Division remained ECOIVRES Area.
Apl. 7th.	Division moved to DAINVILLE Area, and took over TILLOY Front. (ARRAS)
Apl. 8th. - July 13th.	Division remained in Line.
July 14th.	Division moved to DIEVAL Area.
July 15th - Aug. 19th.	Division continually on the move between ARRAS and DIEVAL.
Aug. 20th.	Division moved South and took over CROISILLES Front.
Aug. 21st-30th.	BULLECOURT and attendant fighting.

Principal Actions.

BOIRY & BOYELLES	...	...	23/8/1918.
SUMMIT TRENCH.	...	...	24/8/1918.
SENSEE & NELLIE AVENUE	...		27/8/1918.
BULLECOURT.	...	...	28th-31st/8/1918.

Aug. 31st.	Division withdrawn to BOISLEUX AU MONT.
Septr. 1st-4th.	Division remained BOISLEUX AU MONT.
Septr. 5th.	QUEANT Area and back.
Septr. 6th.	Division remained in BOISLEUX AU MONT.
Septr. 7th.	Division moved to VIS EN ARTOIS Area.
Septr. 8th.	Division took over Line RECOURT-ETERPIGNY Sector.
Septr. 9th-28th.	Division remained in RECOURT Sector gradually side-stepping South to just north of MARQUION.
Septr. 27th.	Second Battle for CAMBRAI. (SAUCHY LESTREE) (SAUCHY CAUCHY)
Septr. 28th.	Advance continued to CANAL DE LA SENSEE.

1918.

Septr. 29th.	Division remained in line and took over AUBIGNY-AU-BAC. Sector.
Septr. 30th. –) Octr. 13th.)	Division remained in PALLEUL & AUBIGNY-AU-BAC Sector.
Octr. 14th.	Division withdrawn to MARQUION Area.
Octr. 15th.	Division moved to HAUTE AVESNES Area.
Octr. 16th. –) Octr. 29th.)	Division remained HAUTE AVESNES Area.
Octr. 30th.	Division moved by Bus to LIEU ST. AMAND – DOUCHY Area.
Octr. 31st –) Novr. 1st.)	Division remained LIEU ST. AMAND-DOUCHY Area.
Novr. 2nd.	Division took over line SAULTAIN Sector.
Novr. 3rd.	Enemy withdrew and pursued. SAULTAIN Captured.
Novr. 4th.	SEBOURG Captured.
Novr. 5th.	ANGREAU Captured.
Novr. 6th.	Advance checked by Enemy Roadguard. ANGRE Captured.
Novr. 7th–9th.	Advance continued to HARVENGT Area.
Novr. 10th.	Division relieved by 63rd. Division and remained in support
Novr. –11th.	Division in support to 63rd. Division in HARVENGT-ATHIS Area.

ANALYSIS.

Period 5/2/1916 to 11/11/1918.	1010 days.
No. of days spent by Division in Rest.	330 days.
No. of days spent by Division in a quiet Sector.	195 days.
No. of days Spent by Division in an Active Sector.	385 days.
No. of days spent by Division in Active Operations.	100 days.
TOTAL.	1010 days.

10th. April 1919.

Instructions regarding War Diaries and Intelligence Summaries are contained in F. S. Regs., Part II. and the Staff Manual respectively. Title pages will be prepared in manuscript.

WAR DIARY
or
INTELLIGENCE SUMMARY. 280th(City of London) Brigade, R.F.A.

(Erase heading not required.)

Army Form C. 2118.

Place	Date	Hour	Summary of Events and Information MAY 1919.	Remarks and references to Appendices
FLENU.			In the early days of the month Football and other Sports were developed.	
			About the 10th the morale of all ranks was raised to a condition such as was usual whilst the War was in progress, by the more or less definite news that we were in fact to be dispatched home very soon.	
			The Cadre of the Brigade in the meantime was reduced to 131 O.Rs and 5 Officers instead of 185 O.Rs. and 7 Officers.	
			The remaining 4 animals were handed over on the 12th inst. and all odd men eligible for the Army of Occupation were finally dispatched on the 15th inst.	
	24th.		The Brigade from this date came under the administrative control of the 169th Infantry Brigade Group who in turn were under "Mons Cadres" the equivalent of Corps.	
	25th.		It was anticipated that the Brigade would entrain on this day but 2 Batteries of 281st and 1 of 282nd. were ordered to entrain instead.	
			No further developments of any description to note. The weather remained magnificent and the troops to en extent amused themselves by playing football and swimming.	

[signature]

Major,
Commanding 280th Brigade, R.F.A.

D. D. & L., London, E.C.
(10340) Wt W5300/P713 750,000 3/18 E 2688 Forms/C2118/16.

Army Form C. 2118.

Instructions regarding War Diaries and Intelligence Summaries are contained in F. S. Regs., Part II. and the Staff Manual respectively. Title pages will be prepared in manuscript.

WAR DIARY

or

INTELLIGENCE SUMMARY. JUNE 1919

(Erase heading not required.)

Place	Date	Hour	Summary of Events and Information 280th Brigade RFA.	Remarks and references to Appendices
FLENU	1st to 8th		Nothing to record	
"	9th		Commenced entraining at 1500 hours at JEMAPPES Station for ANTWERP	
	10th		Arrived ANTWERP at 0600 hours	
	13th		Departed for ENGLAND. Equipment on the S.S. "Strathclyde" and personnel on S.S. "Arbroath"	

Major
Commanding 280th Brigade RFA.

D. D. & L., London E.C.
(10340) Wt W5300/P713 750,000 5/18 E 2688 Forms/C2118/16.